EXPERIMENT
IN
WORLD ORDER

PAUL McGUIRE

AUTHOR OF "WESTWARD THE COURSE"

EXPERIMENT

IN

WORLD ORDER

NEW YORK, 1948

WILLIAM MORROW AND COMPANY

The lines from "The White Man's Burden" on page 138 are from *The Five Nations*, copyright, 1903, 1931, by Rudyard Kipling, and are reprinted by permission of Mrs. George Bambridge and of Doubleday and Company. The quotation from General Baden-Powell on page 326 is from a paper, "The Development of Colonial Africa," in the *Proceedings of the Royal Colonial Institute* 1895-96, Vol. XXVII, page 223.

*f j l *

CONTENTS

EXPERIMENT
IN
WORLD ORDER

ONE

"INVOLVED IN MANKINDE"

I BEGAN to write this book at some time after midnight in the fall of 1946 in a little place on the borders of Illinois and Indiana. For five hours I had been talking and listening with two hundred men, mostly farmers, who had driven in twenty, thirty, and forty miles. They came from their fields in the midst of the largest harvest and the highest prices of American history. They came because they were haunted by the omens of the times. They had seen a day of triumph. It had gone down in flaming victory. Now the skies had suddenly and strangely darkened, and a new day was coming with signs of disasters unknown to the sons of men from their remotest begetting.

The farmers smelt the trouble in the air as they might have smelt across their plains an impending tornado; and they turned now from their quiet houses and the heaviest harvest ever borne by their fields to talk of it. They knew that I, an Australian, had been busy in London and New

1

York about the new political contrivance called the United Nations. They wanted to know what answers it had to questions put by a distracted and divided world: questions they could shape themselves.

I knew this part of the Middle West in the years before the war. A change had now come to it. For the first time these men understood that they were "involved in mankinde," that no country can live of itself, that their futures and the futures of their children and of their houses and fields were inextricably caught up in a complex of relations which reaches far beyond America.

They saw that in an age when children may starve in Salzburg unless wheat moves from Iowa, the moral responsibilities of men are enlarged. They saw that in an age when a rocket fired seven thousand miles away might blast the marshaling yards at Chicago, the whole shape of politics must be recast. They guessed that the change of mind in their own Middle West might prove a major turning-point of the 20th century.

For them the old isolationism was dead. Some who had served abroad had seen in the complexities of modern war the inter-relationships of states, peoples, and economies. Others working and watching at home had renounced the isolationist philosophy as a thousand facts revealed its errors. All but the memory had been plucked from their minds by the after-blast of the atomic bomb.

But its going had left a gap, an hiatus. Isolationism was not an eccentricity of the old America now passing. It was a central theme apt to the circumstances of that America's life. It was native and even creative in the growth of America: it had been less a dogma than an historic necessity. It had not been a policy as the Monroe Doctrine is policy. It had been implicit in the revolt against European attachments which had evoked the War of Independence. It was motive in the migrations which had peopled the country before and since. It was necessary in the opening of the continent when men's major energies and attention had to be applied here, generation after generation. The whole course of American history was westward and contrariwise to the European orientation.

One might without great fancifulness even consider that these Americans felt the full impact of world politics only when at last in their westward course they collided with hostile power. When the Middle West even after Pearl Harbor looked back towards Europe it looked down a long vista in chiaroscuro. But westward in full light appeared the naked image of power. These Americans had felt the Japanese War more their own than the European. They had towards it a curiously possessive attitude, almost as if it were a private war and in their destined course.

Isolationism was rationalized in a natural objection to entanglement in what seemed (often with justice) Europe's incessant brawling. But the Japanese War was fought at Europe's antipodes. This was unmistakably America's quarrel, even for the *Chicago Tribune* (much read hereabouts in rural Indiana and Illinois): and as the dust cleared from Hiroshima, and a transformed world appeared, the shape of another empire rose visible beyond the ruins of Japan.

Russia in Europe might have continued to seem for many Americans but a remote element in the fantastic European scene. But Russia in Asia stood armed and sullen on frontiers a few miles from Aleutian bases and Alaskan territories: in immediate opposition to the sense of manifest destiny which has been bent through America's history towards the Pacific and on and beyond.

The westward course had carried the Americans like circumnavigators first far from the old world of power politics into regions isolated and remote. But now as their sails expanded in the new winds of history they had come to their

Cathay, and in Cathay and beyond they have met the harshest realities of world politics.

The Russians have precipitated in the American mind a new conception of the world. If the major post-war issues had appeared only in Europe many Americans might again have tried to withdraw. But Russia now appeared in the West as in the East. Eastward she might have seemed remote through the half-lights and shades of European politics. But America could not turn her mind or eyes away from the Power revealed in Asia above the Northwest Pacific, Alaska, and the Arctic coasts.

America is now also deeply engaged in Europe and the Mediterranean Basin and the Middle East. She has come full circle in her course. She has seen that no great issue can be isolated from the whole complex of human relations. She only begins to grasp the implications and she does not clearly see the vast pattern into which her own is now woven. But the fundamental change of mind and mood has come. She understands that no people now can be "an Island intire of its selfe"; and that within each people many alien things may work.

Yet these Americans felt that the trouble with Russia was only one phase of a larger trouble. They sensed that it became an imminent peril only with the dissolution of a wider order.

They saw that here was more than a problem of simple aggression. They understood that a familiar world was dying about them and that the frame in which their own lives and economy had been sheltered was broken. They understood, in a fashion, that even their isolationism had been possible only when the peace had been kept in the world outside.

They had (like the Canadians, Australians, and the peoples generally of the New Worlds) lived for a century and a half within a world-system to which they hardly paid attention except when assaults on it plucked them into the conflicts which at last have cracked it. They had mostly accepted the system as if it belonged to a perennial providence. Actually, it was largely the effect of Briton's adventure in the world; and with the disruption of the British mercantile economy has come the disruption of the system in which it was a central and creative element.

This book is an effort to answer for the farmers of Illinois and Indiana some questions they put: to describe for them one major element of the order which is passing and whose passing has brought to them and to all Americans enormous new responsibilities and dangers.

The transformation of the British System is the major fact of contemporary history. It has consequences of an unprecedented sort for the world at large, because this was the first world-system men have achieved. Britain's part in the world is not ended. Britain and the Commonwealth may still have the major role if their peoples understand their own problems: but the British peoples also (as the recent performances of several of their Governments reveal) lack a clear sense of their situation. They and the Americans alike must understand that the world-system in which the British were the primary creative force is in flux and change. It must be refashioned, perhaps with the United States in the central role, if we are to restore a world economy and establish a firm frame of order for a world peace. The thing can be done. It can be done if peoples and politicians once see what it is that needs to be done.

But to see the problems and their answers, we must first look at the order now in transformation. Hence the approach of this book must be in some sense historical. We cannot understand the present and the emerging shapes of the future unless we understand the past from which they come, and the system which for two centuries was its major political and economic fact.

But the book is not intended as a piece of history. It is

rather an effort to diagnose from some of our immediate symptoms. It is concerned not with the past but with the policies we in the Western World must now pursue. It is concerned with the essentials of American as well as British policy. Both bear on America's domestic life as well as on her external relations.

For the United States there is today only one foreign policy that means anything. It must find expression in an Open World Economy. This is also the fundamental issue of America's domestic politics, because an Open World Economy requires the Open Society at home.

Only in an Open World Economy can America expect to use her full productive power and creative energies. The alternative to it is isolation in the world; and isolation must sooner or later breed war.

America must now take up much of the charge that the British System has borne. She cannot do it alone. But she can give the means and leadership for a combination of the Western peoples if she will see her interests and see them clear and whole.

Through the 19th century, the British kept on the seas and along the world's great routes the peace in which the new countries recruited populations and enlarged their commerce. The British system of trade and investments fed their economies, provided markets, manufactures, and capital goods. Britain's interest checked the growth of Powers which might have been hostile to the young countries. The Louisiana Purchase would not have come cheaply if Napoleon had held the seas.[1] The Monroe Doctrine might with equal appositeness have been named for George Canning. When he "called the New World into existence, to redress the balance of the Old," he gave to the New World guarantees realized by the existence of the Royal Navy. Behind

---

[1] Jefferson saw that if the French should dominate Louisiana "we must marry ourselves to the British Fleet and nation."

the wooden walls of England the Spanish colonies asserted and established their independence. British policy assured in effect that the United States should have as neighbors a group of American republics and not an empire reaching from Cape Horn to Colón or the Rio Grande or even (as it did until 1802) to the Mississippi. The British were pursuing their own concerns. It was America's fortune that hers so often ran with Britain's. But the fortune was not accident. Americans and British shared an intellectual and moral heritage. The meaning of life was much the same to both; for behind both was the traditional faith of Western Europe in the value of the human person and his great destiny.

There have been sharp issues between British and Americans. But they have been few, considering that American affairs have been far more entwined with Britain's than with those of any other Power, and that British territories and influence in Canada, the Caribbean, and Central and South American regions have borne closely on American interests and security.

The differences have worked more in the American mind and imagination than in the British. I doubt whether ten in a hundred Englishmen could recall even the vague outlines of the War of 1812,[2] which is naturally enough a powerful part of the American legend; and in the British world there are no racial groups traditionally hostile to the United States.

Despite the differences and quarrels, America accepted, and came in crisis to defend, the world system which flourished between Trafalgar and the Kaiser's War: for while that system first grew and rested primarily on British power and purposes, its range and benefits extended far beyond the British countries. The British themselves came to take

---

[2] It was a foolish and unnecessary war. The United States declared it on June 18th, five days after the British had withdrawn the *Orders in Council* which were its chief provocation, but before, of course, despatches could reach Washington from London.

it all much for granted. We begin to see its importance only now when it is in change and we find ourselves exposed at countless points to problems and responsibilities which it once bore.

It was least developed in the North and Central Pacific regions, partly because these have only of late revealed their full strategic and economic significance. The Pacific curtain is still rising on its vast stage. Geography and her own increasing power and the bent of history have set America in the forefront of the drama. Here she is protagonist; and here tremendous issues rise. The cultures of the East static through ages are in flux. Old forms dissolve and new forms will appear. Here also, eager to impose its own character on chaos, is a tremendous and militant Power which lies above all Asia and Europe, and across the western frontiers of America.

No great community lives in isolation. Its interests and influence extend far beyond its political and geographic frontiers. Inevitably they meet the interests and influence of other Powers and there must be combination, co-ordination, compromise, or clash. This is the region of foreign policy and diplomacy. In our time the variety and extent of these interests and influences have grown enormously. They reach into every phase of life. Diplomacy is no longer, as with Castlereagh and Canning, an exercise in the *hautmonde* of politics. It must grub and grapple now in every sort of human problem. State Departments and Foreign Offices have tried to meet the new situation by adding to themselves a curious collection of cultural and economic organizations. But these new instruments serve more to point the problems than to meet them.

Political development has fallen grotesquely short of social, economic, and cultural developments where the interests and influences of nations overlap. We have here problems of political education and machinery which the United Nations does not begin to meet. It has failed above all to meet the problems arising from fundamental conflicts of principle, from the clash of moral systems. The United Nations has in operation sedulously avoided them. It has attempted to treat here and there local symptoms. It has overlooked the deep disorder.

The American and Russian interests stand now opposed in the North Pacific world; but behind the local and immediate differences is a fundamental conflict. Unless it is resolved, war (by all the precedents of history) will come. If war does come, the new Russian forts and bases at Paramushiro and in Kamchatka set America somewhat the sort of question once set by the French at Fort Duquesne, Ticonderoga, Niagara, and Crown Point: the question which had its answer at Minden, Quiberon, Quebec, Plassy, and Wandiwash as well as on Lake Champlain and in the Ohio Valley. The Americans did not learn the lesson of world strategy when George Grenville stupidly tried to spank it in with his Stamp Act and tariffs. But today Americans have learnt that the question of the Straits is only geographically remote from the question of Bering Strait. They begin to see that domestic interests are intimately related to foreign policies: that foreign policies must work within the whole vast, complex range of world relationships which is their medium and milieu; and that policy is informed by what men think of life.

This was not all explicit in the minds of the farmers of Illinois and Indiana. Their immediate attention was on the dramatic symbols: the atom bomb, the ruin of war, the Communist aggression, the curious performance then proceeding at Flushing Meadows. Their questions were pointed and shrewd. But behind the questions was a growing sense that the basic problem was not in the threat of atomic warfare or the devastation already spread on the earth. These were symptoms of a disorder more profound, of the break-down in the values by which men live, of a fundamental moral crisis. I repeat that all this was not explicit. But it was implicit and active. They saw that the old bases of order in the world were dangerously weakened. They knew that they must be prepared to pump in cement or to play Atlas. They knew that the old isolationism was scrapped by history. But they still did not know what would replace it.

One said gloomily that politics go from bad to worse. But I was more impressed by another man I met in the Middle West, an old acquaintance with considerable influence in local Republican politics and sensitive to the movements of the Midwestern mind. He was before the war angrily isolationist. But now he looked at me across his table in Missouri. "I see that things largely hang on us. We have the power. But its use requires knowledge. Do we know enough to use it well? I think we can learn a good deal from the British, if we will. But we've also got to learn that power brings responsibilities. That sets us moral problems."

I have had him much in mind as I put together this book.

* 2 *

The British System went far wider and deeper than its political shapes reveal. We mistake it if we try to interpret it only in political terms. It is the nearest approach we have made to a world community. It defines some of the conditions necessary to a world order; and its virtues and vices, successes and errors are instructive when we must create new order or perish. The problems are far larger than the problems of the British System. It also is confounded and confused in the moral crisis which has come on all mankind. But in an effort to interpret that crisis, it provides an essential theme. I have therefore made it the primary argument of this book.

The British System has recognized that the vital interests of peoples and their economic, strategic, social, cultural

frontiers reach far beyond the political frontiers of their
several sovereign states. This is obvious as soon as one looks
at the scene. Yet the operation of the modern National State
in countless ways cuts across the growth of the wider social,
economic, cultural communities; and sets up intolerable
tensions.

In an age when the Basuto buys a bicycle from Birmingham and he and a Yankee in Connecticut both ride on rubber from Malaya, the economic community has obviously
outgrown and overrun political frontiers. Yet the National
State has increasingly resisted every effort to find new political forms which will adequately meet the new economic
facts. Today whole areas of the world are shut off from that
economic community which we might have developed had
narrow nationalisms not swung down their iron curtains,
their trade barriers, restrictions, economic autarchies.

Once also in the world there was some community of
scholarship. The old European order gave free traffic of
ideas among philosophers, moralists, theologians, and natural
scientists. By the end of the 19th century it had grown across
most of the world. But today as in Japan under the Shoguns
iron curtains have come down in the life of the mind. Whole
ranges of knowledge are cut off from whole populations.
Information and ideas are perverted to political prejudices
and plots. We have lately had protest from the physical
scientists whose governments have put them under secrecy
and refused their claim to open publication. But for a
generation other governments have checked under savage
censorships and prohibitions the free play and exchange of
ideas in philosophy, morals, and the social sciences.

The Americans are less prone than most to the modern
superstition of the State. The careful, clear men who shaped
the American Constitution saw the proper limits of politics
and knew the vanities and lusts of politicians. But America
is nevertheless threatened by a narrow nationalism which

crosses not only her traditions but her real interests: for she cannot live of herself alone. She must understand the patterns of life which extend far beyond her visible frontiers if she too is not to work against the growth of the world community.

* 3 *

We lately set up a piece of machinery which we call the United Nations. It is not an organic entity. It has no personality. It is a manufactured thing. It has potential uses as a tool, an instrument. But we cannot expect it to unfold into a world community. Communities grow. They belong to the order of life, not of mechanics. They cannot be created by the pressure of political machinery or according to blueprints. They develop in the wide context of social life and relationships.

The British System as it grew through the 19th century is in sharp contrast with the new political gadget. It has no centralized or uniform political machinery at all. Politically many of its major elements are autonomous and in fact independent. The British System for a century has preserved peace and order among an extraordinary variety of the world's peoples. But it exists less in a political pattern than in a broad social, economic, and human complex. If we remember with Burke that Government is, after all, only a contrivance of human wisdom, if we remember that few things in politics are more ephemeral than political machinery,[3] we shall better understand the problems of world order.

Politics are not enough, as Mr. Bevin knew when he tried through the first meetings of the United Nations Assembly to get its attention for the wider concerns of mankind. He

[3] We have seen two German Reichs and a Republic within one generation. In a century, France was absolute monarchy, limited monarchy, republic, empire, kingdom, republic, empire, and republic.

was defeated by the obsession with politics which has come upon us with the monstrous growth of the State.[4] But his insistence on the broader human values reflects the long experience of British statecraft. The farmers would have understood Mr. Bevin because they understand the difference between life and mechanics. They are familiar with growth. They have knowledge hidden from many moderns: they know that milk comes from a cow before it appears in a can.

Mr. Bevin's voice was lost in the clatter of the machinery and in the cries and counter-cries of the confused mechanics. But in this book I have tried to develop his sense.

The political element has been grossly exaggerated in the modern world. The State has become to many the absolute sole lord of life and death: which is obvious and dangerous nonsense as soon as we remember that the State in operation is machinery managed by men much like ourselves with all their sins and foolishness on them. They may hide remote behind their gray abstractions and persuade the innocent and ignorant to the new idolatry. But it is the essence of responsible democracy that we do not mistake our own devices and servants for Baal and his priesthood.

The men from Eastern Europe at the United Nations encouraged the political and mechanical superstitions. The more intelligent no doubt repeat to their own comfort, *L'État c'est moi.* They belong to sects or cliques which have seized on the machinery of the State. Their insistence on the supremacy of the political arm is understandable.

When Bevin looked towards the wider social and economic interests in which a real community might grow, the Eastern bloc resisted him. The U.S.S.R. refused even to

---

[4] I find it curious that many people who profess the need for an international community still cry up the Great State, its arch-enemy.

enter the United Nations Educational, Scientific and Cultural Organization.

The Russians represent the extreme of those who would subdue to the political interest and its instrument the State every phase of social, economic, personal and cultural life: with them politics have replaced morals and philosophy in the hierarchy of the sciences. They confuse ends and means in the horrible disorder which has come on the modern world. They worship the machines, the instruments.

Politics are out of right order when they are become a final end. This is the fundamental error of totalitarianism and this is why totalitarianism is ultimately destructive. Man is much more than a political animal. Politics cannot meet all the needs of his nature. The State, like the physical sciences, must be ordered within a larger system. If we do not impose a moral order on the conduct of the State and the application of science, they will blow our world to pieces.

When they fall outside the moral order both State and science become monstrous and aberrant growths. They will destroy us and in destroying us destroy themselves. This on the present weight of evidence we may now expect. Our one hope is to restore the hierarchy of values in which all science and all art, including the science and the art of government, find their proper place in a frame of moral reference. Here is the issue before all mankind.

* 4 *

I began to write this book in Illinois. But it first came to my mind in Berlin in the autumn of 1945 where men moved among the jagged ruins as through a nightmare. The debris and the rubble and the ruined streets are also the effects and expression of a more horrible catastrophe, of the ruin of a social and moral community.

The desolation of the wrecked cities and economies is not an episode isolated and ended. It is not a phase apart

from the main course of history and now complete. It is a
local expression of forces still active everywhere in the
world. We have Berlin and all its terrors within us. Hitler
has gone into his legend. We have strung Göring, Ribben-
trop, and Keitel to their gibbets. But we have not laid the
evil which evoked them. We have not cured the sickness of
which they and their wars were symptoms. The herd still
runs violently down a steep place into the sea.

Man's world, like his lesser works of art, expresses and
reveals his values, principles, ambitions, virtues, vices. He
makes it in his image. It is his *chef-d'œuvre,* his major poem.
We look at the world as in a mirror, darkly perhaps. But we
can understand that the great Dom of Cologne and the
tangle of medieval streets that were once about it with their
crafts and guilds and shambles and taverns and oratories
reflected the mind, values, faith, and interests of men. We
can interpret another mind and culture in the Roman Law
and Roman roads and Roman pride of citizenship and Roman circuses: another in Fifth Avenue, Rockefeller Center,
and *Leon and Eddie's.* We read back from their poems
and sonatas, their bridges, houses, racetracks, gardens, con-
venticles, fashions, hotels, salons, and schools the minds
of men and their moral purposes, literally what they make
of life. The great cathedrals which stand above Chartres,
Wells, Salisbury, Milan recall the dominant values of one
age as the insurance buildings and banks which crown the
modern city reveal another's. The smashed streets of Berlin
and the images of ruin spread from the North Cape to Africa
and from Glasgow to Hiroshima are also representative.
They reveal a world which has bent the major effort of a
generation to destruction. They reflect a world which is
thrashing itself to death.

We look in the mirror of art (as Shakespeare knew) for
the captured shapes and images of life, for the values there
each given a local habitation and a name. This is the prime

purpose of art, its social significance: to provide occasion for the examination of consciousness and conscience. So we see in the great mirror of the world our supreme artifact. Here is what we have made. Here is revealed what we are. And here I suppose is the chief theme of this book, its text, and use, as it is of all books that men write and all things that they make.

* 5 *

This is an intensely personal book. I do not know how it could be otherwise when the hierarchy of values within which politics should find their proper place and their moral direction is dismissed.

It is a discursive book and it much returns on its arguments. But life and history are discursive and men's acts turn back on them; and I have striven here to present what have seemed to me realities. The world has moved excessively among abstractions in its social and political thought. Abstractions may take on life and appear embodied in vast and terrible forms: Hegel and Marx between them have had consequences in our time. Man is a creative being. His ideas are bodied forth. Here I have tried to look at the works he has made; and to go beyond the political abstractions to the broad human context in which they are organized with life. The book does not profess to expert attitudes. It tentatively gropes towards some synthesis of facts relevant to its argument.

It has used the British System as a peg for many themes. I have taken the British System as a centerpiece because it has been the major fact of world-politics for two centuries.

Out of it came great colonies and new nations, the Industrial Revolution, Finance Capitalism, the Parliamentary System and Trades-Unions. From and about it grew world-commerce; and within it grew the one authentic society of nations which the world has seen.

The British System as it has appeared in history this hundred years is the nearest we have come to a world community.

It is not merely a political Empire attached to a Commonwealth of Sovereign States. It reaches beyond its political organization to knit peoples in economic, social, and cultural relations.

This book is not a defense of the British System. Much that could be said for it and against it is passed over. It is an attempt to review what in it is useful and relevant to our present problems of world order.

Or let us say that the United States must take up some of the burdens of great power. They must exercise in the world some of the functions of what is properly called empire: functions of law, of order, of economic aid and development. Americans will do well to look at the methods by which responsibilities of the sort have been met.

And this is what I mean by looking at reality instead of at the abstractions.

The League of Nations and the United Nations were shaped in a confusion of realities and abstractions. The British System has grown as a reality.

We may get some notion of historic realities by watching the curious developments of the British System in time and place; but we can stare at the Charter and Constitution of the United Nations from now until world's end without coming to know how men behave and why. Men are the stuff of history, charters and constitutions but their instruments and records; and the British System presents a great pageant of men struggling to make some sense of the surging facts and to bring some order and community among peoples of all creeds and colors.

We may be convinced only of the British System's failure. We may believe that it has been stupid, blind, oppressive. But no other human system in all time has embraced and revealed such a variety of men and conditions. Every problem of order that men can know has had to be met somewhere in it.

We should try to learn at least from its failures. For heaven knows, we must learn all we can of the strange creature *man* who now seems bent on his own destruction.

TWO

THE BRITISH SYSTEM

WHAT we conventionally call the British Commonwealth and Empire is the least understood politico-social system in human history. The foreigner can hardly be blamed if he mistakes and misunderstands and misinterprets it, for so do most of its own people. The British should not resent the tone of the Colonel McCormicks. Critics as bilious have flourished in the King's Dominions: and in truth the British System had and has grave and glaring weaknesses. It has operated sometimes with gross injustice and more often with stupidity, for men, as Bacon observed, are more fools than wise; and the British System is a very human affair. But the urgent matter now is not to defend or attack the record but to discover what its uses and lessons are for a world which must find international order or perish.

The British System includes the most advanced and prolonged examples of international co-operation. Moreover, it is still a part of the pattern of men's daily lives (whether they realize it or not) in Oshkosh, Tulsa, Baltimore, Brooklyn, Marseille, Oslo, Tehran, Saigon, Pernambuco, Callao, Tangiers, Batavia, Canton, Hankow, and Lincoln, Nebraska, as well as in London, Ottawa, Canberra, Christchurch, Cape Town, Colombo, Aden, Zanzibar, Hong Kong, Rabaul, Mauritius, Rangoon, the Scilly Isles, Wigan, Esquimault, Halifax, Tooting Bec, Woolloomoolloo, and Clapham Junction.

Its immensity and the extraordinary range and variety of its influence have perhaps discouraged study. Objectivity is difficult when the theme is much with us: and this establishes our styles in tweeds, Manchester cotton goods, and the procedure of the law-courts and legislatures of half the world, while it supplies Canadian salmon to the Kikuyu of Kenya, Indian jute to coffee planters in Brazil, and the Oxford Dictionary to schoolteachers in Burlington, Vermont. Naturally enough this vast pervasive fact has appealed to publicists less than the inwardness of Europe or the love lives of dictators or the Utopias of the Steppes or those tidier themes which can be treated with nice academic detachment and where the pleasures of speculation are not too much oppressed by the constant surge and flow of multitudinous realities. Nevertheless, we must (if we are to make sense of our world) have a general understanding of what the British System has been and is and yet may be.

As an object of study, it is a pother and vexation. Even its terminology is ambiguous and confused. Regarded merely as a political system (it is actually much more a socio-economic system) the word "empire" has been applicable only at some of its times and places. Even "system" is too neat and precise, for the British Thing includes almost every known variety of political organization and relationship.

It is at one plane a loose-working arrangement between autonomous States; to some of which are linked other Governments and peoples in the relations of colonies, dependencies, protectorates, and mandates or trusteeships. If you look at it through time and then in contemporary cross-section you find no single constant element. The British Crown is commonly and rightly taken as its centerpiece. But the relations of the Crown with the constituents vary now and through history. India was in fact and practice incorporated in the system long before the Crown had much more than cognizance. The Chartered Companies, though composed of his Majesty's liege and licensed subjects, went off for long passages on their own careers to acquire rights and territories abroad often as mere by-products of their mercantile activities. Eire renounces for its people British subjecthood but retains its own peculiar link with the Crown. In Sarawak until lately an independent Rajah was also a British subject. It is all very confusing and one can understand why it has irritated the logical and temperate men who conduct the *Chicago Tribune.*

The British System spread far beyond the map's bold reds. Most conscientious map-makers long ago despaired of one unqualified crimson and drifted off into pinks and old-rose and hatched patterns to represent its different sorts of association. But no map-maker could attempt the further marches of the British System; the extension of its influence and investment into other sovereignties; its parts at Kabul and Buenos Aires, in Baluchistan, Persia, Peru, Portugal, and along the Union Pacific, its role in the building of the United States, in California, China, and on all the great routes of the world.

With India, its political frontiers included a quarter of the earth's surface and over two hundred distinguishable units. It runs from the Arctic to the Antarctic and is massively established in every continent. It coils across oceans on its archipelagos and commands the capes or offshore islands at every major turning point of the world's traffic: at the gates of the Mediterranean and the toes of Italy and India, at the

Leeuwin, Good Hope, and the Falklands off the Horn, at
the southeastern tip of Asia and the eastern capes of North
America and the western thrust of Africa and the vents of
the Red Sea and Persian Gulf. It includes large elements of
most human stocks at almost every level of culture: English, Irish, Scots, Welsh, French, Dutch, Chinese, Negroes,
Semites, Hindus, Polynesians, Melanesians, Red Indians,
Malays, Sakais, Australian aborigines. The Anglo-Saxons
were in 1939 perhaps 11 per cent of its population. Its religions range from Animism to Buddhism. It has been with
India the first Moslem Power. It is in point of nominal
numbers the first or second Christian Power: and in India
it, of course, embraced a third of the four great world-
religions. It speaks most tongues that came from Babel and
their dialects and sub-dialects. It reveals every phase of
economic life and growth: nomadic hunters, fisher-peoples,
pastoralists, peasants, planters, traders, merchant companies
and all varieties of industrialists from charcoal burners and
boomerang makers to Courtauld's, the Broken Hill Pro-
prietary, and Imperial Chemical Industries. It uses every
sort of money known to men from checks to cowrie shells
and rum. It produces all the staples of commerce and almost all known minerals. It travels by the *Queen Elizabeth,*
dugouts, prahus, rafts, and canoes, aircraft, trains, automobiles, camels, oxen, mules, and sleighs; and sometimes it
just walks. Its exports and imports were in 1939 nearly two-
fifths of all the world's.

It has almost every variety of political organization and
social experiment except Totalitarianism. One or other of
its parts has pioneered in every phase of labor organization
and legislation, in social services, co-operative enterprises,
electoral franchises, free and compulsory education, industrial arbitration, and the rest. It embraces the most advanced
and the most primitive of social modes and ways of life.

Yet the British Empire as a political unit hardly exists at

all: it has nothing resembling a unitary or federal constitution. The political bogey which affrights so many people belongs to the class of chimera and cockatrice. The actual System has no resemblance to classic empires: no one center of government, no uniform pattern of law or administration, no common citizenship. It is less a political empire than a loose mesh of economic, cultural, and social interests. No single common bond appears among its parts unless it is that England has always belonged to it. It is just somehow strung together. But its broad human influence and (by one attachment and another) its economic, social, cultural and moral fibers are spread through all its varieties of peoples and beyond. If the British System withered or was wrenched out of mankind it would leave large parts of the world loose, leaderless, astray, with their politics awry and their economies in collapse.

International trade, traffic, communications, investment, markets are mostly intertwined with the British System or looped across it. The enormous expansion and organization of the world economy during the last century and a half has grown from or in or about the British System. It could not be subtracted from the world system as if two separate entities existed. If the British System withers or snaps, the world system that we have known will perish with it. We should have to attempt something altogether new. It is doubtful whether we could succeed within measurable time: for these are matters of life and growth, not of mechanics only.

The British System was the chief element of growth in that curious phase of human history which has produced the modern world. It is still the chief element of such coherence as we have. It is integral and organic. Babies are sometimes thrown out with the bathwater; but no one yet has successfully ejected his central sympathetic nervous system and survived.

The wars in which the British are heavily involved become world-wars because the whole world is involved in the British System. The recent wars were in one view revolts against this prevalent pattern. They failed because the world at large could not afford successful rebellion against the chief organizing element of its general economy. But the instinct of the rebels was sound enough when they saw Britain as the first enemy of their ambitions.

One may have a powerful distaste for the British System. One may (like an acquaintance of mine in Milwaukee) see it as a sort of cancer which has crept through all the world. But it must be dealt with as a fact of enormous consequence to all the peoples of the world.

We must understand it in its historic context and in the context of our own lives as it enters our igloos, wigwams, kraals, or apartments on Park Avenue; as it influences our tastes, foods, social habits, prejudices, bank-accounts, bookshelves, cotton prices, and party politics. It is a lion in the way and in the streets: yet politically (let us work at this point until we have it clear) it is a most diffuse and scattered sort of beast; which is perhaps why Herr Hitler, and his Kaiser before him, and other people of urgent, tidy minds who attach great significance to social discipline have mistaken it for a sawdust lion or a lion dismembered and reduced to a somewhat moth-eaten rug.

Its parts have, of course, each their own political structures. Some have written constitutions. All accept the King of the United Kingdom and of the Dominions Overseas as their king. There is still some reference in legal courses to the Privy Council. Some machinery (grown considerably of late) exists for consultation on specific issues. The Governments hold occasional conferences and regularly exchange views and information. But the political relations between the Dominions are otherwise slender. They appoint to one another High Commissioners. But the ties between the self-governing Dominions are interests and sentiments broadly human and social rather than political.

All this may seem trite to those familiar with the system, but it is precisely the character which foreigners most frequently mistake. Many Americans still do not understand that Canada is mistress in her own house. During the Pacific War, Australians and New Zealanders were frequently advised by American acquaintances to follow the example of 1776 and cast off the tyrant's yoke. But they have no yoke to cast. The Dominions do not contribute even to the King's support, though he is King of Australia, New Zealand, and Canada as well as of the United Kingdom. Their equivalents of the Privy Purse and Civil List [1] go to maintain their Governors-General, who may be local citizens.

In some parts of the System the Royal Writ has run absolute. In others, authority belongs to representative, though not responsible, legislatures and to appointed executives. Others are autonomous States exercising sovereign power. Australia, Canada, New Zealand, South Africa might properly be called kingdoms; but the vocabulary of this curious system has not found a generic word. South Africa is a Union. New Zealand and Canada are still called Dominions (though not discreetly within earshot of Mr. Mackenzie King). Eire sends its diplomats abroad under credentials from the Crown, though it insists that it is a Republic. "Dominion" implies precisely what the Dominions are not: territorial lordships. "Kingdom" is the proper word but it might provoke sensitive if illogical democrats in the Dominions. "Realm" perhaps would serve, as a word of historic dignity which suggests without emphasis the royal note. The United Kingdom has lately changed the ministerial and departmental title of Dominions Affairs to Commonwealth Affairs.

[1] The Civil List is the British Parliamentary Allowance for the King's Household and pensions; the Privy Purse is the allowance from public revenue for the King's private expenses.

"Commonwealth" at a pinch serves to describe the group, although as inhabitants of Massachusetts will recognize it is not very apt. Federated Australia calls itself a Commonwealth, but a Commonwealth of Commonwealths would sound a trifle silly. The reality is a Society of Realms.

But the British System resists every effort at simplification and is consequently much exposed to rash judgments.

The point here is that the System as a whole has no single political structure, no single pattern of law, no single center of sovereign power as had the Roman Empire, the Czardom, or the great Empires of the East. No comprehensive principle of unity appears. The characters visible in a state or nation as we commonly understand them are missing. It presents almost every variety of political constitution while at the center the United Kingdom has no comprehensive constitution at all. The British System has no official tongue. It has no one order of defense, no common economic program, no universal qualifications for citizenship. Even the accepted symbol of the Crown has various meanings for various parts. Politically, in short, the British Commonwealth is little more than a series of working arrangements. They operate when they exist *ad hoc* and for particular issues; but no authority exists to impose general agreement. The self-governing Dominions no longer declare war together. The issue of war or peace is for each to determine. They have fought their wars side by side until now. But wars are conceivable in which one might engage and others not. The obligations which all members have accepted to the United Nations are more considerable than those which the self-governing Dominions accept within the British System.

Nevertheless, there is in the world a recognizable being which we call the British Commonwealth and Empire. The roots and prime realities of the association, though they have great political consequences, are for the most part outside and beyond mere political arrangements. Yet this association has been extremely strong. Twice in one generation the whole team has gone into war together, welding its fighting forces, drawing from its peoples prodigious efforts in the general defense. But even in the crisis of 1940 the System effectively resisted any formal political development. A proposal for a joint War Cabinet with headquarters in London was rejected. Rejecting it, Mr. Mackenzie King expressed the curious character of the System's diversity in unity with one neat phrase. "I feel," he said, "that the captains should be each on his own bridge and not assembled in the flagship." Even this measure of co-ordination exists only by free assent of all the parties and on specific occasion.

I labor the point because this is the prime fact about the British System as it now exists; and because the example of this curious community is worth attention in a world which must somehow grope towards a world system if it is to be saved. The British Commonwealth is the nearest humanity has come to a world community. The classic Roman Empire was within its range much more highly organized politically with a common center of administration and one fount of sovereign power and one official language, one system of law, one official creed, one military structure. The medieval ideal of the Holy Roman Empire would have come nearer (if it had been realized) to what we need in way of world polity. But the range of one and the achievement of the other were far short of the British System. The British System has knit peoples of the most various races, faiths, tongues, and economies. Generally it has kept peace among them and it has provided some of the conditions for their orderly progress. In its experience with one quarter of the world, it has urgent significance to what we dream of for the whole.

The lack of central or co-ordinating political machinery (it has now become an excessive lack) demonstrates that the political interest has often lagged far in the wake of other interests; as in India where a hundred years of Company control preceded the Imperial symbols, which came at last, we may notice, from the brilliant oriental imagination of the least English of English statesmen, Benjamin Disraeli. The flag has often followed trade reluctantly. The initiatives of empire were more with private groups or individuals than with Government. Clive and Hastings were disgraced. Raffles (the most prescient of empire builders) who created Singapore was neglected and browbeaten. Many of the major figures of British expansion were not politicians or officials but merchants and missionaries. Through the 19th century, authority at home and colonists abroad contemplated with something more than equanimity their ultimate separation.

The British System is an astonishing example of the much-neglected fact that a living community does not depend on political uniformity. Its major links are not political; they are in broader fields of human interest. It has at times and in one place and another attempted to impose fixed forms and rigid settlements. These attempts have in the long run always failed where they lacked assent: as in America and Ireland.

Where the British System gave freedom it has endured.

It stands in contrast to the autocratic and authoritarian systems. We are all nowadays willy-nilly much influenced by the concept of the highly centralized State. But it has yet to prove that it can provide as the British System has for multifarious peoples a reign of both liberty and order.

The Police State is in historic fact a gigantic fraud on human nature. It may survive through long passages of time by brute force. Successful rebellion against a modern tyranny armed with secret police and all the instruments of war is practically impossible. The peasant's hayfork was once as handy as the soldier's pike; a New England musketman could compete with a Hanoverian mercenary or a Grenadier. But the peasant cannot beat his plowshares into amphibious tanks or poison-gas or rocket-bombs.

We have seen an exceptional crop of tyrannies in our times. Some have already come to catastrophic ends. Others may survive. But while they live their victims rot. They so distort and pervert, cabin, crib, and confine, bind in saucy doubts and fears that their peoples' intellectual and moral energies wither. They sink to fellaheen; and even the State itself in time crumbles away, for where there is no liberty all grows corrupt. Great empires and their peoples have thus gone into decay; and the sands have come in over their fields and cities; and the Lion and the Lizard keep the Courts where Jamshyd gloried.

In our approach to the problems of world order we should be careful not to exaggerate the value of the central machinery; we should look for a healthy distribution of responsibilities. The British System has survived its changes, its losses and gains since it learnt (with Burke and from the American Revolution) the uses of a "wise and salutary neglect" and the need to "pardon something to the spirit of liberty."

THREE

CROWN, COMMONWEALTH,

AND COLONIES

THE forms of government and administration within the British System vary with each of its units. They defy general description; and the System is at one point or another constantly in change. But a brief review is useful for the picture of variety in unity and for the lessons in political adaptability. The British System avoids arbitrary prescription: its elements evolve in local needs and circumstances. Its test has been pragmatic: *Does the thing work?*

The System is now in one of its great passages of flux and change. But an account of its essential character need not wait on the resolution. The historic meaning of the System can be seen in what it was as it went into war in 1939.

With the omission of the mandates, which as special creations of the Treaty of Versailles are not organic members, it has been conventionally divided into three principal groups: the Commonwealth, the Colonial Empire, and the Empire of India. With the final transfer of power in 1947, the Indian Empire ended, and the Emperor of India renounced his title. If self-governing India remains in the British System, it will be with the Commonwealth.

The Commonwealth found definition at the Imperial Conferences of 1926 and 1930. Seven Governments were represented: the United Kingdom, Canada, Australia, New Zealand, South Africa, the Irish Free State, and Newfoundland. They interpreted themselves thus: Great Britain and the Dominions are "autonomous communities within the British Empire, equal in status, in no way subordinate to one another in any aspect of their domestic or external affairs, though united by a common allegiance to the Crown and freely associated as members of the British Commonwealth of Nations. . . . Every self-governing member of the Empire is now the master of its destiny. In fact, if not always in form, it is subject to no more compulsion whatever. . . . Equality of status, so far as Britain and the Dominions are concerned, is thus the root principle governing our interimperial relations."

This was the sense enacted in the Statute of Westminster passed by the British Parliament in 1931.[1]

The Crown as the one great remaining symbol of the association will endure while the Commonwealth endures: for, as Smuts once pointed out, a substitute would pass the wit of man to devise.

Symbolism is native and natural to men. They find their meanings in the imagination as well as by reason. Social groups cohere in their traditions and devices as well as for

[1] The Statute at its passage was applicable to Canada, the Irish Free State, and South Africa as well as the United Kingdom; though South Africa took action of her own for special reasons. Australia ratified only in October, 1942. New Zealand and Newfoundland did not bother.

evident interests. Men die for a flag as they die for a creed. The republic is still prolific of Grand Knights and Supreme Rulers and Worshipful Masters, of regalia and tokens, football colors, college songs. The armies of the Soviets are much bedecked: the cloth caps and workman's tunics (themselves symbols) of its leaders are exchanged for military splendors or diplomatic uniforms.

Symbols quicken the general imagination, and normally the sense of responsibility in those who bear them. In its wiser passages humanity takes precautions against the corruption of its rulers. They may be restrained by checks and balances, or they may be hedged with sanctions, ceremonials, and customs. The kings were anointed in the old Christian order to remind them of their own subjection to a King of Kings. Their dignities were meant to symbolize their office but also to invoke a discipline. The king might still prove a blackguard, and very often did, for power has great temptations. But at least he and his people usually knew him for a blackguard. It is not a mere simplification of history that we remember medieval kings as "good" kings and "bad" kings. They lived in a milieu where moral judgments were still powerful and impressive.

Great office should carry appropriate dignities and disciplines. A man sensible of them is often raised out of himself. He is caught up in the strong texture of traditional values. Those with wide acquaintance in the world of affairs will have noticed often this salutary phenomenon.

Men who come to power in ill-ordered, demoralized communities are much more open to the corruption which Acton described than those who come to offices supported and defined within a stable order. Successful revolutionaries seldom resist the corruptions of power. Its burdens and temptations are almost always too much if the man is not at once sustained and restrained by a context of law and custom, discipline and dignity. Caesars come by violence and commonly in megalomania, as our age notably re-affirms.

The British have thought it well to separate the supreme symbol of the Nation and the Commonwealth from controversial politics and to set the man who embodies it beyond the meaner temptations of power, profit, and vainglory. His position must be curiously uncomfortable; but it is a fascinating projection of the poetry and the pragmatism which combine to produce the peculiar character of British history.

The King reigns. He does not govern. The government is conducted in the King's name but always on the decisions of his Ministers. These in the practice of the British System must have the confidence of a majority of members of the Parliaments in which they sit.

The authority of the Crown is exercised separately by each Government of the autonomous Dominions. When the King acts as King of Australia or of Canada or South Africa or New Zealand, he acts not on the advice of the British Government but of the Australian or Canadian or South African or New Zealand Government. They each conduct in the name of the Crown their own affairs. As Smuts once said to a British audience: "The King is not your King but the King of all of us, ruling over every part of the whole Commonwealth."

If the King is in a Dominion he acts there as King: thus in 1947, King George VI presided over a meeting of his Executive Council in South Africa and he opened the South African Parliament and delivered the Speech from the Throne (which in all his Parliaments reviews the state of the country as the Government sees it and sets out the Government's policy).

In his absence the King is represented in each Dominion by a Governor-General or in the United Kingdom by a Council of State. These give the Royal Assent to laws passed by the Parliament, issue the King's Commissions, appoint Governments and accept their resignations, and conduct in general the business which still formally belongs to the Crown. The Governor-General in each Overseas Dominion is appointed by the King on the advice of the local Prime Minister and without reference to the Government of the United Kingdom. The local Prime Minister actually selects the Governor-General, as we saw in 1947 when the Australian Prime Minister put forward an Australian politician and offered the King no alternative name.

From all this, the innocent abroad might imagine that the King and his Governors-General are reduced to ciphers or public Seals; but again we have a paradox within a paradox. The King is unlikely to use again his formal powers against a Government which has the confidence of Parliament and people. The Crown would probably accept legislation to abolish itself. But the King may wield great personal influence. The Crown is still the pinnacle and center of social life in the British System, and it has tremendous popular prestige. This is due partly to the quality of those who have worn the Crown in the last century, partly to the evolution of the institution itself.

The predecessors of Queen Victoria were as much a butt of public criticism and sometimes of ridicule as the holders of most great offices. Their subjects were capable of such amiable epigrams as this:

> "George the First was always reckoned
> Vile, but viler George the Second;
> And what mortal ever heard
> Any good of George the Third?
> When from earth the Fourth descended
> God be praised, the Georges ended!"

The Throne was still considered fair game for criticism through the first half of the Queen's reign. Even the long seclusion of her widowhood drew caustic comment. It was bad for trade. But the Queen's devotion to the routine of her job, her capacity, her sheer endurance won respect, affection, ultimately awe. Through the latter half of her reign the Crown became more and more a necessary symbol of unity in the new System which was developing. It became a symbol also of the imperial splendor which for a decade or two in the era of her Jubilees caught the reluctant imaginations of her peoples. Events and the Queen's shrewdness combined to withdraw the Crown further from executive responsibilities. She might speak her mind to Ministers: but the Ministers now bore the public responsibilities and all the odium of Government.

Yet through the last quarter-century of her reign she was in political experience unapproached by any of her Ministers. Political experience is a great asset of the Kingship. Parties rise and fall, Governments come and go, Prime Ministers usually can expect only a few years on the Front Bench. But the King stays. If he lives long enough, he acquires from his incomparable observation-post a knowledge of state affairs, state papers and statesmen which no Minister can hope to equal in his briefer visits to the chambers of the sun.

In the stress of modern administration most Ministers must concentrate on their own departmental responsibilities; but the King like his Prime Minister surveys the whole field of government. As his reign lengthens he will pass with different Ministries through their crises and the Nation's troubles. He will come to know in their triumphs and depressions the leading men of all parties. He will meet thousands of people from all walks of life. The inner passages of history as they are known to his Governments will be open to him.

The King is expected in his progresses to be sufficiently conversant with the conditions of his people, their major industries, their problems of health, housing, employment and the rest. He must dip in all their bowls and sample all their brews. He acquires an extraordinary experience in public matters. If he is intellectually competent to organize and use it, his personal influence is inevitably powerful.

The Ministers are in the theory of the constitution the King's advisers. In practice the King sometimes usefully advises his Ministers.

Anomaly has existed since the Statute of Westminster in the Crown's relations with its different Governments. The King, though equally King of the United Kingdom, Canada, Australia, New Zealand and South Africa, normally has a much more intimate and active relation with the Government of Great Britain than with the others.

It can at least be argued that since the Statute of Westminster the Crown's relations with the United Kingdom and the Dominions overseas should go *pari passu:* that the Crown as an Imperial symbol should normally appoint a representative to Great Britain as to the Dominions. The King would in this case give much more time to the Dominions Overseas, and the wide Imperial interests would be his primary concern. This might be an excellent arrangement if anything corresponding to a general government or permanent conference should appear in the British System: but, as matters are, the Crown would be excessively remote from the realities of government. The anomaly can be resolved only in a general development of Commonwealth relations.

But a Crown thus detached from the special interests of any one Government might provide a center of allegiance for a wider circle. Eire conceivably might be more at ease with the Commonwealth if the Imperial Crown seemed to Irishmen less a symbol of British hegemony than of equal partnership.

It is most curious that Samuel Adams during his long agitation (and his was the loudest voice in America to call up Revolution) took much the attitude which has since been taken in Commonwealth relationships. Adams held that the Crown was the center and source of union in the British Empire. He repudiated the Westminster Parliament and declared that the Revolution of 1688 had been a domestic affair which could not modify the old contractual relations of Crown and Colonies. The Colonies had been founded under Royal patents and charters. Their link was with the Crown. They were entitled to deal with it direct. The Crown, but not the British Parliament, had authority to act for the Colonies in international affairs, and to order inter-Colonial relations. The Crown should govern in the Colonies with the consent of their representative assemblies and not on the advice of British Ministers. The Westminster Parliament could have no sovereign authority in the Empire at large unless it was transformed by the inclusion of Colonial representatives: without them it certainly had no rights of taxation. (Adams thus touched the theme of a Federal Empire which was widely canvassed four generations later.)

The British Commonwealth has since gone on and beyond Adams without dissolution; and we must allow that angry man a strange perception denied to his contemporaries of one element at least of its genius. Adams has been described by James Truslow Adams in *The Epic of America* as a fanatic with "a fanatical hatred of England"; and his argument may have been chiefly tactical. But he seemed to pluck it from beyond the veil of the future, as men sometimes may when they are soundly grounded in the principles of the past: the principle of taxation without representation upon which Adams seized has been for centuries a clue to the English mystery.

The Crown has become the *sine qua non* of the Commonwealth; and it serves in the Colonial Empire as an incomparable sign and image which peoples at all cultural levels can grasp. It gives a personal object to the loyalties of men unaccustomed to abstractions. Bagehot thought the best argument for Monarchy is its intelligibility: "the mass of mankind understand it." But Monarchy also has tremendous strength in the affective life of men. Where it does not exist, something like it must often be invented. Against the tawdry trappings of the absolutists who infest our times there seems much to say for the decent usages of traditional and constitutional Monarchy.

* 2 *

The seven countries represented at the Imperial Conference of 1926 were each completely self-governing with their own constitutional structure: no two precisely alike.[2] The Dominions of Pakistan and India are now self-governing also; and so is Southern Rhodesia, although it has not yet pressed for acknowledgment or separate place in the international theater as a Dominion.

The Colonies are variously organized under the Colonial Office. Almost all have some measures of self-government and legislative councils, assemblies or both which provide the foundations and frame of parliamentary systems, to be completed by the peoples as their political and social development requires. The British System presents a constant effort to find the forms of government most appropriate to local circumstances and the local pattern of social development.

A single arbitrary pattern of government is manifestly impossible for all the varieties of peoples, creeds, and cultures which compose the British System. A pattern preconceived and perhaps alien to all their habits and customs and beyond their understandings cannot be clapped down upon them. Humanity was not all designed to the model of the Sixth Ward, as Mr. Dooley unquestionably suspected. I do

[2] For specific variations in governmental structure in the Dominions and Colonies, see Appendix, Note I, page 389.

not know what a ballot-box might seem to some pleasant people I once met in Sumatra who lived high in the jungle trees and came to earth only on notable occasion.

The British have believed that only in experiment and by trial and error can be found the methods suited best to the various peoples. There must be constant recognition of local problems and prerogatives, prejudices, philosophies, interests, and customs; and a wide distribution of responsibilities.

The British have worked also in the understanding that time is necessary for political development. Peasants who have for uncounted centuries accepted without question their local autocrats as divine are not readily persuaded to prefer the parliamentary system. Only the more naïve or cynical among us would expect to find a good democrat in the happy matriarchist who sees an advancing crocodile as his great-aunt revisiting these glimpses of the moon and proffers her in decent family loyalty his favorite son.

Pre-war Malaya was a remarkable instance of British regard for local customs and susceptibilities and of a Fabian "inevitability of gradualness." The administration in Malaya has been caustically criticized for its failure to produce an effective military machine. Perhaps this should have been the prime purpose, but it would have required an authoritarian system which most of its critics would have equally abused as gross imperialism and blatant tyranny. But criticism comes now more from prejudices than from an industrious application to multifarious facts.

The facts of Malaya certainly were multifarious and so were the administrative schemes designed to meet them. The Malay was notoriously one of nature's gentlemen and little given to labor but much to hunting heads. If in good hunting weather he found himself out of enemies, he made them. Let me hasten to add that he was and is a likable and intelligent man apart from these idiosyncrasies, which are not, after all, unique in him. But they set prob-

lems for Sir Stamford Raffles and his officers and their successors. The British had to wean the Malays from their
excessive taste for blood-sports. They succeeded astonishingly. The atmosphere of the Malays' Malaya came to
suggest an English Sunday afternoon. I never in peace
saw a Civil Servant armed with more than a walking-stick
as he went his rounds even in remote jungle villages. If an
administrative method is designed to reduce head-hunters
to peaceful citizens and if this is its chief preoccupation for
a hundred years, it cannot reasonably be expected suddenly
to evoke armies organized for modern war. The handfuls of
officials [3] in any case were not warlike sorts of men. They
were often plump and sometimes scholarly. They were experts in Chinese or native laws and customs, irrigation
engineers or doctors. They included, as I remember, several
poets *manqués*.

The Malay likes to sit in the sun and to hire out his land
to a Chinese or Indian. Chinese have been in Malaya immemorially, but the opportunities created by the British
drew them in new floods until they threatened to swamp
the Malays. The British had, therefore, to develop a political
structure which would sufficiently protect the Malays
against their own feckless habits. Otherwise their lands and
properties would long have gone to the shrewd Chinese
and the Indian money-lenders. Raffles defined in 1823 the
terms of reference.

"Let the principles of British Law be applied not only with
mildness, but with a patriarchal kindness and indulgent consid-
eration for the prejudices of each tribe as far as natural justice
will allow, but also with reference to their reasoning powers,
however weak, and that moral principle which, however often
disregarded, still exists in the consciences of all men.

[3] A notion prevails that the Orient gave fat livings to large hordes of
British Civil Servants: actually both the Malayan Civil Service and the
Indian Civil Service proper had only a few hundred Europeans each.

"Let all the native institutions, as far as regards religious ceremonies, marriage, and inheritances, be respected when they may not be inconsistent with justice and humanity and injurious to the peace and morals of society.

"Let all men be considered equal in the eye of the law."

* 3 *

India inevitably has been an Empire within an Empire. She now presents massive problems to a world grown very small. The fate of what may presently be 500,000,000 people must bear and weigh on the whole human fabric.

India cannot solve her problems alone. She will revert to the disorders of the pre-British era unless she finds support and aid in some new system of relations. Long before the British renunciation of power in 1947 it was evident that the nationalistic temper might force the British out but that it had in it no real principle of unity. Order seldom is the child of agitation.

Its area is half that of the United States. Its population increased by 50 millions to 388,997,955 between the census of 1931 and that of 1941. British India (after the separation of Burma) was only about 57 per cent of the whole area; the rest was divided among 562 Native States [4] with about 25 per cent of the population.

The peoples speak over 200 recognized vernaculars of 47 principal languages. They are divided into about 2,400 castes. Racially, they are far more diverse than Europeans. Their two great religions are in fundamental conflict.[5]

The literates are 12.5 per cent (the figure almost doubled between 1931 and 1941) although over 15,600,000 were at schools and colleges in late years. The Central Government's revenues in 1940 were less than $1.50 by head of

[4] Few are older than the British Raj. They mostly grew among the ruins of the Mogul Empire. The youngest of them was formed in 1910.

[5] Hindus are 65.5 per cent, Moslems 24.3, Christians 1.6, Sikhs 1.5, Buddhists .06, Parsees .03.

population: a figure which cramps the style of public expenditure, but which cannot be much increased when seven-eighths of the population are immediately dependent on the land for their subsistence and have practically no surplus income.

Government in India has been paternalistic. It has had to provide not only for security on the frontiers and internal order but for railways, irrigation, and public works on a gigantic scale. India has the fourth railroad mileage of the world (twice Great Britain's) and its areas irrigated by public works exceed those of the United States. Only Government could have provided in India the transport and irrigation essential against famine and necessary to meet the tremendous pressure of populations expanding in the security the British brought.[6]

From the Battle of Plassey in 1757 the East India Company was the paramount power in India until 1858. But Government in India was set the most complex and difficult of administration problems, and the Company could not carry the constantly increasing burden.

The Crown assumed after the Mutiny sovereignty over British India and suzerainty over the Indian States. Within three years, the Crown began to devolve responsibilities. Provincial Councils were restored or authorized with rights of local legislation and new High Courts were established. In 1877, the Queen assumed the title of Empress of India and thus established a distinction which was designed among other purposes to encourage a sense of Indian national unity. During the eighties, broad measures of local

[6] In India, as in Indonesia, populations grew grotesquely under European regimes which suppressed internecine wars and slavery, and gave some measures of hygiene and economic stability. British India's population grew by 135,000,000 in the 60 years to 1941; Java's five times over between 1860 and 1930. With population constantly pressing on subsistence, it has been extraordinarily difficult to create reserves or margins of capital and income sufficient to pay for the constantly expanding needs of Public Works and Social Services.

government were introduced in district boards and municipal councils.

The British prefer to encourage democratic growth from the grassroots. In occupied Germany in 1945-6 they restored local government to the Germans before they gave them provincial and zonal government. They believe that men learn the responsibilities of government first and best in the affairs of their own township, parish, or district where almost every family has immediate and active interests. Lord Ripon as Viceroy (1880-84) worked for elected representation wherever he properly could in Indian local government: [7] "not primarily," he somewhat ruefully said, "with a view to improvements in administration" but "as a measure of political and popular education."

The Indian States with their hereditary leaders have had varying degrees of autonomy. Their relations with the Crown were established by treaties. They could not make war. They maintained no relations with foreign powers. They accepted direction in some matters common to all India: e.g., posts and telegraphs and customs. The Crown reserved the right to intervene against gross misgovernment. But the inhabitants of these States, although British-protected persons, were not British subjects and the laws of British India and its judicial system did not cross their frontiers; they maintained in many cases their own armed forces. The measure of intervention varied according to treaties and circumstances. Some of the States are little more than village areas, whereas Hyderabad and Kashmir are almost as large as the United Kingdom. Eighty-eight Princes have salutes of 11 guns or more: the guns allowed being as convenient a method as any for classifying this heterogeneous collection. Many Princes are descended from generals of the old Empires. Some States (as those of the

[7] For the development of local government in India, see Appendix, Note II, page 391.

pre-Mogul Rajputana dynasties) resemble feudal monarchies. Some are, but for the British suzerainty, absolutist. Some are governed by associations of local head-men whose chieftainships have been by family custom again and again divided in successive generations. Many of the States have already introduced constitutional reforms: for example, Baroda and Hyderabad have Executive and Legislative Councils, the latter partly elected; Gwalior has part-elected Upper and Lower Houses; Mysore, a Legislative Council and Representative Assembly.

Since 1921, the more considerable States meet in the Chamber of Princes to consult on matters of common or Imperial relevance.

The Act of 1935 offered India the structure of one national State, self-governing, responsible. It was the culmination of the careful advances by which administration had been broadened down and representative, responsible government achieved. It seemed to promise to India as a great Dominion in the British Commonwealth a sufficient frame of external relations to preserve the unity which the British had brought her. But as soon as it was seen that the British seriously meant to withdraw their legions the ancient disintegrative forces came again into violent play: the traditional divisions reappeared and widened rapidly. The work of unification had not been completed. It had been maintained by the British. It evidently could not survive their reign. The Mountbatten Plan of June 1947 did promise to prevent a general disintegration. It was perhaps Britain's last great contribution to the Indian polity.

If British authority had continued in India it (by pressure and persuasion and by the assurances it alone could have given) might have brought Princes and Moslems into a Federal Union. But they would not be won for a State dominated by those articulate Hindus who had shaped the Congress Party.

As India becomes less a British problem and responsibility, it becomes more and more a world-problem of tremendous implications. Those in India and beyond who have worked and agitated to bustle the British out have cut a pretty rod for the world's back. In the long run, perhaps, only the British will have much to be grateful for in their removal.

FOUR

MOTIVES OF EMPIRE

THE tremendous adventure of Empire brought large benefits and profits to Britain. Its cost was also large and less calculable. The millworkers, the miners, the dockers did not grow fat on the proceeds of Empire and it was disastrous to British agriculture. By the end of World War II an accountant might have argued that her great role in the world had at the end impoverished Britain. But figures in ledgers are not the final symbols. Greatness appears in other tallies; and the last balance is not struck. Experience, knowledge, flair, energy are formidable assets. So proverbially is necessity. British industry and intelligence will be quickened by its spur. For Britain, her present difficulties should be a useful bracer. For the outside world, however, they set startling problems, as yet hardly understood.

Great Britain now must conserve and concentrate her resources. She must apply a wise economy to her disposi-

tions of capital and energy. She must give more attention
to the conditions in which her own masses work and live.
She needs now for her immediate problems resources of men
and money which once went to the outer world. She can
take less responsibility for the world economy. She can afford less capital for investment in the backward regions.

Yet human and material resources must still be applied to
vast areas and populations if they are not to revert to the
old evils. Most of Asia and Africa is still desperately in need
of technicians, teachers, commerce, capital. Many peoples
have, of course, passed out of the period of tutelage and
may now stand firmly enough on their own feet. But provision must be made for order and aid in regions politically,
socially, or economically backward.

The British System, with all its deficiencies and failures,
has been creative in the social and economic life of the
regions where it has worked, whether inside or beyond its
political frontiers. The British in their fashion understand
what it is to be a World Power. A nation does not become
a World Power merely because it is materially powerful,
nor does it grow great in contemplation of its potential. It
must trade its talents. It must use its resources shrewdly. It
will inevitably and naturally seek to use them to its own
benefit. But it will not use them wantonly or in blind selfish-
ness. It will take long views and sometimes defer immediate
gains for remoter benefits. It will apply its contributions
widely. Englishmen and English money have for generations been active from Cape Horn to the Caspian and from
Cape Verde to Shanghai. They have hunted the main chance,
but they have leavened the loaf. A World Power is one
which in the whole count raises the general life of mankind
and extends the reign of law.

The British have still a part to play. But others must contribute if that measure of order which was brought out of
chaos is to be held. World Powers must labor to sustain the

structure of the world economy. They must be ready to support and repair it where faults and strains appear. Empire was a rough but ready method of applying national power to the larger problems. If we abhor and reject it, we must find a substitute. The old colonial systems may seem ramshackle affairs. Their subjects may take some pleasure in bringing them down on their own heads. But they are making for themselves a housing problem.

The United Nations will not in its present shape and circumstance meet the case. How will the United Nations aid India to train and support the 3,000,000 teachers India needs if she is to continue in the courses (the dubious courses, perhaps) of the modern world? Where in the policies and personnel of the United Nations is provision for the thousands of administrators, experts, and entrepreneurs needed still in backward regions? [1] The trusteeship principle caters for some. But what of areas emancipated from colonialism? What of autonomous but backward States? Consider the jobs which British agents and officials did in Persia.[2] Will the United Nations Organization take up their tasks? And if it does, on what principles and policies will it proceed; and with what resources?

Backward peoples must have aid and solace if they are not to remain hagridden by poverty and fear. If *imperium* will no longer serve or suit, we need a new model. This was the thesis which Ernest Bevin tried to hammer home at the first session of the United Nations Assembly. The United Nations did make some gesture of recognition with the

[1] The British Colonial Service appointed in the eighteen months after recruiting was resumed in 1945 2,800 officers to 33 territories. They included administrative officers and specialists in education, medicine, dentistry, nutrition, agriculture, forestry, fisheries, engineering, mining, geology, survey, architecture, town planning. Approximately half were University graduates.

[2] Sir Arnold Wilson's remarkable books are an excellent mirror: for example, S. W. *Persia: Letters and Diary of a Young Political Officer 1907-1914.*

Economic and Social Council. The Economic and Social Council was perhaps the seed of a world parliament for social and economic issues. But the seed has fallen on stony ground or was tangled in political thickets. Yet if we could sufficiently detach the great social and economic issues from mere politics we might be shaping a world community while politicians argue. But the Great State and the political interest have so obsessed men's minds that few now can conceive social or economic authorities autonomous except for the general provision (which is the affair of the State and politics) that they be ordered for the general good. Mr. Wells and Mr. Shaw both made argument for social and economic parliaments but they too fell into the confusion of their Socialist politics: and no National State has attempted what was vaguely envisioned for the world at large in the Economic and Social Council. Yet somewhere hereabouts is part of the answer.

* 2 *

In the modern debate, the defense of Imperialism and Colonialism has often been allowed to go by default. The Colonial Powers have piped a low tune; but in their experience we can best grasp great problems of world order and community. The first is always to extend the reign of law.

But the reign of law must not only suppress evils. It must labor in good deeds. The house swept and garnished cannot be left empty. For instance, the abolition of slavery brought new and tremendous difficulties. Almost all Africa was riddled and rotten with slavery. The Elizabethan seamen and their successors who entered the trade engaged in what was already the world's largest commerce: and they were small beer in it. It was everywhere present in the non-Christian world except among a few aborigines. As European sails filled to the strange wind of the 15th, 16th and

17th centuries, they came to worlds old and new; and even to the farthest islands of the Asian archipelagos they met economic systems resting on the slave. The slave was transport, the slave was currency, the slave was the medium of taxation. Through much of the East the effects of slavery were reinforced by rigid caste.[3]

Slavery kept Africa in constant war and poverty. The Arabs raided through the continent for slaves. They were the staple of the Moslem economies in the north. The tribes raided one another for the wherewithal of traffic with the Arab merchants. As the British pressed on into Africa in the mid-19th century they found whole regions utterly wasted by the traffic and its terrors.

Cameron in 1877 saw fifty-two women in chains. To take them, the slavers had destroyed ten villages and fifteen hundred people. Cardinal Lavigerie believed that not more than one-third and often only one-tenth of slaves seized in the interior survived to reach the marts. When the British first took active interest at Zanzibar in the 1850s, two-thirds of the people thereabouts were slaves. Temple speaks of zones a hundred miles wide in Nigeria utterly wasted and emptied of human life: villages and walled cities in decay.[4] Africa in war and slavery was seventy years ago "bleeding out her life-blood at every pore."

Even into the 20th century armies of ten and fifteen thousand slave-hunters yearly laid waste large tracts of West Africa.

In India, where fifty slaves in the 18th century fetched the price of one good horse, Warren Hastings and the East

[3] The European traders usually bought peoples already enslaved. The worst horrors of the traffic were in the original chase and capture. Shipmasters, merchants, and slave-owners were not usually reckless of slaves bought at considerable expense. Thousands of slaves died in the Middle Passage from scurvy and ship-typhus: so did thousands of European seamen.

[4] For an assembly of authorities, see L. C. A. Knowles' remarkable book *The Economic Development of the British Overseas Empire:* Routledge, London.

India Company blocked the export of slaves and stopped where they could the internal traffic.

In 1807, the British prohibited any part in the traffic to their own ships and people. The status of slavery was finally abolished in all British colonies in 1834. In 1820, Britain paid Spain £400,000 and Portugal £300,000 to join in suppressing the traffic. For fifty years at heavy aggregate cost in men and money, the Royal Navy's chief occupation was a world-wide campaign against piracy and slavers. We forget too readily that the peace on the seas in which modern commerce grew has been a brief passage and hard won: and we have seen since the end of the Pacific War that both piracy and the slave-traffic could quickly reappear if the Western Navies ceased their constant police-patrols.

Madagascar was a tremendous *entrepôt* of the slave-traffic until the French moved in between 1883 and 1896. When the British occupied Uganda and Nyasaland and Kitchener marched into the Sudan in the 1890s, they cut at three corners a vast triangle of the trade and sliced its major routes in Africa.

As with slavery, so with internecine war. War, massacre, pillage were endemic from the Gold Coast to Timor until the European appeared. The merchants and agents who went to India in the 17th century report peoples brought by tyranny to the final depths of misery. Whole provinces were reduced to deserts. The terrorized peasants hardly dared to cultivate their fields. What the local tyrant left was swallowed by repeated invasions. Within twenty-three years of the 18th century, the Afghans made five major invasions and a Persian army swept the Punjab and destroyed Delhi. Freebooting companies of Mahrattas plundered and slaughtered through the country. The Sikhs even to the mid-19th century were raiding harvests every year, burning and killing. Raids from the Hills were constant: rich lands for fifteen hundred miles along the borders were derelict and deserted save for prowling tigers and hillsmen hunting towards the plains.

Before the British began to rule, Indian politics were, in Sir A. Lyall's words, "a mere tearing and rending of the prostrate carcass, a free fight with little definite aim or purpose beyond plunder and annexation of land revenue." [5]

With slavery and war, superstitions lay like miasmas on the mind and spirit to produce a dreadful apathy.

Disease and deprivation brought a corresponding physical lassitude and rot. Ross estimated that in a normal year 1,300,000 Indians died of malaria before its cause was discovered, and tens of millions were debilitated. His reports suggested that over half the children under five in Africa already had the enlarged spleens of malaria.

Plague swept off millions in Asia and Africa almost every year. The physical, moral, and mental lassitude opened the way to other evils. Drought was one cause only of recurrent famines: fecklessness and the failure to provide roads and transport were others.

The backwardness of the black and brown peoples was not an inescapable character of race. It was of the malaria in their blood, the hookworm in their stomach-walls, the sleeping sickness. It came from the superstitions which corrupted the life of the mind, and left (as the blood-sucking insects and the cutting hookworm left in the body) vile sores into which other evils entered to fester and enlarge.

European man has lost belief in his works. He despoils and ravages his own civilization and corrupts it with dreary doubts and cynicisms. Yet in a century he transformed the life of Asia and Africa: much for evil (as his own publicists now insist), but much for good, as the history of tropical medicine sufficiently shows.

The Colonial Powers at first believed that natural man

<hr />

[5] Quoted by Knowles, *op. cit.*

once freed from the worst evils which lay on him would respond and take on the habit of civilization. It was a delusion from the 18th century Rationalists and the French Revolution which still hung about the notions of belated men like Mr. Wells and Mr. Shaw. A little experience in the Colonial Administrations would have instructed both.

Economies collapsed for lack of labor.[6] Freed slaves sat in the sun or gathered in idle or mischievous groups. The accustomed frame of their life was gone. Government had to reorganize their lives. It had to find them land and train them to cultivate it and themselves. It had to form somehow in them skill and ambition enough for their own necessities. It had to induce some responsible sense of law and order to replace the discipline of knout and knife. Freedom could be proclaimed from Exeter Hall or William Lloyd Garrison's *Liberator*. But the moral reconstruction of the emancipated slave was work for the men on the spot: the missionaries and the administrators, now both much blasted in the mouths of ignorance.

In 1902, slaving armies were still out in West Africa. A few years later, a British Commissioner traveled where he had extended law and found one case of robbery in a thousand miles. Slaves in India and Africa often could not be persuaded even to claim their freedom until the administrators came to pay wages for work on roads and railways. The establishment of a wage-fund was in fact a practical necessity if slavery was to go. For it the imperialist exploiter made the provision. In Malaya, the British were still battling with slavery (debt-slavery especially) into the 20th century. They made its abolition a condition of the protection extended to the Malay States. But abolition always brought the need for social and economic measures

[6] The British West Indies were a notable case: while Cuba and Brazil with slave-labor took their sugar trade, the B.W.I. went into a decline from which they have not recovered.

to replace the system broken and to re-employ the emancipated.

The British Empire in Africa and Asia grew mostly from
chartered companies designed originally for trade. But trade
requires some stability. You may plunder chaos but you
cannot sustain a ·steady commerce with it. The merchant
must cultivate his prospect as well as reap it, if he wants
to stay in business. The Companies were compelled to deal
in local politics. They lent support to those who could give
order and they began themselves to impose order. They
were more and more drawn in and on. Empire came to
them as one damn thing after another, so to speak: until
at last the weight of political and human responsibilities
was too much for any private association and the Crown
had to lift loads which could hardly have been dropped
without disaster.

First, the problem was order. Then it was marketable
products to produce a money economy for trade, taxes,
and services. Then it was communications, and then education, health and all the matters which have become themes
for government.

The British expansion was always on the skeleton of
communications. The British sought less than the French
for vast territorial gains, especially after the loss of the
American Colonies. They looked for ports and markets and
coaling-bases: Singapore, the Cape, Colombo, Gibraltar,
Malta. Their System rested on the sea-routes. As they were
drawn into the hinterlands of Africa and Asia, they still
thought always in terms of communications. Like the Romans, they made roads. They made roads (in the old tag)
as the Germans built barracks and the French opened *cafés*.
Among the matters which we forget too readily in all this
is that the road makers have been rare among the peoples
of mankind. Roads, like the Roman law, were a heritage
mostly to the Western peoples. Man elsewhere has moved

more by the waterways or horse and camel, and found his
way less by settled paths than by remembered landmarks
and stars.

Except with Europeans, the traders and the travelers have
not been many even among the sea-peoples. The great migrations of whole tribes or nations have been rare in historic
times and usually under extreme pressure of hunger or of
hungry hordes behind. Since men learnt to break ground for
seed, they have mostly clung while the soil held to their
patch of native earth and moved but a few versts or paals
in all the days of their lives.

The Japanese were a fisher-people, but they threw no lines
of empire beyond their narrow seas. They made nothing of
America or the rich islands southward, if they had news of
them. For the Chinese, China was the heart of the world,
the Middle Kingdom. Men leaving China left their souls
behind and continued only in the living death of the outer
darkness. From India Buddhist missionaries and Brahmin
merchants spread empire of a sort east and south; and the
Moslem message ran (but more as the motion of a wave
through water than as a movement of mass) from Arabia
to Java and Seville and from Cancer to Capricorn. The
Polynesians went on their prodigious passages of the Pacific.
But none of these put empire out as did the Europeans to
open and people whole continents and set the seal of their
law and custom and commerce on the world.

Roads have been an element of the European mystery, of
that in Western man which moved him in pilgrimage to distant shrines and schools. It marshaled him to the Crusades,[7]
and sent him to seek gold and silver, spices, silks, and souls

[7] The Crusades ended not in Holy Land but when the Portuguese turned
Good Hope and went up by Africa and Asia to slash at flank and rear the
long routes of trade which fed the Moslem Power. For eight hundred years
the Christian had hammered at the front of Islam and failed to break it.
In one generation the Portuguese brought it down by cutting in the Red
Sea and Persian Gulf, in India and Malaya, its main artery and the sinews
of its traffic.

in the lands of Prester John and the Great Khan, in Cathay and Cipango, Calicut and the Americas. The European had adventure in him. There was Alexander, from whom half the dynasties of Asia still claim descent. There were the Romans, powerfully ambitious to extend the Roman law and Roman roads. There was the Christian mission to teach all nations. At the very fount of the Christian tradition and remembered at the Christmas Crib, in carols, stones, stained-glass and sermons were the glowing figures of the Magi working, like their own magic, in men's dreams of other worlds whose symbols were gold, frankincense, and myrrh.

The combination of adventure and order, of law and liberty set Western men to making roads.

They were drawn over the hills and far away; but they paved the routes and set up the signs. The British pre-eminently among Europeans had this synthesis of poetry and pragmatism. They built roads with a kind of dogged passion. Then they built railways. They opened to trade regions inaccessible through all history; and down their long avenues could blow the winds of change. The roads are at once a sign of advancing order and a course for freedom. Roads like arteries feed the whole social body. Swettenham, the great administrator of Malaya and its historian, recalls that even a bridle road "was no sooner completed than small houses, plantations, and fruit and vegetable gardens sprang up along its whole length." In the United States, Australia, Canada, population grew along the advancing railroads like a vine along a stick. At halts by the routes people clustered to form new growing points. China had in 1940 about 8,000 miles of railroads, India 41,000. There at once is a great argument of empire.

Work on roads and railways induces in idle or apathetic peoples habits of industry. They discover new commodities and tastes, learn the tricks of money, labor to acquire it. The process is often ugly and carries with it many of our

Western evils. But it brings to the primitive a larger, if not always a better, life: and the jungle villages, the kampongs by the muddy rivers, the long-houses reeking in the palms, the verminous, malarial, and leprous life of countless communities needed to be opened to the sun and wind.

* 3 *

The major regions of colonial exploitation were mostly very poor when the European came to them. Commerce has not been a matter of exchange only. It has been creative. It has prompted the production of goods for exchange. When the European went first to the fabulous East he most sought spices to flavor his dull winter diet.[8] He had little to barter for them. The blue cloth of Porlock in Somerset became a useful trade in Oriental courts; but when da Gama opened the first door in the East to our seaborne trade he had nothing more to offer the Zamorin at Pandarana than a box of sugar, a pot of honey, two barrels of oil, and six Lisbon hats.

The Eastern potentates desired gold, silver, tin, ivory, copper, and the like. The Europeans bought ivory in Africa with Eastern cotton goods and paid for their spices with coral from the Persian Gulf and silver from the sale of slaves in the Americas. The demand for exportable manufactures stimulated the British textile industries; and as these grew they came to need imported raw materials. Merchants began to plan their trade ahead and to promote production. Factors were left in the East by the Companies between the voyages. They established gardens for the fresh food needed by themselves and the ships. They extended the gardens to plantations. Presently the crops of commerce were grown there and encouraged in the country round about.

[8] The green eyes of little yellow gods were, of course, hard to come by: spices, cotton cloth, indigo, saltpeter, and later tea, coffee, cocoa were more significant staples of trade.

Thus the Dutch East India Company, whose motto was *Plow the Seas,* began to cultivate the land; and the plantations of sugar, tea, camphor, and coffee to climb the hills of Java. The factory with its stone walls, its guns, its markets, its shrewd hard men of business inevitably acquired influence and power in the lands about it. Warring chieftains and rival princes competed for the factor's aid by treaties guaranteeing delivery of pepper, rice, cotton yarn, or indigo extorted from their peasantry. If war or disorders threatened these supplies (for which the factor came to budget) he was strongly tempted to apply pressure. Local politics as much as local climate became a constant item in his calculations. As trade increased and the cultivation of his market-crops extended so did his political interest and his need for communications adequate to the traffic. The thing grew by what it fed upon.

In the 19th century the whole process was accelerated by the Industrial Revolution with its vast range of new manufactures and its insatiable demand for raw materials to feed the maws of the expensive new machinery whose every idle moment was dead loss to the capitalist.

Cotton opened Central Africa and changed the agronomy of Central India and Egypt and the Southern States. The dry throats of the industrial workers crowding into factories where the air was filled with fluff made tea a great Indian crop.[9] The sensibilities of missionaries and man's native taste for novelties put millions hitherto unwrapped into shirtings and made fortunes for Australia's shepherds; and "squatter" became there a synonym for wealth and power. Jute was first spun in Scotland in the 1830s, and the demand for sacking in the Crimean and American Civil Wars set India growing jute presently worth to her millions a year. Canned food first came into large demand for the

[9] It was brought from China and first planted in India in 1835, in Ceylon forty years later.

armies of the Union in the War between the States. The
tin-coated cans were treated with coconut oil; and copra
began to make its way also into soap and presently lipstick
and gasmasks, oil-cake and margarine.

Scientific planning began. Rubber seeds went out from
Kew to all Britain's tropical colonies in 1876. Agricultural
Departments with their research scientists and teachers
appeared. Joseph Chamberlain opened the London School
of Tropical Medicine in 1899. Health had become an essential condition of developing economies. Little could be done
in the tropics while a white man who took appointment
there gambled desperately with death. One of the marvels
of the imperial story is that men should have taken its
risks and endured its tediums. Consider the boredom of an
18th-century Dutchman living twenty years at Koepang in
a constant greasy sweat. He was an old, yellow, aguey man
at forty if he so long survived (few did) the fevers, malnu-
trition, and the Timorese. The pay was poor and the
plunder has been vastly exaggerated. Some "nabobs" of
both the East India Companies made fortunes in the Companies' happier days; but the expenses of government left
little in the till of either the Dutch or the English Company
at the end, and through their history the factor or official
in the East seldom made much from it all.

West Africa was until the other day "the white man's
grave." An official appointed to the Gold Coast or Sierra
Leone was thought spendthrift if he took a return ticket.

Clearly too the tropical colonies would not operate while
the labor-force was riddled with hookworm or malaria. Even
those who see in the imperial effort only gross exploitation
of the colonial areas and peoples may at least admit that
the exploiters dealt with the tsetse fly. Theodore Roosevelt's
deal for the Panama Canal Zone clearly was a flagrant piece
of power and dollar politics. But in the balance of history
we may think humanity gained there more than it lost, for

the chance given to General Gorgas. Gorgas and Ross were both servants of imperial order. Uncounted millions owe their lives to them.[10]

The new colonial economies called also for bookkeepers, cashiers, tally-clerks, accountants, stenographers; the foremen, engine-drivers, policemen had to read instructions and fill in reports. The three R's had to be provided.

Tradesmen and craftsmen were needed; and technical education became an urgent concern of colonial administrations.

Macaulay in the 1830s advanced a scheme of education for India. Its bias was perhaps excessively literary. It produced a host of white-collar people, too many for the jobs available. While the Company and the Crown had use for many clerks they could not employ all these. Those denied the careers which they felt their educators owed them turned to bitter cliques and hostile claques. India needed fewer Babus and more doctors, engineers, agricultural scientists, and skilled technicians. But these are more expensive to produce than ordinary or even honors Bachelors of Arts. Administrations had to borrow money or wait on expanding revenues to equip medical and engineering schools and technical colleges.

Schemes for universal and technical education require sufficient schools and teachers. The problem of finance is tremendous for a country of low average income. British India had nearly 220,000 [11] educational institutions in 1945, including 15 universities, 455 arts, science and professional colleges, 176,000 primary schools: but over 80 per cent of Indians were still illiterate.

[10] But for them the Pacific War might have cost ten times the human toll it took.

[11] Against 226,000 in the U.S.A. (193,400 primary schools) and about 180,000 in pre-war Russia. These figures are offered not in comparison of school standards or populations, but only to suggest that India's education has not been wholly neglected and to indicate the problem's immensity.

A World Power must be prepared for more than pump-priming. It must lay out enormous sums. For a century or more Great Britain was banker to most of Asia, Africa, and the New Worlds. The profits ultimately were great. So were the losses. Money has lost value through the period of financial empire. Ventures have failed. Loans and investments have been repudiated.[12] But however little sympathy the misfortunes of a banker earn, we may still recognize that the whole course of development in Asia, Africa, the Americas and Australia would have been inestimably delayed if Britain had not found the cash. British money went into the railways, ports and public works of the larger part of the world. In 1934 (when her proportion of the world's investment had, of course, much declined as other Powers engaged in it) Britain had out in loan to Dominion and Colonial Governments much over £1,000,000,000. Foreign Governments had perhaps £400,000,000. British companies abroad had £1,200,000,000. Foreign and Dominions companies had nearly £700,000,000 of British capital. To visible investments must be added the other charges of Empire: the costs of defense [13] and of diplomatic, consular, commercial and social services and of expert advice and administration rendered by Britain free. For items of this sort Hitler charged occupied territories such as Czechoslovakia what he called "incorporation dues."

Britain's investment in the United States was colossal: two World Wars were needed to liquidate it. Americans who know the methods of capitalism should understand, if others do not, the part which Britain played in their material expansion.

The range of investment indicates how far and formidably the British System spread beyond its political frontiers.

---

[12] Notably after World War I.

[13] The United Kingdom has always borne in total and per capita by far the heaviest burdens in defense of the imperial system.

British capital was sown into railways, factories, harbor-works, roads, plantations from China to Peru.[14] Everyone who wanted money for major enterprises went to London for it in the 19th century. The great Colonies usually had it cheaper than anyone else. Membership in what was still called the Empire saved millions a year in interest to Colonies borrowing for development. The bankers had per-haps some sense of policy in offering lower rates within the Empire; and perhaps they agreed with the widows in Brighton and Balham who preferred to trust their savings to the Empire family. The judgment has been sound. There have been no gross defaults within the Empire or Common-wealth. But the British may whistle for much of the money owed them elsewhere.[15]

Britain came out of World War II with an adverse bal-ance of £6,000,000,000.

The great part of the Commonwealth and Empire is now self-supporting. But the progress of its quarter of the world and much beyond it was largely due to steady irrigation from the reservoir of British capital.

The British masses benefited when interest and capital repayments appeared as eggs and butter on the breakfast table, as material for British mills or cargoes for British ships. But the vast sums which sank through foreign sands might have wiped out the slums of British cities and en-larged and enlightened the lives of British workers. The British garden was far from lovely: the kitchen garden was left derelict as cheap food flowed from abroad. But the manure of British capital was spread in Malaya, Ar-

[14] For example, Argentina in 1945 still had £252,000,000 of British money in her railroads alone (half of it was in default).

[15] Russia's debt (repudiated in 1918) would by 1941 have amounted to over £1,600,000,000. Britain is owed much more than she owes abroad in the ways of both public loans and private investment. France in 1945 owed Britain in war debt £756,000,000. Italy owed £253,000,000 before the war. Private British investors have, of course, lost colossal sums in many countries.

gentina, South Australia, the Valleys of the Nile and Niger; and prairie states and provinces expanded to provide the British loaf.

Brown men and black men and yellow men began to use oil lamps. Bicycles appeared in the villages and top hats on the chiefs. The peasant began to eat more food, smoke more tobacco. Canned salmon and jams, umbrellas, brooms, brass pots, birdcages, Oat Flakes, collar-studs, and portraits of Deanna Durbin in the course of time reached the native markets. The motor-bus became the familiar excitement of millions. The village clinic appeared and district hospitals and trained midwives and *mantris*. The living standards, though they may seem low to Western eyes, throughout the colonial areas have risen more in two generations than in all history before. The worst evils of usury, which had ground the Asiatic peasant from antiquity, were countered by government advances, by rural and rice banks. He was given new security of tenure in his land. Countrysides long waste were brought back into production.[16] The enormous growth of populations in Asia was an effect in part at least of imperial order. If life and life abounding is evidence, something may still be said for the imperial systems.

* 4 *

With all said against the imperial systems they at least imposed a measure of unity and community. We may believe (if we carry ideological predilections to the top of our bent) that the peoples emancipated in 1919 from the Austro-Hungarian Empire have since grown in wisdom, tolerance, prosperity and freedom; but we can hardly say that they have grown in community.

[16] In the 18th century the Indian ryot yielded half of his gross production to local tyrants large and small, and to his "taxes" was added forced labor-service. Half of the fertile lands of India had been abandoned and left waste when the British moved in.

The British System has offered peoples development towards autonomy and freedom within a general unity. It has been an extraordinary experiment in political method and human behavior. If it is now to decline, its own peoples and politicians are much to blame. They did not clearly see the thing which had appeared under their hands; and they latterly lost confidence in their effort. The men of the 19th century developed a strange conceit of themselves. In that rapidly expanding world, loud with the triumphs of scientific method and its applications, they suddenly saw themselves as like gods. They rejected the traditional faiths and the accumulated experience of countless generations. They swore to a new religion. They called it Progress. It has had the briefest life of all the great heresies.

It was long corrupt in 1939. But it was still poisoning the air. Its infection even now produces strange delusions. Men who have lived through two world wars and grown beyond skepticism to cynicism and despair can still hunt mirages. Their skepticism and cynicism reject the substantial achievements of their kind because these, like all men's works, reveal inadequacies and errors. They reject the realities but they clutch at illusions: the belief that political machinery of itself can answer human problems is typical. We are in search of philosophers' stones and panaceas. When abracadabra fails, we plunge into new depths of cynicism and despair.

There is one way only of human progress. It comes in moral effort, in the long, stubborn struggle towards ends perceived but never wholly realized.

We have been seduced by images of an Earthly Paradise. Men deprived of hope and faith in a Providence beyond themselves succumb, because all men have in their hearts a strange yearning for other worlds than this of their daily habitation. But the Earthly Paradise is constantly defeated by the World, the Flesh, and the Devil, its ancient enemies.

Men with no hopes beyond themselves are soured. Their cynicism is as false to the human facts as their escapist dreams.

The politician has no prescription by which our world can be born again even in the blood and fire of revolution. It remains a place of labor, pain, swift joys, adventures, heroism, love, death. The stuff of society, the material of politics is still the old Adam, dark of understanding, weak of will, but capable also of greatness beyond his own dream and devising.

He is the reality to which we must return in our political thinking and judgment. We must shake off the mood of illusion in which every bush becomes a bear and handsaws are seen as hawks however the wind blows.

The great merit of the British System is that it has on the whole dealt with people as realities: not with Economic Man or with Political Man, but with John and Ahmad, Wang and Pierre. It has taken man for what he is, a fool, a saint, a coward, a being of passionate loyalties and fantastic prejudices, a clamorous belly, a lusting thing, a creature of such parts that at his end he does perhaps seek and find pardon between the saddle and the ground.

The British System adapts itself sooner or later to human needs and conditions: which is why it has little of uniformity and few blue-prints. It works in the medium of experience. The world is turning away from the methods of the British System because it is turning away from the principles of growth to a harsh mechanical interpretation of man and his societies. But men will not perform like machines. They will not run smoothly or with the precise and calculable power of pistons. We suffer from the perfectionist delusion and the mechanical delusion. Men lost in these abstractions mistake the nature of their kind because they mistake themselves and are blind to their own stupidities and sins.

These seek for mechanical perfection in society: and when they do not find in their fellows what is not in themselves they turn in despair or rage or blind pride to the instruments of oppression. They would shorten mankind by a head to fit their formulae.

Even in India and Africa, the British System was not a rigorous frame, an authoritarian vise. It now normally provides from its founts of authority only discipline enough for local order. When this prevails its people are encouraged to take responsibility for their own administrations and in an enlarging liberty. Liberty is slowly broadened down from precedent to precedent: too slowly perhaps for the eager and the cynics. But the System goes at the tempo of all great institutions which have endured many generations of men. The innocent young and the revolutionary want all refashioned to their prescriptions while the swallow is in flight across the room. But the British System has learnt that life is brief and all things subject to change, and that it is more difficult to preserve what should be preserved than to innovate and invent. The task of the present is but to be the nexus between what was and what will be: and seasoned experience knows that changes seldom fall as men expect and never precisely as they plan. The play of human affairs is too various for nice calculation. They flow from the different moods and beliefs and purposes of countless men each in action and interaction and counteraction with all his fellows in the vast complex of human life. "No man is an Island intire of its selfe" nor is any generation. We are caught up in all mankind from its beginnings.

The most subtle politics can only here and there command reality; the most rough and ready tyranny cannot canalize the whole life of man. Politicians who think to command that tide work, like most of us, perhaps, in a world largely of their own illusions.

The British System inclines to wait on the emerging

realities before it blueprints or plots them. It believes that
political systems should be made for men, not men for
political.systems: hence its curious variety of forms. It has
failed again and again and again and again. Its failures
have almost always followed some presumption, some effort
to force men beyond their gait and understanding. But
through blunders, changes, gains, and losses it has endured;
and the endurance in human institutions suggests sufficient
conformity to the nature of things.

Let us be clear about this because it bears on our larger
problems. The British System is not Machiavellian and not
intelligent. Systems never are intelligent. Men are intelligent. The more elaborate the system, the more it resists the
free play of intelligence. It develops machinery which will
not roll and cross-tangles of administrative relationships
which harden into hopeless knots.

The British Colonial System has most of the bureaucratic
features, but it does produce in a sound tradition a number
of highly skilled and devoted men who sometimes buck the
machine. More important, it sometimes leaves, though less
now than once it did, large measures of responsibility and
initiative to the man on the ground if he is prepared to take
them. The old Chartered Companies perhaps preferred it
so, for under criticism they could and often did repudiate
him. The work of the British Empire was never done or
even properly planned in London. It has been carved out
by handfuls of men scattered as lonely individuals across
the immensities: the merchants, factors, agents, the District
Commissioners and Assistant District Commissioners and
Deputy Assistant District Commissioners. They built the
roads and bridges, cleaned the towns and killed the tigers,
renewed the forests, taught hygiene, built dams, irrigated,
reformed agriculture, fought erosion, murrains, the tsetse
fly, suttee, slavery, and moral apathy, protected, policed,
established order, extended law. "There be of them, that

have left a name behind them; and some there be, which have no memorial." But they are part of the thing which we call empire and they should not be forgotten in its final account, or in its interim statements.

Empire is an expression of men in their historic needs. It has in it what we are, our virtues and our sins. It works at all levels of our life. It expresses our political purposes, our economic purposes, our moral purposes. There is an empire of the mind and spirit which works also for good and ill. Lugard, the great authority on Colonial Africa, insisted that there the pioneer work of missionaries and philanthropists like Livingstone and Moffat was the largest single factor in the development of the British possessions. They gave not only religious and moral instruction: they educated the natives in trades and crafts, in habits of health and industry. They pioneered and explored the strange lands and the minds and cultures among which they came.

Behind them runs the tide of Western ideas, turbid but strong. We put out this phase of empire in a thousand forms: in books, films, and all the curious merchandise which have worked on the minds and imaginations of other peoples to modify or melt away their traditional values and habits. We have confused, distracted, and demoralized. We have perverted consciences. The impact of the Western mind and morals has broken immemorial forms of thought and faith in countless peoples. It has brought them new beliefs, new thoughts, new superstitions. Empire has worked and woven endlessly new patterns of life and knowledge and social habit and economic interest. It has organized gradually with its flying shuttles cultures and races disjoined since Babel.

With all its evils it has brought some measure of organization into a divided and distracted world. It may be a poor thing, but we have yet to better it.

FIVE

THE FIRST EMPIRE

THE British System, let me repeat, belongs more to the nature of life than of mechanics. It persists through time and like an organism grows and changes, spreads and withers, and spreads again. Elements of all its pasts continue in its present. It is often mistaken for what it was. The popular mind in the United States still views it with suspicions and misgivings which have their prime occasion in the 18th century; which is much as if the British were now alarmed at the ambitions of President Polk or in protest at the behavior of Sam Houston.

The Empire of George III is as distant from the Commonwealth of autonomous Dominions as from the United States.

The British System is at one point or another in constant change. Phase merges into phase. But one may for convenience distinguish several major passages.

The Islands had considerable experience of empires before they set up in the imperial business themselves. Southern Britain was for four hundred years a province of Rome. Parts of Ireland, Scotland, and Eastern England were in desultory fashion subdued to a Scandinavian reign during the Viking centuries. The Norman Conquest brought England within a minor Empire of the West: and the image of it haunted English mind and policy until the Stuarts. The effort to shape an Atlantic Empire persisted from the Angevins to the Ulster Plantations. It faded only under a greater Atlantic theme, but not until it had knit the Islands themselves.

The medieval Empire and especially the adventures of Edward III and Henry V in France left their strong mark on the English. These were their first challenge to the large world. They had little hard profit of them, but they brought triumphs which still glow like a glory in the minds and imaginations of the race. At Crecy and Poitiers and Agincourt the English won their strong belief that on one pair of English legs did march three Frenchmen. Clive at Plassey recalled Agincourt: and St. Crispin's Day still stirs the English blood. Those wars with their scintillating chivalry and blazoned fields perhaps brought to the English their curious sense of history as high drama. No people has been as conscious of history. The ancients were indifferent to it. But to England, history has been a poem which sang in the blood; and what eloquence it has had:

> "This story shall the good man teach his son;
> And Crispin Crispian shall ne'er go by,
> From this day to the ending of the world,
> But we in it shall be remembered;
> We few, we happy few, we band of brothers. . . ."

and

> "Be copy now to men of grosser blood,
> And teach them how to war. And you, good yeomen,
> Whose limbs were made in England, show us here
> The mettle of your pasture. . . ."

At Crecy and Agincourt was the source of England's vaunt in the world. The English have been the least military and the most militant of peoples. And they have delighted in the whole great play.

The reserved and taciturn Englishman is a temporary aberration of the late and lower middle classes: the English clod is, in fact, a cunning fellow filled with humors. The bold, boastful, emotional Drake was as little like the stock or stage Englishman as Mr. de Valera is like the stage Irishman.

Empires are won by adventurers: merchant-adventurers and poets of action whose imaginations are caught by the mysteries of distant seas and the marvels of rumored kingdoms.

> "Tom, Tom, the piper's son,
> Learned to play when he was young,
> And the only tune that he could play
> Was: 'Over the hills and far away' . . ."

Even in their nursery-rhymes, the English were off to Banbury Cross or counting miles to Babylon, and their cows notoriously jumped over the moon.

But empires are consolidated and held by men of a strong corporate sense who believe in themselves and in the values of their community. The Portuguese and Spaniards like all Europeans of the seaboard had the quality of adventure, but they missed the tremendous self-assurance and sense of order of the English. Little Jack Horner was a compatriot of the piper's son, and Jack was never more English than when he picked out his plum to a note of self-commendation; for the English have always found great virtue in themselves.

At the entrance to English literature stand the great figures who still hold mirrors up to the English pageant: Malory, whose wonders seem matters of familiar fact; Chaucer, who looked down the common highways which

the English love to travel and saw them filled with humors
and marvels; and Langland, who peopled the English meads
and hills with moral images. They reflect what is essential
of England still.

The stern, censorial, and somewhat self-righteous theme
which Langland sounded twists and turns through English
history. It and the tightness of the island give the sense of
order. England was the first of modern nations to consolidate, in spite of the racial variety which Defoe in sourer
accents than Lord Tennyson's noted:

> "The *Romans* first with *Julius Caesar* came,
> Including all the Nations of that Name,
> *Gauls, Greeks,* and *Lombards;* and by Computation,
> Auxiliaries or Slaves of ev'ry Nation.
> With *Hengist, Saxons; Danes* with *Sueno* came,
> In search of Plunder, not in search of Fame.
> *Scots, Picts,* and *Irish* from th' *Hibernian* Shore:
> And Conqu'ring *William* brought the *Normans* o're.
> All these their Barb'rous Offspring left behind,
> The Dregs of Armies, they of all Mankind;
> Blended with *Britains* who before were here,
> Of whom the *Welsh* ha' blest the Character.
> From this Amphibious Ill-born Mob began
> *That vain ill-natur'd thing, an* Englishman."

However that may be, the sense of order gives a curious
equanimity to English proceedings. Chaucer and Langland
would both have understood the old lady (Alice, indeed,
through the Looking Glass) who set out to visit relatives on
the morning of September 3, 1939. The sirens suddenly
sounded in the first hour of war. She crossed to a policeman
and spoke: "Excuse me, officer, but have I time, do you
think, to reach Victoria before the devastation begins?"

The ambition for continental empire ended with the loss
of Calais. The English attempted no conquest on the European mainland after it (Gibraltar belongs to the oceanic

system). But from this first Empire remained the union with Wales and the way to union with the Scots. From it was the running trouble with Ireland, the wound which would not heal, the tragic flaw, which Burke, an Irishman, must have had in mind when he spoke of the American matter: "The use of force alone is but temporary. It may subdue for a moment; but it does not remove the necessity of subduing again: and a nation is not governed which is perpetually to be conquered."

Yet the Irish contribution to the British System must not be missed. Burke himself is its greatest expositor. As Shakespeare recalls there were Irish, Welsh, and Scots in the Army of Agincourt. The Irish in more than their proportion went to the peopling of the Empire overseas. Men of Ireland's breeding commanded at Waterloo and in North Africa. The Irish were a powerful element in the American Revolution and also in the making of the Dominions. Through the centuries of Britain's power in the world they have been inextricably involved, here contributing and there resisting, but always influencing the course and character of this strange history.

The obvious motives for the foundation of the American Colonies and the Merchant Companies were religious freedom, trade, and plantations. The Pilgrim Fathers may have conceived religious freedom chiefly as freedom for themselves. But Catholics went to Maryland and Quakers to Pennsylvania. There was often more than the desire to find room for the play of conscience. The more devout of those who went had a larger passion for a community of saints. They believed in the *Civitas Dei:* and perhaps the recurrent English romance of Utopia was in their heads.

Thomas More had powerfully moved the social conscience of his countrymen. More himself was no Utopian. As a saint he was too aware of sin to accept the perfectionist delusion. But his *Respublica* was packed with social criticisms and suggestions which still lie at the roots of English social thinking. The Utopian theme was to appear and reappear in the history of British colonization from Raleigh through the Pantisocrats to Lang's strange 19th-century experiment of a New Australia in Paraguay. It was to work in Godwin, Shelley and the young Coleridge, in a score of American prophets. It was a motive, however obscured, among other motives in more pragmatic men.

The Portuguese and Spaniards sought for silver, spices, souls. "We come to seek Christian souls and spice," said Vasco da Gama's men in India. The British also had their moral purposes. We miss much of the meaning if we forget the evangelic part in the expansion of Europe. The dynamic character of European civilization which brought the expansion comes in some measure from the Christian sense of life as a struggle, a pilgrimage, an adventure. The Christian is an activist even in his orisons and contemplation. His is a religion of energy, movement, growth, power, unending creation. It enormously influenced his view of the world and his way in it. The religions of Asia (Mohammedanism derives sufficiently from Christianity to take some of its character) were mostly quietist. Their influence on social forms was to subdue, reduce, stabilize. India's social basis of caste was set two thousand years ago. The great societies of Asia tended to turn in on themselves, as the Middle Kingdom. At the first firm prod from the outer world the Japanese curled back into their carapace. They had no sense of mission to the world, no jargon then of co-prosperity spheres. But the Christian had still ringing in his ears the injunction to go and to teach the nations. Francis Xavier is a symbol, with Albuquerque and the pilots of the power which Europe put out, of the tremendous thrust which carried the peoples of one peninsula to empire about the world and to colonize three continents. He is a fool and blind who sees the course of empire only in the terms of trade.

But the traders had their large part. Trade was the special skill of the Dutch and a knack that the English acquired. They came slowly to it for an island people. But during what Seeley neatly called the Thalassic Age they had been at the edge of the world. The Dutch lay across the mouths of the rivers which were highways into Middle Europe. They held the portals between the inland waters and the sea. They were from their dim origins notable coastal seamen; and they learnt their oceanic skill from the Portuguese when both were subject to Spain and the Dutch had charter to carry and sell through northern Europe the wares of two empires already spread from Brazil to Batavia and from China to Peru. When the Dutch broke from Spain, the tough, shrewd merchants of the Scheldt, Rhine, Rotter and Amster sent their tough, shrewd seamen to crack the old monopolies of the Iberian Kingdoms.

As Spain and Portugal declined and England rose, the main issue lay between the Dutch and the English. It raged from Amboina in the East Indies to the Basin of London. The Dutch had long experience and skill in finance and trade, and they had access to the markets of the rich German lands from the Baltic to the Danube and from the North Sea to Poland. Half were Protestants but the Dutch retained the immensely useful trade in salt fish for Fridays through the Catholic north and west.

The English over all had the better of their wars with the Dutch, although Tromp burned ships within sight of London. But the English could not acquire by force of arms the special skill and experience in European commerce of the burghers and Dutch bankers. These came in with William of Orange to found the Bank of England and add their character to the Age of Walpole. The new men who had risen in 17th-century England were wise in their generation, and subtle in their alliances.

But the century from the Armada to the coming in of

William had seen great things. Here was America founded. There is much of 17th-century England in America still, much that you will not now find in England.

The Puritanism which made New England was the Puritanism which four generations before the American Revolution revolted in England. There is a powerful likeness between John Hampden's eighteen shillings and the tea-party in Boston Harbor. The army of stubborn Roundheads with their multiplying sects, their prophetic propensities, their twanging pieties, their given names which ring in praise or admonition have had more heirs in America than England. John Brown belonged to that stern nation. One need not ask where Webster or the Adamses would have stood at Naseby, or the allegiance Lenthall and Ireton would have chosen after Lexington.

The American foundations owed little to the State. They came largely from private initiatives. The concept of free associations and private enterprise has remained a major motif of the American polity and economy. On free associations and private enterprises the British System grew through the 17th century both in the Colonies and in the Merchant Companies. Loot from the Spanish treasure ships and ports went into the early merchant adventures. The profits of the Levant Company fed the East India voyages. Profits from the East India Company went into the Virginia Company. The increment of the ventures overseas flowed freely from one trial of fortune to another; and the men who found the money for the expansion (whether from the Spaniard or by mortgage of their estates) were ready to try a toss with fortune at long odds.

The British System thus acquired the resilience necessary for the range and variety of its efforts. It could take risks and absorb losses while the profits of adventures flowed freely into new adventures. With Spain, profits of empire were drained into the coffers of the State for the extravagant and unfruitful campaigns of European politics. With France, the Companies were controlled by the State and it also sucked up such profits as there were for its own purposes. But the British plowed back their profits into the business of empire; and they had the harvest. The capital needed to support slow, laborious development in North America largely came from the quicker profits of the Eastern trades. Only the African Company had aid from the public funds of Great Britain, and that generations after its first foundation.

Government was in fact cautious, chary, and suspicious of its enterprising subjects and it remained so, except perhaps under Disraeli and the first Chamberlain. British Ministers still incline to flinch away from any suggestions for development or enlargement of the Imperial relationships; and their guardians at the Office for Commonwealth Relations seem as sad as angels for men's sin. Drake spoke for more than himself and to more than his Queen when he said: "Commit us afterwards for pirates if you will . . . you will have the gold and silver mines and the profit of the lands." Clive, Warren Hastings, Raffles might all have grimly echoed him.

Yet, the State *should* proceed with precaution and discretion. Its first function is to protect and preserve the vital interests and security of its people. It should not gamble with destiny or play history's long shots or experiment with human nature. Enterprise is not its forte. It either strangles enterprise or pushes it too far. The Spanish bureaucracy slowly choked out the energies of empire. The Nazi State tried to do business by force of arms. The Crown of France went in the 17th century earnestly to work at empire-making. It prescribed policies and master plans and minute directions. But the infinite and intricate problems which seamen, privateers, traders, and colonists had to meet at countless points remote could be properly met only from their own experience and on their own responsibility. The French Empire was defeated by Clive and Wolfe and by its own jacks-in-offices at Paris pressing their tedious prescriptions on men whose work was in worlds the clerks had never known.

The British Empire had no Five-Year Plan. It, with the North Americas, grew to its great state in the world by the initiative and energy and enterprise of unnumbered men now mostly forgotten. Neither Elizabeth nor Cecil could see beyond Drake into the secret seas where he was to go. Even King James—that calculating man—could not provide a pattern of behavior for shipmasters to the Indies or explorers in the Virginian woods. When Government did interfere it usually confused or confounded. It was wiser in restraint, and when it accepted the timely device of the Chartered Companies. By charters it could hold substantial men responsible for general policy under its hand at home, while their agents in the field and across the months of seas could proceed with wide discretion.

The British System allowed political as well as economic latitude. The local jurisdiction of Company Officers and Council usually was followed rapidly by elective assemblies with power to legislate for local needs. In 1619, the first colonial Parliament met at Jamestown: "That they might have a hand in the governing of themselves yt was graunted that a general Assemblie should be helde yearly once, whereat were to be present the Governor and Counsell, with two Burgesses from each plantation, freely to be elected by the inhabitants thereof, this Assemblie to have power to make and ordain whatsoever laws and orders should by them be thought good and profitable for our subsistence." [1]

Though the Virginia Company fell into confusion and was ended in 1624 the principle of distributed responsibility was established: and the settlers kept their council. The British

---

[1] *The Briefe Declaration.*

System was not to be clamped in a centralized machine. There was to be responsibility and authority in all its parts: and because it had no single comprehensive plan it had room for variety. At one point or another great principles found ground to strike root. The legislature of Catholic Maryland in 1649 declared (first in the world) for religious toleration "the better to preserve mutuall love and unity." [2] New England emphasized that the polity and economy must live within a moral context: that a true community is more than a political association or a public company. "It concerneth New England always to remember that they were originally a plantation of religions, not a plantation of trade. And if any man among us make religion twelve and the world as thirteen, such an one hath not the spirit of a true New Englander." [3]

Ideas emigrated as well as men: and many which were slow to make head in the tangle of customs and traditions of the old culture struck swiftly in the virgin earth. Connecticut drafted its own constitution in 1639 to provide for election by its freemen not only of the legislature but of the Governor and his Council. Four years later, the United Colonies of New England with their federal council presaged what was to come not only in the United States but in the federal structures of Canada and Australia. There has been an almost constant interplay of principles and ideas. When the Australian Colonies joined to form their federation they drew a constitution from the experience of both the great English-speaking peoples.

The democratic thesis was developed again under Penn with his government "for the support of power in reverence with the people, and to secure the people from the abuse of power." In Georgia Oglethorpe introduced the philan-

[2] Maryland's Toleration Act was suspended by the Puritans under the Commonwealth, but re-enacted in 1657.

[3] Higginson: the Election Sermon of 1663.

thropic theme which was to recur in Wakefield's plans for
South Australia and New Zealand. The United States were
to break with the British polity; but the themes and threads
are interwoven still in a wider historical pattern where
William Penn and Oglethorpe are not divided by alien
allegiances from Washington and Lincoln, but are of one
community.

* 2 *

The British Empire since the death of Mary Tudor has
had three major phases, each sufficiently distinct to suggest
as useful terms First, Second, and Third Empire. These
need not mislead if we remember that the three are not
three entities but variations on one theme: the adventures
of the British peoples in the world.

They are now entered on a fourth major phase. It may
prove perhaps the "last scene of all, that ends this strange
eventful history"; or it may provide another of those curious
recruitments and renewals which at least twice before have
followed reports of imminent collapse. Conceivably, the
British System is still the first Power in the world if its
politicians and peoples have wit and will enough to realize
it.

The death of Mary Tudor marks as clearly as a single
event can a vast historic change: the end of the England
which had for 1,400 years since the coming of the Romans
been orientated towards the Continent. Mary's death was
prelude to the final breach with Rome: the Rome which
had sent Augustine and Reginald Pole to Canterbury and
the other Rome which had once established unity in Europe,
a unity still held in recollection by the figures and signs of
the Holy Roman Empire. The Holy Roman Empire under
Charles V was something more than an occasion for epigrams; and Mary had married Charles' son.

Mary's loss of Calais was a vivid omen. Calais had been

the last foothold in Europe of the English: to her it must
have seemed their last anchor-hold. Mary was not mourn-
ing for a mile or two of ground when she said that the name
of Calais would be found burnt on her heart, but for the
breach which she foresaw between England and the
Christian order in which England had been formed and
from which it had received its civilization.

The Elizabethan Reformation was in essence a revolt
against the established order of Europe. It much resembled
the American Revolution of two hundred years later. Both
Revolutions (whatever their rights and wrongs) were ex-
plosions of rising energies, and at the beginnings of tremendous expansions.

The First British Empire was born with the formation in
1562 by London merchants of an African Company to
finance John Hawkins in the slave trade. The Companies
for Trade or for Colonization or both were to be favorite
devices of the three Empires. The merchants risked the
money, and the seamen their necks. The Companies carried
all the losses, but the whole kingdom was enlarged in their
prosperity.

They began with a loss. Hawkins sold live slaves in Santo
Domingo for dead hides which he shipped to Cadiz. There
they were seized by the Spaniards for Hawkins' breach of
Spain's monopoly: and the great quarrel of the English
seamen and merchants with Spain was on.

It was resolved off Gravelines in 1588. The loss of the
Armada was catastrophic and cataclysmic for Spain. Spain
was already stretched desperately thin. Eight years before
the Armada, Spain had absorbed Portugal and its half of
the world. Both Spain and Portugal had worked miracles
with the resources at their disposal. Portugal (its population then was only about one million) built in a generation
an empire which ran down both sides of the Atlantic in
Brazil and West Africa, turned Good Hope and went up by

East African forts and ports to the Red Sea and Persian Gulf: and thence by India and Malacca to Java, the Celebes, and Timor just above Australia; and about the corner of Asia on to the China Coast and Japan. The effort was too much.

The Spanish Empire grew with tremendous sweep and power until its resources were constrained to the central treasury at Madrid. It is not true that the Spaniards merely mined their colonies while the English farmed theirs. Many millions of people were living in the Spanish colonies on developed agriculture while the English were struggling to clear ground and the French in Canada were still importing food. The rapidity of Spanish development was largely due to the incorporation of the Indian population in the new communities. Indians in thousands were at universities already generations old in Spanish America when the Pilgrims came to Plymouth Rock.

The Spanish expansion was until the late 18th century much more extensive than the English. It spread from the Horn to San Francisco. But the resources of the Iberian Peninsula, this one peninsula of the peninsula of Europe, were not enough to encompass and organize the vast areas of the world it seized upon while the British Empire was still an "empire of outposts" (the phrase is Professor Knowles'); and the Spanish effort was constantly sapped and distracted, as we have already marked, by the strain of the ponderous misshapen Spanish lordship in Europe. The English by the character of their island situation and the caution of their kings were much more detached from the national, dynastic, and religious struggles of Europe.

They achieved another immeasurable advantage: as Bacon noted, "he that commands the sea is at great liberty, and may take as much and as little of the war as he will."

Philip II was no fool. The Armada was not thrown against England wantonly. He knew that Spain needed much time

to shift the economic basis of her imperial development.
But she could not gain time unless she could check the
English excursions into a world too vast for Spain to
protect and police.

Philip threw the Armada in the teeth of advancing history. History devoured it.[4]

Gravelines was more than a victory over the Spaniards.
It was a domestic triumph also for the new men who had
the money, owned the ships, and paid the seamen. They
might cheerfully have anticipated the eminent Mr. Hunt
and his music-hall vaunt: "We've got the ships, we've got
the men, we've got the money too." The Armada put
effective end to the Tudor despotism in a way which Philip
(he was not so prescient) hardly foresaw but perhaps Elizabeth did, for her long reluctance to permit open war was
designed not only to husband England's strength but to
preserve the Crown's. From the victory of 1588, power in
England perceptibly shifted. Henceforward the new men's
Parliament rapidly rose. Half-a-century later it broke the
Crown and killed the King.

Hot from the Spanish action, the merchants began to
push their ventures out. In 1591, Lancaster made his voyage to the East Indies for a London group; and in 1600,
they had Charter for their East India Company. The new
men provoked rebellion in Ireland; and with rebellion
crushed, they confiscated lands and settled their people on
them: "The Eagles took wing for the Spanish Main; the
Vultures descended upon Ireland." [5]

In 1605, Barbados was acquired. In 1606, the Virginia

[4] It is worth noting that even with the tremendous and concentrated
effort to produce the Armada, the Spaniards were already weaker at sea
than the English. Medina-Sidonia had larger but less suitable ships for battle
in narrow seas (many were merely transports) and only 120 against nearly
200 English. The Spanish ships were ill-provisioned and ill-manned, with
only 12,000 seamen against the English 16,000.

[5] Goldwin Smith, quoted by Marriott in *The Evolution of the British
Empire and Commonwealth:* Nicholson and Watson, London. 1939.

Company was chartered. In April 1607, Virginia was after much trial, error, and tribulation at last founded. The substantial business of Empire began.

The First Empire ran for five generations. It died when the Second was already some years grown, and the most convenient date for its memorial is at the loss of the American Colonies. The foundation and growth of the American Colonies and the rise of the East India Company to dominion are the great themes of the First Empire. Both owed something to the ambition of the Government and merchants for an *entrepôt* trade. "We shall rear merchant ships both fair and tall so that nothing that swimmeth shall make them vail nor stoop, which shall make this little corner of the world the richest storehouse for merchandise in all Christendom." [6]

The *entrepôt* trade has always touched the English fancy. It requires imagination and a delight in the curious. The English created Singapore and Hong Kong where they played shop with half Asia. The touch of the English poetry is on it; the poets were in fact moved by the merchants' revelation of the world and their verse alludes repeatedly to its riches.

In this mood colonies were seen as estates to be worked for raw materials and tropical products. The colonists were to provide sugar and spice and other items notoriously nice and to receive the manufactures of the Mother Country. Their trade was to be the core of a maritime traffic which would encompass the earth.

The dominant economic policy of the first Empire was this "Mercantilism" with its effort to control colonial production and to raise a great Marine by monopolizing for its own shipping the trade between the parent country and its hopeful sprigs. The English controls were much more

[6] A quotation repeated from Knowles: *The Economic Development of the British Overseas Empire.*

liberal than the Spanish, French, or Dutch: nevertheless English law and regulation (Navigation Acts, provisions of the Company Charters, and the like) sought a measure of economic planning and control in striking contrast to the free-trade policies and laissez-aller, laissez-faire attitudes which were to dominate the economic life of the Second British Empire.

The First sought trading-posts and ports and bases along the trade-routes rather than territorial expansion. That came only in America and slowly enough through the early generations. The Chartered Companies all had trade in mind. The East India, Hudson's Bay,[7] and African Companies were embarrassed and often resistant as history thrust dominion on them. The Companies of Virginia, New England, Guiana, and a score of other territorial designations were founded to colonize, but they too looked for their ultimate profit in commerce which would grow with the colonies (the immediate profit usually was sought in the sale of land). The largest parts by far of the First, Second, and Third British Empires came from the enterprise of the Companies: American Colonies, India, Malaya, New Zealand, South Australia, British East Africa, the Gold Coast, Uganda, Rhodesia, Nigeria, North Borneo, Malacca and Ceylon came from the Netherlands East India Company, of which Cape Colony also was a foundation.

In spite of Mercantilism (and perhaps because of it, for the merchants who were its progenitors were Parliament men, and Cromwell, their man turned master, fathered the Navigation Act of 1651) the British Colonies had their own political institutions from the beginning. The General Assembly of Virginia was the first child of the Mother of Parliaments. When the *Mayflower* pilgrims made their simple compact of common assent they were expressing at its purest the democratic concept.

[7] Incorporated (as a tag on my pajamas informs me) in May 1670.

The democratic impulse was enormously strengthened by the character of the New England colonies. Here were men come at desperate hazard to worship as they wished, come not for quick profits but for permanent settlement in a climate and conditions apt to the exercise of the sterner moral virtues.

The seamen and the merchants and the factors might learn strange sins in the East. The Puritans of Massachusetts were singularly indifferent to the spiritual and material welfare of the Red Indians (the "devilish men" and certainly not Elect) who at least survived and multiplied under Papist Spain. But the First British Empire nevertheless was braced in a powerful if narrow sense of God's immanence and governorship.

The early migrants to America were mostly artisans and working people. Royalists, including some authentic Cavaliers, went to the Southern Colonies and the islands after the King was taken; but in the north and elsewhere America grew from a working people. Those who had not labored with their hands before they came turned perforce to the hoe and ax and adze in America. During the decades and generations when the life of small settlements might hang on the chances of a harvest, the plowman, the food-getter and food-grower were men of first consequence.

Democracy (though many New England champions hated its name) was inevitable where government was largely the affair of small communities which, remote from higher authority, had to deal with the more pressing problems as they came. As these mostly bore on every family, men were active to assert their views and votes.

The colonists were carving a new nation out of the forests; and as the trees fell before their axes, they must have had a powerful and intimate sense of the creative role of man. Men who shape a civilization with their own hands and in their own sweat are not much given to the mechanical superstition. They think of the world more in terms of brawn and brain than of tendencies and influences. Men who make the venture of "the wat'ry Maze" to fight the forests and bring the deserts under plow know that authority resides in guts and muscle; in their own gray matter rather than in the gray abstractions of the State. They see the machinery of government as their creation, like the fenced fields and log cabins. Government is their contrivance for specific social purposes, a tool and instrument, not a Master or a Monster.

Men thinking thus gave its fundamental pattern to American society, to the American Soul. These were not the Merchants or the Governors or the garrisons. These had come to stay, to inhabit their creation, to give it in heritage to their sons and their sons' sons. This, after all, was the great end of empire to which the rest was means; and if it was not always from the first so seen, it has appeared in the developed theme as the proper use and purport of the adventure. We can make no sense of anything (or of ourselves) until we know the use and end. This was the end shaped, rough-hewn though it was: and in it appears the true meaning and tale of imperial dominion.

It is this enlargement of man which is the real theme: enlargement in numbers and resources, enlargement of the mind and spirit. To the strange problem of man's darkness and weakness there is but one answer and it comes out of the primeval: "Be fruitful, and multiply, and replenish the earth, and subdue it." For we were given a dominion.

* 3 *

The loss of the American Colonies concludes the first phase of the British System. The second, we can now recognize, had already begun to grow from many seeds. The Quebec Act of 1774, for instance, had in it as it was administered by Governor Carleton a new tolerance and latitude. These applied to the Colonies a generation earlier might have released energies which, once compressed, made head for revolution. But the American issue was decided before the new temper could be recognized. The First Empire and its men had not acquired the flexibility, the play, the facility which in the Commonwealth have developed the concept of equal sovereign status among the several parts. The machinery was still too stiff: and so were necks—on both sides of the Atlantic.

The issue between Britain and the English-speaking colonies has been paraded through an immense literature; but several factors are worth touching again for the present purpose.

The general mind of Britain was not much interested in empire at all. When its attention was finally caught by the American problem it was still enmeshed in the First Empire. The Revolution in wrenching America from the British System also wrenched the British from an obsolete idea of empire. Perhaps (as so often in human affairs) resistance and violence were necessary to clear away a litter of outmoded notions and conventions.

The First Empire with its mercantilist notions of plantation, regulation, and control was indifferent to continental territories as such. Only the poet and philosopher had foreseen the promise of new nations. In 1764, at the end of the great war, argument was high in England from those who wanted to retain at the peace settlement Guadeloupe and Martinique (as potentially profitable tropical plantations) rather than Canada.

The British also, at the end of the Seven Years' War, were somewhat impatient with the problems of defense set by continental colonies. Britain has always come reluctantly to land warfare on a massive scale. She has preferred to employ her genius and resources where she could use them with nicer economy, at sea. The Seven Years' War had in

large part been fought to prevent the threatened French
encirclement of the American Colonies. It was an expensive
war and long-drawn. It produced at its end the reversal of
feeling which usually appears when great efforts have been
made to defend distant peoples, who seldom show much
substantial gratitude. The British by 1765 (like the Americans in 1921 and in 1947) were inclined to shrug their
shoulders and mutter: "Cui bono?"

The Americans for their part, like others before and since,
were quick to turn their attention from the perils past to the
problems and possibilities of the new situation. The smash-
ing of the French barriers opened the view beyond the
Alleghenies: the vast rivers, the immense rich lands, the
prospects which seemed illimitable. Were they to be cribbed
and confined by a system of controls which did not even
efficiently control?

The drive of American history westward was enormously
strengthened by the new opportunity; and as it swept up
over the mountains and by the great rivers towards the heart
of America, immense distances were put between it and the
old world; even between it and the eastern seaboard whence
seaborne traffic sustained the old relationships. The frontier
was for a hundred years henceforward the growing-point
not only of material advance but of the American mind and
character. The young men of ideas and energy were going
west with a vengeance, leaning across its urgent bosom.
Within fifty years of the Revolution their new political
force was to replace the dynasty of Virginian gentlemen
and the New England merchants and lawyers at the center
of government with men from the western woods and
waters. "Old Hickory" came to the White House in 1829;
and his advent is the advent of a New America. It had at
the core something different and strange from the British
world-view and that which had prevailed in the tidewater
colonies. It had a continental mind and outlook. It was

turned from the sea and from all that lay beyond it. It was absorbed and held by the great land-mass. It would understand less and less the character of the insular and pelagic system whence it had sprung. The British System was to grow on a world-wide web of sea-communications. The British were to depend on a world-order and to realize more and more the interrelations of mankind. But the American empire was to march along the land-trails, developing with its own resources and as a geographic bloc rather than by the organization of heterogeneous peoples dispersed throughout the world. The Americans were to take in enormous numbers from other human stocks; but their problem was to co-ordinate, consolidate, compress to the American pattern. Until her own immense regions were peopled America was to be sufficient to herself, or as near sufficient as any people could be.

Isolationism was thus not an aberration, but an inevitable character of this American world which began with the victory of the Seven Years' War and ended only with another World War three long lifetimes later: when America had come again to the sea, which can never henceforward be for her a mere barrier or moat, but the highroad of world responsibilities and history.

Continental peoples tend to isolationism while they have still space to people and resources to expand. But when they reach from sea to sea and have filled all the lands between, they become again as islanders, with need to cast abroad for markets and materials. Further, man must grow, work, and create while his moral and intellectual and physical energies are potent.

The Russian isolationism has a curious, though not complete, likeness to American isolationism. The major strain in the Russian System comes from the conflict of its continental character with the world-ambitions of an ideological power superimposed on it. A corresponding strain in the

American System comes from the surviving strength of isolationism in a situation which has developed far beyond it.
Both are conflicts between conscious policies and the almost
instinctive habits of the social body.

The Power which first resolves its argument will have the
greater influence in the oncoming world. The Russians are
in one sense better equipped. Their decisions are still taken
by a small group of men who seek the world-stage and
dragoon their people for it. In America, the men who understand must persuade the democracy, which in a free society
is subject to counter-propagandas and the argument of
competing parties. On the other hand, America is better
equipped in the general education of its people. They cannot be dragooned, but they have open to them the information and education necessary for judgment; and America
is superbly equipped in technical and material resources.

Her enormous industries now need export-markets to
keep them fully employed. Her financial resources must find
new outlets. She can no longer absorb all her own abounding power. The facts force expansion on her; and her people
will learn from urgent facts. But Russia still is in desperate
need of her own fat. Unless the Americans refuse the role
which the century requires of them (and to refuse it will
bring on them unprecedented domestic catastrophes of de-
flation, unemployment, economic and moral and intellectual
depression), Russia's time is not yet. One sometimes thinks
the Russian leaders see that clearly: hence their resistance
to a new world-system centered perhaps about the United
Nations, in which America's influence might prevail as
Britain's has in the world systems of the last two centuries.

It is sometimes said that wars settle nothing. That is the
sheerest nonsense. Beyond the vast changes immediately
visible (the fates of lordships and regimes, the facts of
death and destruction) they bring to all the systems and
peoples concerned changes sometimes of a sort utterly un-

foreseen. The First British Empire's greatest war was sealed by its greatest triumph at Paris in 1763. France was crushed in India and North America and the whole outer world seemed at Britain's disposition. Yet within twenty years the First British Empire was in dissolution.

The Third British Empire came to victory almost as splendid in 1945. Again, the battle thunder had hardly died when the Third Empire entered a phase of disintegration comparable to that which ushered out the First. The passages of change in which India is parted may usher in the Fourth Empire already long shadowed forth. But we have seen the end of the Third Empire as clearly as the men of 1783 saw the end of the First.

Mr. Churchill watching India must have reflected often on the last years of another triumphant War Minister, William Pitt.

English statesmen and English public opinion were for the most part blind to what was happening in the depths of American life: to the stirring national spirit upon which Samuel Adams worked with passionate skill. But American statesmen were not always more alert. At the end of the Seven Years' War, Franklin held it ridiculous to imagine a combination of the Colonies against "their own nation"; and in 1774, months after the Boston Tea-Party, George Washington could still declare in all honesty: "I am well satisfied that no such thing as independence is desired by any thinking man in all North America; on the contrary, that it is the ardent wish of the warmest advocates for liberty, that peace and tranquillity on constitutional grounds should be restored and the horrors of civil discord be prevented." So well may the shrewdest and most careful men read the future.[8] (Nothing comes clearer from a study of

---

[8] There was one seer (we recall him in vindication of the professional diplomats for he was perhaps the ablest France produced in the 18th century), Vergennes, who said of the American Colonies, after the Peace of

history than the unpredictability of its courses: nothing more stamps the *parvenu* and bumpkin in politics than his belief that he can prescribe the future. Policies must be attempted; but an educated electorate will be always watchful for presumption in its planners.)

Franklin and Washington belonged to the educated society of the East. They did not understand the forces working among the poor and on the frontiers. Samuel Adams did. He played upon social grievances. In 1770 when Britain had withdrawn practically all the legislation to which the men of substance in the East had objected, Adams was still proclaiming that the Colonies were to be reduced to slavery and poverty. He played also on the resentment of the frontiersmen at any effort of the government to control or confine their westward march. The pioneer depended on himself and his immediate fellows for protection. He felt that he owed little to government. He was in bent anarchistic. He felt himself expressed when Adams cried that "the natural liberty of man is to be free from any superior power on earth, and not to be under the will or legislative authority of man, but only to have the law of nature for his rule." [9]

This intense distaste for political and legal order worked against the settled systems of the seaboard Colonies; but its most obvious and major mark was the Imperial System.

It is important to remember that, if the Revolution cost Britain thirteen Colonies, it cost the Colonies a lively and vigorous strain which left for territories under the British flag. The Loyalists went to make English-speaking Canada. Nova Scotia, New Brunswick, Cape Breton Island, and Prince Edward Island were largely peopled by them. Upper

Paris: "England will presently regret having removed the check that held her colonies in awe. They no longer need her protection. She will ask them to aid with the burdens they have helped to bring on her. They will reply by striking off their dependence."

[9] Quoted by James Truslow Adams: *The Epic of America.*

Canada took being from 30,000 of them. Thousands more went into Quebec.[10]

The Revolution gave Canada its first great impulse since the French had settled; and it was progenitive also in the foundation of Australia.

The first public proposals for settlement in Australia were drafted by James Maria Matra, the son of an American Loyalist.[11] Matra had sailed with Cook and Banks in the *Endeavour* on the voyage which first defined the east coast of Australia. He argued for settlement "to atone for the loss of our American colonies," and to provide for the refugees. James de Lancey, once the largest landholder in Southern New York, was ardent for it and promised to procure colonists from the United Empire Loyalists in Nova Scotia. The British Government was less inspired. Australia had to wait until the overcrowding of the jails and prison-hulks (an effect also of the Revolution in America and the end of transportation thence) forced government to decision. Even so, the First Fleet anchored in Sydney Cove on 26th January, 1788: only five years and four months after the Treaty of Paris had recognized American independence. Here again was one of history's unpredictable and incalculable turns. Of all the consequences flowing from the agitation of Samuel Adams, the Townshend Acts, and the Tea-Party, few are stranger than the growth of a little convict settlement at the ends of the earth into another great democracy speaking the tongue of George III and George Washington.

Australia has in her ancestry (if from the wrong side of the blanket) the American Revolutionaries. Five genera-

[10] If Alexander Hamilton was right, only half the population of the 13 Colonies was in 1775 for separation. New York was notably against it; and many thousands went to Canada from there. Most in Pennsylvania were against the war and independence throughout; and the prosperous classes of New England were generally hostile to a revolution which had social elements they feared.

[11] The family derived from Corsica. Matra was born in New York.

tions after them, the United States and Australia formed the most intimate political and military association either had ever entered with a foreign power, to fight a war in seas and islands whose names were hardly known to the Founding Fathers. Strangely too, America growing to world power in the 20th century was to find that her structure of defense north and west would need the new pillars of British power in the self-governing Dominions which the American Revolution had all unknowing helped to bring into being.

SIX

THE SECOND EMPIRE

THE Second British Empire was, even in terms of territory, largely a new creation. Of the Empire which William Pitt was called to defend, Barbados, Bermuda, the Bahamas, Jamaica, the Leewards, Newfoundland, Nova Scotia, St. Helena, and some points in Gambia and on the Gold Coast were all that remained after the American Colonies marched out.

But from the Seven Years' War the East India Company's reign in India was firmly founded, and from that war came Canada into the British System. The rest of the vast Second and Third Empires was recruited after the Americans had gone.

Napoleon forced much of this new growth. France's plotting with Tipu of Mysore compelled the British in India to raise allies and crush the French and their friends, a few months after Nelson had checked at the Nile Napoleon's own eastward march. French intrigues evoked in India Wellesley's "forward" policy, which was extremely unpopular at home. The first British Mission to Persia and the occupation of Ceylon, Malacca, and the Netherlands East Indies were all to counter Napoleon. Stamford Raffles ruled in Java until Britain restored the N.E.I. to Holland after Waterloo. But Ceylon she kept; and from Malacca and Raffles' foundation at Singapore, British power grew in Malaya. Cape Colony was occupied at the suggestion of the Dutch Stadtholder lest Napoleon's puppet, the Batavian Republic, should secure it.[1] The Knights of St. John were relieved, as a precaution against French invasion, of their sovereign tasks in Malta. Mauritius was collected, with the Seychelles, directly from the French; and Trinidad from Spain.

When Napoleon was dead, the French rivalry continued to spur Britain on. South Australia, Western Australia, and New Zealand were all settled and incorporated partly to forestall ambitions the French sometimes seemed to entertain. The French might also be said to have forced a shotgun wedding on the British and their Second Empire. The British unquestionably were reluctant. The extent of the territories returned by Britain to Napoleon's unhappy allies at the end of his wars is perhaps less evidence of magnanimity than of boredom with the imperial affair. The British retained points primarily useful to their sea-borne commerce (as the Cape, Ceylon, Malta, Mauritius); and they used their overwhelming power to declare what were to be dogmas of the Second Empire: their rights upon the seas, especially the rights of blockade and search. The British mind was still on trade and its naval protection rather than dominion.

The Navy was at the height of its prestige. Rodney's great victories against the Spaniards and French more than compensated in British eyes for the defeats of the American War. His action off Martinique in April 1782 answered

---

[1] Subsequently, the Dutch were paid £6,000,000 for the Colony.

Yorktown and "saved for Britain her ocean sceptre."[2] It established firmly the sea-power which was the basic fact and necessary condition of the Second British Empire. After Rodney came the glories of Jervis and Nelson: St. Vincent, the Nile, and Trafalgar.

From 1782 until 1943, British power at sea was also the prime fact of world-politics: the hold from which Napoleon, the Kaiser Wilhelm, and Hitler could not break loose. By 1943, the new naval power of the United States was joined to confirm the Anglo-American command of all the oceans. Sea-power may count somewhat less in the future than in the ages gone. But it will remain a tremendous factor in human affairs while the weight of the world's cargoes must be carried on the buoyant element; and while a hundred aircraft built and serviced and fueled at tremendous cost cannot together lift the payload of one tramp steamer.

Sea-power does not mean merely the possession of a powerful force of fighting ships. It might be, and in fact has been, exerted without a specialized naval force at all. Sea-power is the power to use the seas and to deny them to an enemy. The chief strategic end of a naval force is to protect its coasts and the ports and routes essential for its national traffic. The end may be best secured in action to seek out the enemy and to destroy him. This is in the tradition of British naval strategy. But the Royal Navy in its last two great wars has achieved its strategic end, although the enemy has avoided decisive action and retained (even after Jutland) the main strength of his fleet intact.

The effects of sea-power are sometimes missed in the melodrama.[3] But in World War II, all other operations

---

[2] Froude.

[3] In the war against Japan, the essential part of the British Eastern Fleet is hardly known because it lacked dramatic event. But its presence (the Japanese only once challenged it) in the Indian Ocean denied to the Japanese all the waters west of 90° East and the approaches to India, the Red Sea, Africa, and Western Australia.

ultimately depended on sea-power. The British could not have held the Middle East or the Island itself but for sea-power. Men and material could not have been drawn from their world-wide System to the battle-fronts and factories without sea-power. The Americans could not have crossed the Atlantic or Pacific without sea-power. The air offensives against Germany and Japan, the invasions of Italy and France, the operations from New Guinea to Tokyo, from Alamein to Berlin could not have been mounted if the Allies had lacked ships to move the men, guns, aircraft, gasoline, and all the gear and tackle and trim of modern war. Sea-power, as the Emperor Charles V observed, is a bridge of ships. Whoever commands the bridge commands the resources of the wide world. The great armies of Napoleon, the Kaiser, and Hitler all were swept away by the wind from the sea.[4]

The skeleton of the Roman Empire was its roads. The circulatory system of the British Empire is its ships. The ships in their passages have woven the patterns of British power and of the world-economy. Other marines have contributed, but the master pattern has been the British. The British opened the new trades, made and protected essential ports, created the marts of Asia, Africa, and Australasia. Sea-power and trade, the Royal Navy and the Merchant Marine are the fundamental facts of the Second Empire and the World System it produced.

The migrations of the 19th century which peopled the Americas and Australasia moved under the Red Ensign in the security given by the White. Africa was opened and Asia

---

[4] It is said that Field Marshal von Rundstedt tried to teach his masters before World War II; and that he closed a course of lectures on sea-power with words to this effect: "A mere Land Power cannot defeat a Sea Power. Sea-Power will always in the long run strangle a Continental Power." The hold imposed from the first hour of war by the British blockade compelled Hitler to his drive on Russia and its resources, to the War on Two Fronts which he had vowed to avoid.

organized for its new commerce with the world in the framework of the System. Its expansion and development produced the new markets and methods of trade and finance and investment and exploitation whose demands stimulated the Industrial Revolution. The machines with their demand for raw materials stimulated the primary economies. America's cotton, Australia's wool, India's jute all grew to feed the flying looms and spinning-jennies of Lancashire and Yorkshire. The heavy bales prompted the first rail-tracks, the heavy cargoes the steam-driven ships. The application of science to the socio-economic problems of mankind is the second great character of this Second Empire. In its growth and for its developing necessities came steam-power and the new methods in agriculture, public health, road-making, irrigation, banking. It produced its own appropriate philosophies: Adam Smith on the Wealth of Nations; Laissez-Faire; the Survival of the Fittest.[5]

Its politico-economic character was essentially capitalistic. It came nearer to pure capitalism than any system before or since has come to its ideal conception. If one could forget the miseries of its industrial slums, its theory would be almost irrefutable.

Free trade in the broadest and fullest sense seemed to offer the best prospects for a coherent world-economy that man had ever known. If men were creatures only of economic interests uncrossed by other purposes and passions, the world might then have grown to universal peace and prosperity. But ours is not that sort of world, and man for good and ill does not find all his peace in the pursuit of the main chance.

It is difficult now to recapture the sober but tremendous

---

[5] Appropriately enough, Darwin gathered the mass of his material for *The Origin of Species* while serving in H.M.S. *Beagle* on a world voyage designed for scientific investigation: a proceeding highly characteristic of a Navy which furnished ship and crew to Dampier, and Captain Cook and the *Endeavour* to the Royal Society.

optimism of the Second Empire at its heyday. Perhaps one
is deceived about the sobriety: the stove-pipe hats and black
broadcloth may have been but necessary masks for a fantastic age. The Second British Empire introduced an era of
marvels beyond all man's earlier imaginings. The 19th century transformed our human life more than all the centuries
before it. It worked daily wonders to change the face of
the earth and the familiar relations of time and place.

Populations multiplied beyond all precedents and the
tempo of life and history was immeasurably quickened.
Perhaps the black hats and somber pants and the stiff manners were put on only to reduce a little the adventurous and
enterprising spirit of an era which challenged every tradition and opened immense new ranges of experience and
fortune.

The Second Empire reached its pinnacle at the Great
Exhibition of 1851. Universal peace and prosperity seemed
then about to dawn, with Free Trade as the presiding genius,
and Prince Albert to speak the Prologue.

The Deity was suitably associated with these triumphs:
"We advocate," said Cobden, "nothing but what is agree-
able to the highest behests of Christianity—to buy in the
cheapest market and to sell in the dearest."

If his Christianity seems a trifle odd, he did recognize
that economics require a moral reference. Economics and
the physical sciences had not yet unqualifiedly declared
for their release from the philosophic and moral order. They
had not yet burst on the world as great amoral Anarchs
charged with tremendous power for creation or destruction
(but chiefly, it now seems, for destruction). The old order
was still strong enough to hold an uneasy equilibrium. In it
the British System grew with an unprecedented prosperity
and peace.[6]

[6] From 1815 to 1914, Britain engaged in war only once with a Great
Power. Three generations of young men came to maturity without taking

Laissez-faire, free competition, free trade and "the rigours of the game" mark the Second British Empire. It believed in the Open Society not only for the several sovereign polities and economies but for the world at large. If competition and unrestricted enterprise were right in the conduct of domestic business, they were right in the commerce of nations. Tariffs and customs barriers were barbarous relics of the old Mercantilism. An enlightened Capitalism would have nothing of them. The Free Traders believed that protective tariffs flatly contradicted the basic concepts of capitalism, and would lead to conflicts which would finally destroy it. As America is increasingly compelled to find abroad not only markets but raw materials it must learn at least to lisp the tongue that Cobden spoke, even if it rejects the whole faith which John Bright held. It must learn that it can sell abroad only if it buys. It must understand better than Calvin Coolidge did that goods, not money, are hired by foreign borrowers, the money being but a local token. Free trade in the world is, and perhaps always was, a dream; but wisdom is to be had from the disciples.

Tariff and customs controls have fed the growth of the Great State. They are the first phase of the politically protected and planned economy. Bismarck built the German Empire on his German Customs Union. Joseph Chamberlain took note, but failed to emulate him in the British System. Bismarck's successors were bedazzled. They used the State to organize the Nation. When the State identified its interests with the interests of its traders, their competition involved the State. But States, unlike private traders, commonly come (if their conflicts are otherwise unreconciled) to the arbitraments of arms. Hitler's drive for production piled up in German warehouses a volume of exportable

arms (unless, of course, they joined the tiny minority of professionals who conducted Britain's colonial campaigns). A man of the 20th century can grimly note their exceptional fortune.

goods. When the world refused them, he tried to prise markets open with bombs and bayonets. The Nazi master-plan was to subordinate all rival manufactures in Europe to German industry and to create in Europe a "colonial" area of primary industries to feed the German workers and their machines and to absorb the products of German factories. If national economies continue in aggressive competition, we must expect the crisis which developed in Germany to recur elsewhere.

The effort of Powers large and small to become industrially self-supporting has pushed up costs of living almost everywhere, and multiplied its difficulties. British textiles might be purchased cheaply in Cincinnati but for tariff charges. America could sell automobiles abroad at a fraction of their present foreign prices but for tariff obstructions. Tariffs push up costs to the consumer and often pull down quality. Peoples who once wore Cheviot tweeds and Lancashire shirtings no longer recognize good textiles; and they put bodies on their home-made cars which suggest that use has at last been found for old cans.

Strangely, many peoples will not rest until they have reproduced the dark satanic mills in once green and pleasant lands. One Detroit, one Wigan might have seemed enough in a small world. But millions everywhere apparently want to live in industrial slums or semi-slums and work at the dullest and most boring tasks men have ever set themselves. I am always happy to let someone else make my shirts or my car and do the other tedious jobs we find necessary. But nations now all want to do their own dirty work and as much of other peoples' as they can grab. The Germans had themselves killed in still uncounted numbers, and their cities and industries smashed, because of a passionate determination to make typewriters for the Dutch, Diesels for the Czechs, and radio-sets for the Hungarians; while insisting that most of the Dutch, Czechs, and Hungarians spend their time growing tulips, wheat, meat, cream, and butter. It might have seemed a cinch for Dutch, Czechs, and Hungarians. But they wanted to make typewriters too. Cows and cabbages were inferior stuff, and the German methods of persuasion were not tactful; and the pay they offered was poor, with no alternative but the concentration-camp or the gas-chamber. Their business was bound to go bankrupt, for business has at least to look like a fair trade.

The motives behind the craze for industrialization are plain enough. Its thrust and suasions are tremendous, and power and security in the modern world depend on indus-trial equipment. For instance, Australia's "protection" was a forced and extravagant affair which slowed her primary development and drained her countrysides to overcrowd dull and dreary cities. But it did produce the secondary econ-omy essential to her defense against Japan and to the Allied counter-offensive. No vigorous people will now care to fall far behind in technical and industrial developments and skills. National rivalries are too intense, the necessities of defense too obvious. Yet the strain of competing industrial economies is a constant provocation to the passions which make for war.

The identification of the political and economic commu-nities in the modern State is thus a powerful factor in our confusion. It has led the State to apply all its power (includ-ing its armed power) to conquer markets and capture ma-terials. The State has come to see the aggrandizement of its local industries as necessary to life, liberty, and happiness.

Yet, if we shift our view from the political monster which fascinates us, we see that the economic community is not identical with national polities as they exist. A merchant in Chicago finds his customers or commodities in Canada or Cardiff as well as in Illinois. He knows that he can sell to a farmer in Iowa only if the farmer has been able by his sales or credit to acquire dollars. He must come to see as clearly that he cannot sell in Britain, France, or Patagonia unless they also have access to dollars.

Protection has in most countries been advanced piece-meal. No one wants to divide the world into isolated, closed economies having each no truck or traffic with the others. But this is the end towards which the lobbyists and pressure-groups could push us by their accumulated weight: even though the basic economic facts, the natural facts are in constant conflict with this absurdity. Nature did not design for complete self-sufficiency each region which chooses to set up under its own flag as a national State.

All this was understood by the people who promoted Free Trade in the Second British Empire. They were suspicious of the State. They saw that in a world of free trade, the economic communities would overrun all merely political boundaries. They looked to the growth of a world-economy to which each region would contribute from its natural eco-nomic endowment and acquired skills. Whoever could pro-duce an article for trade should have for it free access to the world's markets, where it would stand on its merits of qual-ity and cheapness. Political barriers and encumbrances should be swept aside. They may have premised a happier sort of world than ours. In their fashion they may have been idealists. They did make too much of the economic factor, and neglected the social and cultural uses of a diversified economy and the natural instinct of men to become in prime necessities self-supporting. But the alternative which appeared was not a balanced relation of free and protected industries. It was a group of economic autarchies; and pro-ductive energies which should have been for use and en-joyment have largely gone into orgiastic agonies of waste and ruin.

The identification of the political and economic interests has led also to the inflation through the whole range of life of the State's authority. The manufacturers and investors

who sought the State's protection for their industries were
inviting the State to a wider intervention. If the State can
protect the capitalist, it can also protect his workmen. Those
it protects, it can control. If the State can fence a fledgling
manufacture it can also direct and discipline it. Tariff-
chasers have no right to complain of State intervention in
their affairs.

The State cannot set tariffs without cognizance of prices
and profits. If the State appoints large numbers of Customs
Officers it begins to acquire a bureaucratic habit. Revenues
swollen by the proceeds of protective tariffs fatten its agen-
cies. These once again grow by what they feed upon. The
bureaucracy becomes a vested interest, a political force: and
like other human groups it strives to enlarge its numbers
and its power. The State in time becomes the servant of its
servants: and they, the masters of the polity. By then the
entrepreneur who sought protection is under the yoke; and
if he is of the wiser sort has sent his sons into the Civil
Service, unless they are already with the ranks (living or
dead) of the *levée en masse* in which the State grown too
gross delights.

The Free Traders were in a political sense Little Eng-
landers.

They disliked empire because it called for expenditures
from taxes on trade or from loans and thus diminished the
capital available to industry and commerce; and because it
required a strong political authority and provision for large
military forces at the disposition of the State. They believed
that all the real benefits of empire could be secured in
peaceful commerce and investment without the expenses,
irritations, and labors of political dominion. They saw also
perhaps that political administrators would be inclined to
push colonial subjects beyond their normal gait and to
force economic development on them, if only to produce

a taxable increment: and thus to raise up prematurely competitors in manufactures and services.

Their attitude was perfectly expressed by McCulloch in 1837: "Nothing, in fact, can be a greater mistake than to suppose, as many have done, that we are mainly indebted for our wealth and the high place we occupy among the nations of the earth, to our colonial possessions. We owe these distinctions to the favorable situation and physical capacities of our native country, the intelligence and enterprise of our people, and the emulation inspired by our free institutions and by the inequality of fortune that subsists amongst us. The truth is that we have derived ten times more advantage from our intercourse with the United States since they achieved their independence than we derived from them while we had a governor in every state, or than we have derived from all our colonies put together. And this advantage has not been accompanied by any drawbacks. We have not been obliged to purchase the timber and other commodities of the United States when we might supply ourselves better elsewhere, and we have not been obliged to keep up armaments for their protection or to encumber ourselves with the government of extensive countries on the other side of the Atlantic." [7]

The laissez-faire school was faithful in its fashion. The Navigation Acts were finally ended in 1849, and free trade proclaimed. Foreigners and colonists were actually made free of the whole establishment: they could trade where they wished and use whatever ships they preferred. Imperial preferences were swept away in Great Britain, and the Colonies were allowed to do what they pleased about tariffs. [8] The foreigner greatly benefited. Germany, in particular, waxed fat on trade with the British Colonies; and her rapid

---

[7] *Statistical Account of the British Empire:* quoted by Knowles.

[8] Canada in 1859 raised a protective tariff which the British might constitutionally have vetoed, but did not.

rise as an industrial and commercial Power after 1871 was largely due to her vigorous dealings through Britain's open doors.

The politicians in the mid-19th century had their cue in a pretty contempt for the Imperial domain. So Lord Palmerston, forming a Ministry and finding no one willing to have the Colonial office, exclaimed: "I suppose I must take the thing myself. Come upstairs with me, Helps. . . . We will look at the maps and you shall show me where these places are."

The Colonies which thought about such things were much of the British mind on the Imperial connection. Respectable pillars of church and state in Australia debated the merits of a republic or an independent kingdom perhaps under one of Victoria's sons. The most eminent of Australian Presbyterians, the Reverend James Dunmore Lang, was ardent for a republic. Two generations later his views would have seemed unspeakable in any kirk or Presbyterian assembly. When Canada received responsible and representative government, British and Canadian politicians, publicists, and people all assumed that it was but a pleasant path to complete separation. "The thing is done," said one of His Majesty's Colonial Secretaries, with obvious satisfaction. "The great colonies are gone. It is but a question of a year or two."

But yet again history, which has, it seems, an ironic providence, refused to perform according to prescription. The Empire in spite of itself remained in being; and laissez-faire and the general latitude were perhaps the prime conditions of its survival and development.

The new liberty left nothing much to quarrel about. There seemed little sense in taking trouble to break bonds which lay so lightly and which obviously could be tossed off if serious occasion rose. Moreover, the advantages of the connection were more and more apparent as the 19th century advanced. Britain was evidently content to carry the main burdens of defense. The enormous and still growing British market was wide open to colonial goods. The primary industries of Canada, Australia, New Zealand, and South Africa grew rapidly to feed the British mills and British workers. British capital was readily available for colonial industries and railways and public works at rates cheaper than foreign borrowers could normally expect. The world-wide system of British finance and trade with all its special skill and long, organized experience (these are still for-midable, if intangible, assets) was at the service of British subjects everywhere.

Colonial commerce operated on the British ports and bases and in the security given by the Royal Navy. The Colonies rapidly built up enormous export trades: *per capita,* and with Great Britain's the highest in the world. The over-seas trade in exports and imports of the British Common-wealth and Empire (omitting the United Kingdom) was in 1938 still considerably in excess of the trade of the United States: Australia, Canada, New Zealand's external trade by head of population was normally about four times the American figure and higher even than Great Britain's.

The British pound and the British passport were keys to all the doors of the world; and the British peace stretched a long arm over its subjects wherever constabulary duty was to be done.

These were solid advantages. To them were added the less tangible ties which can still sway the moods and motions of men.

The British System was unquestionably through the 19th century the first Power in the world and membership gave a sense of safety and, in most of its peoples, of pride. The Colonists shared the glories gathering about Britannia's somewhat portly figure. They were citizens of no mean city. They joined, if vicariously, in the triumphs of the thin red

lines which made and kept the Pax Britannica from Kaffir-
land to the Khyber. They were heirs of great fame: "I the
heir of all the ages, in the foremost files of time," as Lord
Tennyson sang. Sometimes their Englishmen abroad seemed
a little too conscious for others' comfort of the supreme
privilege of being born to a chosen race. But the English
were still (like most peoples) much nicer at home, where
they produced a standard of social habits, manners, and
decorum which the world might envy but mostly sought to
imitate. Their roots were in the English good-temper which
comes from self-confidence, and in what Matthew Arnold
somewhat sourly noted (he thought it marched to excess
in his day) as "the Englishman's heaven-born privilege of
doing as he likes."

The successful combination of these in every level of
English life produced the ordered political progress of the
19th century. It moved through a succession of reform bills
to the liberalizing of the parliamentary structure and the
enlargement of the franchise and the development of co-
operative and labor movements. If Britain first produced
the problems of modern urbanism, of industrialization and
proletarianization, she was also first to produce the sober
instruments of reform: first (in spite of Tolpuddle Martyrs
and such) with trades-unionism and labor legislation and
the sturdy movements for self-help which have been the
special glory of the British workers, who have kept more
than most peoples in the barrack cities their essential native
characters and virtue. The damp, drab, and drear industrial
slums continued to swell, Cobbett's "great wen" of London
to grow, the countrysides and rural populations of Britain
to decline; but the standard-of-living steadily rose, the death-
rate fell, and the mechanical gadgets multiplied. Steam-
power come in and coal-gas and electricity and penny-
postage and the twopenny bus and the new police, who in
England have seemed a symbol of sober order rather than

a symptom of disciplines imposed by the expanding State. With them waxed the British middle classes, the creators and created of the new system; and the middle classes looked on what they had made and found it good. But being of a temper essentially acquisitive and progressive they thought that it might be better. They bent their energies to make it so.

Freedom was good; freedom should be extended. Order was good; order also should be extended. Honesty was the best policy; and they carried a novel measure of integrity into the conduct of business throughout the world and into the administration of their new subjects everywhere. Government immemorially in most of the world has been conducted on the ground by agents privileged to oppress and exploit. Even under the Roman Empire, the taxes were farmed out, to multiply in the exactions of the tax-gatherers who held the concessions.

The Second British Empire at its beginning impeached the greatest servant Britain ever had in India and set his honesty to test in a trial of seven years. Warren Hastings' personal tragedy gave occasion for the enunciation of great principles of public probity. The Second Empire produced for the world the highest model of administrative competence and honesty it has ever known. Order, freedom, and probity flourished under the British flag. The new imperialism crept up on the British middle classes almost unawares. It seeped up from their virtues and their sublime self-confidence. It expressed itself at the religious and philanthropic levels, as well as the commercial. The Free Traders and Liberals suddenly put out a tremendous missionary effort designed to carry the Victorian ethic and (it must be confessed) a somewhat Victorian Gospel into the heart of Africa and the furthest islands of the Pacific. The Church Missionary Society and the British and Foreign Bible Society and Exeter Hall were eminently representative of the new impulse. Christian Europe, Catholic and Protestant, produced the largest missionary effort since the conversion of the Roman Empire at the moment when Europe itself was on the eve of a new materialism and widespread apostasy. The new civilization was already sowing the contradictions which were to produce the whirlwinds of the 20th century.

With missionary effort, and the extension of order, and the growth of trade, and the increasing costs of colonial and imperial defense, a change came gradually in the minds of the British middle classes. It brought a new sense of responsibility to backward peoples, which no cynicism can discredit. "Darkest Africa" and Asia called some of the finest spirits Britain has produced to sweat out their lives in fever-holes. They sought for the natives spiritual freedom. They were prepared for its political consequences.

The expenses of Empire also perhaps prompted interest in men who still took a balanced budget as a term of moral virtue: and saw (with moral arguments) an income-tax as iniquity. The costs of Empire shocked them.

In 1850, the Privy Council announced the Orange River Colony as positively and without exception the last acquisition Britain would make in Africa. British officers were "interdicted in terms as explicit as can be employed and under sanctions as grave as can be devised from making any additions, whether permanent or provisional, of any territory, however small." [9] The Ionian Isles might be given away and proposals advanced for presenting the West Indies to the United States. But the thing still grew.

It grew because the British, once engaged, had little option but to advance in most colonial areas. Anarchy could not be tolerated on the frontiers of order. The raiding Kaffir, Zulu, and Afghan had to be reduced to some sense of discretion, if not of propriety.

[9] Report of the Privy Council: quoted from Knowles.

The native peoples themselves had to be protected from the disorders which ran ahead of European expansion. In Africa and Asia and the Pacific the lawless white adventurer had to be brought to heel and under control. In the Pacific especially, Empire moved too slowly rather than too quickly. Whole populations were decimated, massacred, or corrupted by wandering adventurers and outlaws and the passions and diseases they carried with them. The villages rotted with influenza, tuberculosis and syphilis; the beaches ran red with wanton murder until the Law came. Imperialism had to grow unless great areas of the world and large populations were to be the prey of licentious and rapacious freebooters, the scum of Europe, Asia, and America. The barriers were down. There were to be no more *terra incognita* or primitive Arcadias. The alternative to Empire was exploitation, ruin, death, and slavery.

The colonists could not be pinned to narrow coastal regions in Africa or Australia any more than the Americans could have been constrained behind the Alleghenies. Individuals and groups were always forcing the hand of government. Australia was not content to remain a little convict settlement. It drove its increasing flocks across the eastern mountains to spread on the vast plains. Count Streleczki finding gold during his scientific travels in Australia did at the request of authority suppress his news. But it could not be perpetually hidden, and population poured in with the great finds of the Fifties. His Majesty's Ministers might regard with distaste proposals for new colonies and settlements, but the colonists demanded that the British flag forestall the French in Tasmania, New Zealand, Western and South Australia.

Mr. Edward Gibbon Wakefield was especially provocative. He had a new scheme for colonization, and whether Government liked it or not he and his friends were determined to try it in Australia and New Zealand. The British

Government was especially reluctant to acquire New Zealand. But Samuel Marsden, the great missionary, was determined to force its hand if only to prevent the seamen, whalers and the like from taking Maori heads; [10] while Wakefield, who had once eloped with a ward in Chancery and later with the heiress of a wealthy manufacturer, now compelled the Government to make an honest woman of his New Zealand enterprise.

Wakefield was a Quaker with the passion for ordered liberty and the enterprising spirit which perhaps derives from William Penn. He was a catalytic influence in Canada, as well as in Australia and New Zealand; for he was Secretary to Lord Durham in the mission of 1838, and one of the authors of the Durham Report, a cornerstone of the Commonwealth System.

French Canada had been organized in the 17th century on the seignorial system and as a Royal Province with Governor, Bishop, Intendant, and a Sovereign Council corresponding to the old provincial *parlements*. The first thoughts of the English were to convert Lower Canada into a Colony of the English type. But in 1774, the Quebec Act gave the French an enlarged Council on which Catholics might sit. In 1791, Upper and Lower Canada each received its own Legislature and Lieutenant-Governor under the Governor-General. The French system of land-tenures and the traditional tithes and privileges of the clergy were allowed to Quebec.

The Legislatures lacked responsible executives; but for a generation neither Upper nor Lower Canada was much concerned. The French had little enthusiasm for the British allegiance. But they liked the French Revolution less; and the British had not grossly interfered with what were already

[10] Freelancing shipmasters before the Law arrived sometimes selected on one passage living heads to be severed and shriveled for delivery as trade by the chiefs on the return.

the traditional characters and social values of the French-Canadian culture. The French chiefly wished to be left alone. They had no sense of community with the English of the Maritimes or Upper Canada. These were mostly exiles from the revolted Colonies, and they had brought north with them their old suspicion and dislike of the French. In 1810 the prospects of a real national unity in Canada seemed immeasurably remote. By 1814, the two Canadas had grown at least one common interest. They had successfully held off American attack, and their minds and tempers had been steeled against American ambitions. But for the War of 1812 Canada might have joined with the United States at almost any time in the half-century of British indifference. But now to the French distaste for the Protestant values of the culture to the southward was added the indignation of English-speaking Canada. The War left bitter memories in the States of the burning of Washington; but the Canadians remembered that Toronto and Newark had been fired by invaders before Ross landed in Chesapeake Bay.

The Canadians, moreover, had felt their muscle in the successes of their militia troops. Canadian nationhood was born to Upper Canada in the forces under Sir Isaac Brock. In 1838, Durham found Canada still two countries; but he could call them nations.

Lord Durham came out as Governor-General on the heels of rebellions in the two Canadas. Both were rebellions against local abuses; and neither had any substantial promise of union with the United States or separation from Britain, though each gave its own twist to Canadian life and politics.[11] The rebellions were brief; the remedies,

[11] The rebellion in Upper Canada was led by the Scots journalist, William Lyon Mackenzie; and his memory has had influence on the career of his grandson, William Lyon Mackenzie King. The family probably derives by the Lyon branch from the same stock as Queen Elizabeth, born Bowes-Lyon.

effective. The Durham Report (a contemporary said: "Wakefield thought it; Butler wrote it; Durham signed it") proposed the union of the Canadas in a bicameral legislature, the surrender to it of Crown revenues, and responsible government. It expressed a principle of development which has always since influenced the political progress of British Dominions. The Crown must "submit to the necessary consequence of representative institutions; and if it has to carry on the government in unison with a representative body, it must consent to carry it on by means of those in whom that representative body has confidence. . . ."

Here was the exact description of the Cabinet System of Government as it had developed in the Mother Parliament at Westminster and as it has since been reproduced in all the self-governing Dominions of the Crown. The Union Act of 1840 did not explicitly provide for this Responsible Executive; but the Governors-General henceforward accepted it in practice and after 1847 in principle by a direction from the Crown.

In similar fashion the Second British Empire produced a string about the world of self-governing States or what we should now call Dominions: seven in the South Pacific countries, two in America, one in Africa. In something under one hundred years four new nations had come into being under the Second British Empire: two in the primeval wastes and two from small primary settlements on the marge of the primeval. We may allow that the Second Empire was not uncreative.

With self-government the family was rapidly growing up: and its members, as they will in families, seemed to be separating and drifting apart. Though the two Canadas had been unified, the general movement of the System was apparently centrifugal and eccentric. The six Australian Colonies toyed for undeciding decades with the theme of federation. In Arthur Mill's phrases the Colonies were apparently being rapidly and happily ripened "by all the appliances within the reach of the parent state for present self-government and eventual independence": this being in the 1850s "the universally admitted aim of our Colonial policy."

No one had yet caught the paradox which was to appear of a group of States effectively independent and yet (as two World Wars were to show) effectively united. Perhaps the only man of the mid-century who could have foreseen this prodigy was Lewis Carroll: although most of the English, like his Queen, are quite prepared in their normal practice to believe as many as six impossible things before breakfast. "When I use a word," Humpty Dumpty said in a rather scornful tone, "it means just what I choose it to mean— neither more nor less." Humpty has the authentic note: and Carroll, the pure juice and distillation of Englishry.

Its wind might be blowing due east; but like the Bellman's ship, the British System was headed west into the teeth of all probabilities.

* 2 *

It carried strange cargo.

Laissez-faire in its prime promised to liberalize all the economies and polities of the world. It seemed to the earnest Nonconformists and Low Churchmen, who were its chief disciples, to correspond in the secular world with the Reformation, to extend into the economic and political life its principle of private judgment and initiative, its refusal of traditional authority. The more devout still recognized a moral order. Thus Cobden's appeal to "the highest behests of Christianity." But the increasing inclination was to autonomy for economics. In economic action, the good became the economic good and indifferent to morals. It was good to buy in the cheapest markets, even in the cheapest labor markets. If a child or a woman could be had for a

man's work at half a man's wage, it was good. The manufacturers and mine-owners came to believe (conveniently,
of course) that the general economic good was served best
in the cheapest possible production and the highest possible
profits. Men who were not monsters on other counts defended zealously the use of child-labor in the mills and
mines, and resisted fanatically every effort to protect the
worker and his family from the appalling exploitation of
the decades between Waterloo and the Crimea. The spirit
of Puritan Protestantism did enter largely into the capitalist
expansion; as we can see in the rolls of the new industrialists and, by converse, in the comparative backwardness of
Catholic regions (though other factors from coal to the
weather were, of course, contributory). Puritan Protestantism brought a sturdy independence. It put emphasis on industry as a moral discipline. Man realized himself in work.
Wits and the sense of policy had been sharpened in the long
issues of Nonconformity. To the Puritan, the elect were
marked in this world as well as for the next by the Divine
patronage. Success in the material order became to him a
sign of his calling. He strove that he should shine before
men. And the stern regime of his life with its prohibitions
of many amiable pleasures and distractions left work as
almost his only recourse against the tedium of time, and
that other Enemy.

> "In works of labour or of skill,
>   I would be busy too;
>   For Satan finds some mischief still
>   For idle hands to do."

The proverbs and catches of the new temper are reveal-
ing. Mr. Smiles was much admired and Mr. Franklin's maxims were a sign of grace in America. The busy bee improved
each shining hour and time was money to the thrusting,
energetic men who transformed the world. But they were

acquiring a more secular and earthly note. For William Penn, as he expressed it in his *Reflections and Maxims,* "the moral man is he that loves God above all, and his neighbour as himself." For the serious-minded of the later age, honesty is the best policy (they missed Archbishop Whately's powerful addendum: "but he who is governed by that maxim is not an honest man"). The useful and the practical were becoming the highest that we know. In spite of church- and chapel-going, the new men were declaring for the autonomy of economics, not only as against the State but as against the moral system which they still professed and often in a private way practiced. They set religion and personal morality in one compartment, economics in another. Each sought its own good or end without reference to the other. They had completely lost the traditional sense that the activities of man have a hierarchic order and unity and that all are subject to the moral discipline which directs man to his final end.

The Reformation was indeed fulfilled in them; but its fulfillment finally broke the control of Christian morals over the social and economic life of man. In England, the State had with Henry VIII and Elizabeth brought religion under the political direction and interest. The Temporal Arm had asserted its supremacy over the Spiritual: the Church was rendered unto Caesar; and to the impulse of nationalism, which has largely usurped the emotive role of religion in the modern world. Now the new economic power was demanding its autonomy against the State, setting its own interest and good apart from the political interest; and inevitably apart from the religious and moral influence also. Men did not see what they were claiming any more than the physicists or chemists who today defend the autonomy and independence of their sciences always see clearly what they claim. It is true that within its own sphere each science or art should have a proper freedom to pursue its end. But its end must be defined and ordered in relation with the other ends of man. Man has a proper right to seek his food, an economic end. But he has not a right to murder other men in seeking it. Thus economic activity must be ordered to the larger good of the community. The physicist has a proper right to pursue the range of knowledge open and appropriate to his science. But he has not the right in his pursuit of physical truths to blow the world to pieces or to betray his brother to death and ruin. The activities of the physical sciences or the economic arts are not the highest activities of man or their ends his dominant and final ends: nor can they be isolated from his other pursuits and ends if right order is to be maintained in life and society. "If the foot should say: Because I am not the hand, I am not of the body: is it therefore not of the body?"

We nowadays complain that moral philosophy has lagged behind our technical progress as if in some curious way the fault was not in ourselves but of the moral order. In fact, we threw off moral philosophy. Ethics was pushed into a Sunday corner, set aside and apart from our economic and technical efforts. What had "The Iron Law of Wages" to do with justice, or the moralists with the application of science?

Utilitarianism held the social field. But it produced its reaction, which has obscured the proper arguments for laissez-faire within a moral order and depreciated its gigantic material achievements. The reaction equally rejected morals. It accepted the autonomy of economics. It went further. It insisted that the fundamental meanings of life and history could be found only in an economic interpretation. It reduced the whole social life of man, his religions and his arts to a flickering nimbus about the mode of production.

This reaction in its major manifestation we know as Socialism; and its great exponent was Karl Marx. History again produces with Marx one of its ironic symbols. Marx, though a German Jew, did his work in England because it was only in the liberal society of England that he could freely agitate against the whole concept of the liberal society.

Marx's elaborate thesis (stripped of its romanticism and wishful thinking) meant the reassertion of the State's supremacy over all life. He was, though abjured of Israel and committed to a sublimated materialism, of messianic bent; and the State is an alternative to men who reject God but still seek a Providence. Much of his language has a cabalistic character. In a palpable reading "the dictatorship of the proletariat" is meaningless. Dictatorships are not divided among the multitudes. Marxism (as we have seen wherever its principles have been applied) means in practice a highly centralized political authority in absolute command of life. It promises at an indeterminable date the resolution of conflicts between classes and nations in the universal dominance of one great State. Marx's conception of life and politics when translated into reality is not remote from those of Machiavelli, Thomas Cromwell, or the Cecils.

Two powerful factors worked for Marxism. First, the abuses of laissez-faire capitalism provoked hostile reaction. Marx himself saw the opportunity in terms of thesis and antithesis. He would have been surprised to find that in Russia his doctrine provided an alternative also to autocracy and feudalism; a curious fact which his followers have never adequately reconciled with their orthodox determinism.

Secondly, Marx gave to misery a sort of metaphysic, to rancor and resentment, a rationale: his mystique and his apocalyptic note have drawn, if they have not fed (in the de-Christianized) the religious sense, man's appetite for God. This in the 18th and 19th centuries had been increasingly starved or perverted.

The divisions of the Reformation and the influence of

Nationalism on religious sentiment and organization had gravely weakened the influence and prestige of the Churches. The Rationalism of the 18th century had gnawed at the roots of Christian belief. In the French Revolution, Rationalism and Nationalism had combined to produce the curious cult of *La Patrie* and the Goddess of Reason.

But more significantly (especially in Britain) the machinery of the Churches failed to meet the new conditions of industrial urbanism. The majority of Christian pastors were settled in comfortable ways. But the masses of the industrial towns had been ripped out of small communities ordered by ancient and familiar values and traditions. There men had grown in a settled moral climate, absorbing their beliefs and values from the social context in which they were born and informed and nurtured. The new barrack-towns of the Industrial Revolution had no such social order. The uprooted men were thrown into the heaving mass, whose only principle of social organization was by factory, shop, or mine. The new towns were not communities, but aggregates of individuals. Many kept some measure of traditional moral values by their personal tenacity and courage. But they lacked the support and sustenance of a coherent social and moral community. We notice as one symptom of the new situation the appearance of large professional police-forces.

At this moment when the uprooted workers were torn from their immemorial communities, they also lost their old crafts and skills: the accumulated experience of their generations which had passed as heritage from father to son, and carried the satisfactions which lie in responsible work and the prides of craftsmanship. They became machine-minders, the more intelligent elements of mechanical processes. They became employees making other people's goods with other people's gadgets to other people's ideas. Being men, most did in time again acquire some satisfaction in work, but never to the old degree; for they did not recover responsibility. Irresponsibility was increasingly a character of the industrial masses. Irresponsibility in work (which is properly a constant influence in moral education) induced irresponsibility elsewhere. They came to look to mechanical processes for entertainment and to external provisions for social security. Their attitudes began to be dependent. They became appropriate subjects for the Social Service State; and it became inevitable, because propertyless workers could not be left without some social frame. They were no longer men living an adequate social life with personal satisfactions in their own work and responsibilities. The village craftsmen may have been illiterate (a surprising proportion actually were soundly read in great books, and Cromwell's Army was not illiterate), but they were richly educated in their people's lore and their crafts and by the constant exercise of mind and will in personal work. The popular arts of Europe, their music, song, dance, drama, local architectures do not suggest a race of boors and bumpkins. But all these were lost to the industrial workers. They slowly developed new resources of a kind. But for decades, the gin-palaces and less respectable venues were the chief resorts of such leisure as they had.

Schools were in time organized as substitutes for the formative influences of organic communities. But popular education has never adequately recovered the intimate relationship between life, work, and learning which most men need for intellectual and moral growth. The schools were usually organized on pseudo-academic principles, and the children of the new slums and suburbs had little spiritual or mental profit of them. They made literates of a sort: a reading public for a vulgar literature which destroyed the integrity of letters and corrupted the instruments of thought.

Men were no longer living responsible and proper personal or social lives. They were socially significant only as "hands"; but the individual "hand" had no necessary or organic relation to the social body. He was expendable. His economic life hung by a thread which any whim of the employer or freak of the economy might sever. His insecurity, his irresponsibility, his loss of creative work and of a social context in which he was supported and sustained have all gone to produce the vast unquiet of modern society, its fevers, frets, anxieties. Industrial man is on the loose, astray, uprooted, and he blows where the wind listeth.

The vast growth and concentrations of populations which came with the Industrial Revolution burst the old orders of society. The instruments of cultural and moral values grow slowly. They could not contain the human flood.

The modern masses (in collars or collarless) were left uninstructed and uninformed by the intellectual and moral traditions of the West. In all history there is no comparable loss of a cultural heritage unless at the barbarian invasions. The frame of social life, the accumulated organized experience of fifteen centuries was lost to the majority. They were left open to shallow and superficial winds of opinion; they succumbed to superstitions, some ridiculous, some sinister. Ignorance let in, as it always does, conceit and intellectual arrogance: the masses succumbed to charlatans in the arts, the arts of living as well as the representational arts. The sciolists, the cunning demagogues, came in time to their kingdoms. Fantastic propagandas raised clever knaves to dizzy heights in politics and brought great nations down to ruin. People no longer knew what they wanted: advertising came to tell them even what to eat and how to eat. Tastes, inclinations, and ambitions were formed and directed by the crudest propagandas. Hitler and ballyhoo could become at last major influences in society because men were less and less responsible mentally, morally and socially.

The great Churches had been for the masses the principal instrument of instruction at the higher levels of the old culture. But they had been organized on regional bases appropriate to the dispersed populations of a rural Europe. As populations were sucked from the countrysides and rural parishes into the industrial warrens to multiply like rabbits, the ecclesiastical organization was left to limp slowly after, if it came on at all. In England, the Established Church seemed bogged in its pleasant pastures. Only a few devoted men ran after the multitudes with the good tidings. Wesley and later Booth strove heroically. Those industrial workers who held to Christianity found it mostly with them, or with the Nonconformist sects already established in the towns.

The Church of England retained some hold in the countrysides and it kept its social prestige. But as social disintegration developed and the rifts widened between the classes and the masses this proved its disaster. The soured stomachs of the mill-hands and miners turned from it as the resort of privilege. The Church of England has not since recovered the proportion of communicants in the British population it then lost, though it has given of its best men and energies to the effort.

On the Continent, industrialism came more slowly. But there too the Christian machinery lagged; and Pope Pius XI could describe the losses among the industrial masses as the greatest tragedy of the 19th century.

Christianity declined partly in the default and confusion of its preachers and teachers, partly in its failure to penetrate the new social milieux. The hungry sheep looked up and were not fed. Wandering, they ate weeds and bred sour vapors. Sheep and men will find something to stay the pangs even if they eat dirt; and all man's history attests that he has a spiritual and intellectual hunger which he will somehow strive to stay.

As the traditional beliefs retreated, others were drawn in by the vacuum. Darwin's revision of the theory of evolution acquired a startling significance its predecessors had missed.

From a hypothesis or series of hypotheses in the order of physical science it was quite unscientifically enlarged in the popular sense to embrace man's ultimate origins and ends and meanings. It filled a 19th-century bill with extraordinary success. It especially met the needs of the devoted capitalist, rentier, and entrepreneur. These had not yet wholly thrown off the unease of the conflict between what they remembered of Christian teachings and the doctrines of the laissez-faire economists. Adam Smith may have insisted that economics must pursue its own good. The steelmasters may have felt themselves elect in the new dispensation. But still they heard echoes of strange doctrines: *blessed are the meek for they shall inherit the earth; blessed are the poor in spirit for theirs is the kingdom of heaven.* The new rich with their family Bibles on the occasional tables among the antimacassars were yet sometimes disturbed by curious talk of a camel and the eye of a needle, of Dives and Lazarus. But one phrase of Darwin's broke suddenly on them, one great chord not lost but found and like a grand Amen. He himself had introduced it quietly as "the expression often used by Mr. Herbert Spencer of the Survival of the Fittest." It became a new and passionate faith. The Survival of the Fittest, Natural Selection: here were answers to such difficulties as might remain in the consciences of mill-owners; here were hints for a new racist doctrine of Herrenvolk; here was the first sketch for the "mercy killers," for gas-chambers and concentration camps. At once, Mr. Darwin's discoveries seemed immeasurably more apt than the Beatitudes to the facts as the masters knew or made them. Their ownership of land and factories and mines and ships was not now an obstacle to salvation. They were already elect and justified; they were the fit who had survived.

Mr. Darwin's triumph was immense, though not entirely respectable (the Throne and Church were dubious and his monkey-stuff still had to have its edge blunted in the music-halls). Many disciples began to make lively and profitable careers by deploying his principles against the general front of conventional thought and values. Evolution explained such a number of difficulties and almost always in an optimistic sense, if Mr. Darwin was correctly interpreted by his popularizers. These, rather than Mr. Darwin, had the public ear; for *The Origin of Species* was a very hefty book and most people preferred to take it predigested. The great matter was that Science now confirmed the strong suspicion that we were Progressing.

Prince Albert's Exhibition in Hyde Park was eminently vindicated. The new railways and the *Great Eastern* were no delusions. Man really was getting on in the world. We could happily assume that the post-Darwinian Age would bring a universal peace and prosperity now that we had answered all those old nagging questions about whence and why we came and whither we were going. Even the Vicar probably felt (underneath his surplice, of course, unless he boldly stood with Bishop Colenso) somewhat comforted that the Serpent was only a figurative Serpent in a symbolic Garden and the Day of Judgment unlikely to arrive for some time yet and perhaps not quite as Saint John would have it.

The new ideas coiled swiftly down through every level of society; for they were ease to many consciences and answers to many questions and they filled many vacuums. Christian dogma took a fearful beating.[12] Christian dogmas were seldom met on rational ground. They were not overthrown by logic. They were attacked by a general notion that dogmas were bad sorts of things to have about, obstacles in the path of progress. The rational character of theology and philosophy were anyhow caviar to the general; and they had few immediate or tangible benefits to offer. The physical sciences, on the other hand, were rich in useful application

[12] I believe it was Mr. D. B. Wyndham Lewis who remarked that any stigma would do to beat a dogma.

and by-products. The physical scientist became the new prophet of Progress. If he set up in a philosophic or moral line as he went, people hardly questioned his competence. The physicist and chemist had become the wise men of the tribe; and people who would not have listened to a plumber on God (unless for entertainment in Hyde Park) took Mr. Huxley's dicta as the latest thing in revelations. The philosophers were isolated in their ivory towers; the theologians were forgotten except as quaint survivals of a human mode outworn. Their influence, which properly should inform the whole intellectual life, was lost, stolen, or astray.

Our fathers might with equal flightiness have arbitrarily dismissed the dogmas of geometry. In the increasing confusion they no longer recognized the rational element. In the increasing ignorance they no longer remembered the gains of patient centuries in the moral sciences and metaphysics. Religion became a mere matter of "good feeling," philanthropy its chief social expression. Reason seemed irrelevant to such religious experience as they still cared to cultivate. Science (and again, this now meant the physical sciences only) had swept the intellectual board. It had all the answers, even to questions with which it could in right order have no concern. The scientists themselves were dazzled and to many the mantle of the prophet was a powerful temptation. Some snatched at it.

Science seeks to know. But the technique of knowledge in the field of physics does not fit a man to prescribe rules for the arts of life. The physicist may become a competent moralist, as may the clerk or plumber. But skill and competence among the drains or atoms do not of themselves equip a man in moral philosophy: as we may see by glancing about us. Our intellectual controls passed to a race of specialists and technicians. But the tasks of synthesis were neglected. Knowledge became departmentalized and sectionalized. There was no longer a comprehensive system. Confusion spread from the realms of ideas to quicken processes of disintegration in the social body.

The rejection of the rational and dogmatic elements of religion is understandable. They were no longer taught or required in half the churches. When Newman tried to vindicate the rational status of religious belief, people deplored a stylist wasted on such unprofitable themes. And working perennially against the Christian Argument was men's distaste for its moral disciplines. The Christian life is a trial and a Cross; and men will take it up only if they are convinced that its demands are rational.

Luther's influence had in general been hostile to "that whore, Reason"; and neither Rome nor Canterbury had much encouraged laymen to theological learning. The promise of the Renaissance, of the broad and lively Christian Humanism of More, Erasmus, and Fisher had been dissipated.

But Christian morals must rest on Christian beliefs; and Christian beliefs must be sustained by Christian doctrines. If Christian doctrines were shed, Christian morals would remain only as conventions surviving at convenience. This was precisely what happened. If we dismissed the Law Giver, why should we keep the Law? Man's higher behavior has always been governed by reasons and sanctions. But if the universe is irrational and has no judge, why should not man do as he pleases? Why should not little Johnny raid the family jam if he can come clean away? Why should we be constrained by moral principles if these have no dogmatic bases, but are rooted only in primitive fears and tribal tabus? Let us gambol at our pleasure about the Golden Bough in *fin-de-siècle* jollity.

All this of course did not at once penetrate the minds of the masses. The English workman still mostly lived as a decent, solid sort of man, with his pipe and his pub. The English middle classes continued in a passage of conventions: for the first instinct when moral bases are rotting is to stiffen the conventions, to prop the tottering roofs and walls. It is a temporary expedient. They will be about the ears sooner or later. But for a moment the weaknesses may be disguised and the dangers hid. The Victorian world proceeded on a majestic way to two world wars and confusion now growing more confounded. But the new notions were percolating through the social fabric.

The symptoms could be seen by the discerning. Carlyle, Ruskin, Morris, Marx each pointed to some or others. But none went to the root or saw the matter whole. The Victorian public shrugged them off and continued on its way to the pub or club. But the ordinary honest man was being changed in spite of himself and perhaps without his knowledge. The values of his milieu were changing. He was moving into a new moral climate. The working-man might not be much acquainted with the notions of more literate classes. But they soaked down through the social structure, modifying manners and morals. A change in mood and character is noticeable. It appears for example in the curious, strained nostalgia of Dickens for a merrier sort of England. The English took their pleasures sadly. The Victorian world in spite of its vast achievements and creative energies has a shadow over it and not only over its slums. It is from a darkening of the spirit. The lights were beginning to flicker in Europe long before the night of August 1914 when Sir Edward Grey watched them going out.[13]

From the shadows straining, were faces pale and intent, the faces of the dispossessed, the desocialized, the de-

[13] The 19th century shed the old moral system and with it the social being it had informed. The advanced among us have gone further. The old prohibitions became in our parlance inhibitions. It was not enough to shake them off. They must be confounded. It became desirable to break the spell of the Commandments and other items of the sort by breaking them: for nothing so reduced the life of man as his inhibitions. It was right, it was good, it was necessary to enjoy the rich experiences of adultery, theft, and

spiritualized, the uprooted peoples of the dirty towns and the dormitory suburbs. Standing over from them beside the pillars of society, pressing on these, testing them, was Marx, an unshorn Samson: a figure far less respectable than Mr. Darwin but as formidable, and with no comfort in him for the men of property.

The poor had heard of Mr. Darwin's monkeys and sometimes as they looked at the dwarfed, undernourished, rickety children about them they may have suspected that he had something there. But they did not wholly swallow the other pill: the Survival of the Fittest. It was not sugared for them. For they clearly were not the Fit in this world of harsh competition and shrewd practice. Yet they wanted to survive. They were (as they thought more of it) determined to survive: and if they could not be the Surviving Fit of this environment, then (they began to think) they might try another.

They caught Marx's eye; and though they mostly still looked hastily away, they remembered, and Marx spat on his hands and tried again the strength of the pillars.

All this was born or conceived in the Second Empire even as it reached across the seas and continents. This seed also it was to scatter in its commerce of ideas and its cultural dominion: and perhaps here was its most formidable meaning in the world; because ideas will work through history to remotest time when the bridges are long broken and the railroads are forgotten and men wonder for what purposes we shaped our steel and stones thus.

(why not as we progressed and could get away with it?) of murder. This new reverse or perverse of the old morality made rapid head. It climbed into high places, it rode into seats of power, it launched upon the world unprecedented slaughter. Its first great orgasm has ended and the world lies prostrate from it, quivering. But it has not done with us yet. For it goes on working through society. It is no longer a prerogative of the privileged classes.

SEVEN

THE THIRD EMPIRE: THE FIRST

PASSAGE

THE Third British Empire grew in this changing moral and intellectual climate. It grew in part from the philanthropic and missionary impulse which was quickening even while the faith of Western Europe itself was in decline: as if again the stone rejected by the builders were to become elsewhere the headstone of the corner.[1]

In Britain, as in America, the missionary energy came largely from the middle classes who had prospered under

---

[1] Yet the Christian population of the world has increased more rapidly in the last century than in any other of history: perhaps by 300,000,000. Catholicism (its figures are the handiest to come by) has grown by approximately 200,000,000. This increase has come, of course, with the general growth of world-population; but the Christian Churches have made remarkable gains in Asia, Africa, and Oceania.

laissez-faire. They were hardly conscious yet of what was happening to belief, even in themselves; the *mores* still survived, reinforced by the stiffened conventions of the mid-Victorian age. Perhaps deep within themselves they found in missionary propaganda some compensation for the loosening of their belief. Protestantism had not been remarkable for the works of mercy. It had made until the 19th century little effort to convert the Red Indian, the Hindu, the African. It had not restored or adequately maintained the public hospitals and refuges of pre-Reformation times. It had restricted the old public schools to the children of privilege. But in the 19th century it took a strong philanthropic turn. Ultimately Protestantism, in reverse of its original position, was to count works more than faith. William Wilberforce and Florence Nightingale are the pre-eminent figures of Protestant Humanism. Its emphases gradually outweighed the doctrinal heritage of Luther, Calvin, Knox; now few English-speaking Protestants could give a coherent account of the beliefs they nominally profess. The philanthropic mood combined readily with Liberalism even though it was ultimately in conflict with laissez-faire. Wilberforce's campaign against slavery was the first of the great modern efforts to elevate the masses. It was strongly supported by the Low Church or Nonconformist Liberals who were also the pith and energy of utilitarian capitalism; and they again were the chief support of the foreign and colonial missions and of such enterprises as the Society for the Promotion of Christian Knowledge. Men are much more complex than the trends and tendencies which historians love to abstract. Individuals sometimes seem microcosms and to include the oppositions and contradictions of their times.

The anti-slavery movements, the missions, and the Bible Societies reveal a fresh appreciation of the world outside and an acceptance of the widening responsibilities. More conscious attention was being given to the implications of Empire. The campaigns against slavery required and encouraged increasing intervention by the State in colonial affairs. Parliament voted £20,000,000 in 1833, an enormous figure in the budgets of those days, for emancipation; and emancipation set problems of economic reconstruction which the State could not ignore.

Even in the heyday of laissez-faire the factors which would make for more political intervention were steadily accumulating. The Indian Mutiny compelled Parliament at last to take over completely the governmental functions of the East India Company. Perhaps the deepening mood of doubt and question also prompted a new awareness of imperial problems. A planned regimen is usually in human affairs an answer to some weakness observed or suspected. We apply a plaster to a toe when it aches. The Imperialism of Joseph Chamberlain which dominates the thinking and debate of the first passage of the Third Empire was a symptom. Britain was beginning to feel the competition of industrial rivals and, for the first time since the 18th century, to find other powers advancing in the colonial fields.

One can detect also a certain brittleness in the new Imperialism. The England of Chamberlain had not the superb self-confidence of the England of Castlereagh and Palmerston. The motives of Imperialism were under acute criticism at home. The Boer Wars ultimately were to split British opinion. The Empire as attention turned upon it needed explanation and defense. Marryat could take it all for granted. Kipling became its propagandist and apologist.

But it was beginning to be prized. The majority no longer wanted to be rid of it. Their investment in it had grown and so had their pride. In the colonies which were to be Dominions the movement towards integration quickened. They were growing up sufficiently to understand their own problems, and of these the first was obviously security. It became urgent in the face of rival and expanding imperialisms.

Interest in the Empire grew also as communications and instruments of information were multiplied and speeded, and as more men from all classes came to move about the world or to read newspapers and books. In 1820, only a handful of Englishmen had acquaintance with India or the great Colonies. Sixty years later hundreds of thousands of soldiers and seamen had footslogged over Africa or shipped "somewheres east of Suez," gone "to fetch you your bread and your butter, your beef, pork, and mutton, eggs, apples, and cheese": they had known the scud and the palm-trees and the road to Mandalay. Every hamlet in the Islands from Banff to Bantry Bay had sent emigrants abroad. Year by year harvesters went to Canada and returned.

The people were learning "an imperial lesson," and as Kipling added, "it might make us an Empire yet."

The Second Empire had been chiefly an affair of the trading and merchant classes and of "the younger sons." The Third Empire engaged the people in the great migrations, in the vast increase of traffic and the extended policing. By the 20th century, one often found a wider knowledge of the Dominions in the farm-laborers' cottages and the East End pubs than in the suburban villas and the counting-houses. Millions of laborers and artisans had at least contemplated emigration and formed some notion of the prospects. The outer world became a familiar topic in the minds of the many; and as they looked abroad, they saw with something of a shock that a large part of it was colored their British red.

With general literacy and some book-learning in history and geography, with a popular press, workingmen's institutes, and the like came the new note of criticism, but also a natural and general pride in the British achievement. This was notably fed in popular literature. *The Boy's Own Paper* and later *Chums* had a profound effect on the young British male. They caught his imagination with remarkably well-written stories of the Canadian prairies, forests, and waterways, of the Northwest Frontier, the Australian plains, the Niger and Zambesi, the veldt, the coral islands, the ocean vasts. They peopled his mind with trappers and hunters, prospectors, boundary-riders, Gurkhas, Sikhs, Zulus, Red Indians, Fuzzy-Wuzzies, Dyaks, and the Royal Northwest Mounted Police. They prompted him with careful directions to outdoor enterprises, to the care of his health, the use of his hands. They taught him to make canoes and nets and to knock up sheds. Dr. Gordon Stables must have been responsible for enormous sales of hammers, nails, knives, fish-hooks and Indian clubs; and for more emigrants than any other man in England. He made straight the paths for Baden-Powell and the Boy Scouts: one of the greatest international movements of a voluntary and moral character in modern times, and the first of the youth movements with which we are still beset. But the literature of which Stables was the dean was not escapist. It had useful, positive, and powerful influence on the youthful Britain which came at his heels.[2]

Reading has immense effect on imaginations yet unjaded and on minds which still largely learn by parables. Whoever has dealt with adults in the way of education knows that their ideas, information, values, judgments, prejudices largely derive from childhood miscellanea. *The Boy's Own Paper* and its kind were genuinely instructive, and aptly designed for children or young adolescents. We probably have since made a colossal blunder by allowing young fancies and feelings to be flooded through cinema and radio

[2] A little later the penny or twopenny weeklies of the *Gem* and *Magnet* sort, with their stories of life in public schools, spread through the English masses the code by which the British upper classes "play the game."

with images and ideas intended for the adult sense, experience, and appetites. The youth of the 1880s do seem to have been free of psychoses which are spreading darkly across our world.

A more sophisticated literature took up for adults the themes of Dr. Stables and his authors. Rudyard Kipling presented the pageant and people of Empire to the London clerks and the country parsons, the businessmen, the butchers, bakers, and grocers, and the circulating-library readers in the suburbs.

Within his range, Kipling was a master of human character and social fact. He evoked the common soldier and the artisan, the tradesmen and the technicians of Empire. He described its mechanics and he invested its common tasks and tools, its ships, railway engines, bridges, roads, and regiments with wonder. Men blinked a little as their familiar round was touched with the glory. The shipping-clerk in Liverpool saw his dull routine and staid manifests as part of the magnificent scenario. The sweating engineer suddenly knew his work as creative. The shipmaster or trainman caught some sense of vocation. Kipling turned their eyes back from the light of common day towards the trailing clouds of glory. He raised the imperial theme to passionate utterance. He was its poet and prophet and propagandist and phrase-maker.[3]

He held it in the mirror for men to look on and know. He was, with all the deficiencies which critics of delicate taste observe, a proper artist with a proper social function. The Empire that was in Hind will be remembered as Kipling saw it; and he saw it primarily (and honestly, for no considerable artist can be persistently perverse, even if he tries) as a service:

[3] He has more space in *The Oxford Dictionary of Quotations* than any other writer except Shakespeare, Milton, and Tennyson.

"Take up the White Man's burden—
Send forth the best ye breed—
Go, bind your sons to exile
To serve your captives' need."

This was not perhaps the happiest way of putting it, and there were all too obvious ripostes. But service, obligation, duty, competence, toughness, shrewdness, loyalty, discipline, order, creativeness, courage, craftsmanship were the merits of Kipling's Empire; and he did not wholly miss the vices. The virtues bent on God do not much appear, but Kipling grasped very clearly the social obligations. He could see at least the human values of Paul's great teaching that we are every one members one of another: a truth most obvious in every phase of life, for we live in a vast social context reaching far beyond our own perceptions and are born, fed, clothed, instructed, nursed, sheltered, and transported only because countless others through time and space contribute to our being. Of all evident facts this is the one most neglected in "practical" politics. But it and the urgent sense of vocation, of responsibility, and of competence give to Kipling's Empire almost a religious note, and certainly a philosophy: a philosophy for the man of affairs, the executive, the administrator, the engineer, mechanic, craftsman. Perhaps the reality of Empire was never quite on land or sea as Kipling saw it; but his pageant has a representational and symbolic truth.

We may come closer to the inner meanings and character of the Third Empire in Kipling's verse and prose than in the bluebooks and statistics, though he catches, of course, but one man's view and that not of the broadest or most generous sort.

Too much, of course, may be made of the awakening to Empire. Macaulay's complaint still had validity: "It might have been expected that every Englishman who takes any

interest in any part of history would be anxious to know
how a handful of his countrymen separated from their home
by an immense ocean, subjugated in the course of a few
years one of the greatest empires in the world. Yet unless
we greatly err, this subject is to most readers not only
insipid but positively distasteful."

The truth is that the whole story was too prodigious, too
bizarre. As Seeley said: "Never did any nation certainly,
since the world began, assume anything like so much responsibility. Never did so many vast questions in all parts
of the globe, questions calling for all sorts of special knowledge and special training, depend upon the decision of a
single public." The Thing as a whole was too much for
the imagination of the ordinary Briton who lacks the French
passion for *le jour de gloire,* and thinks more of beer. He
was content to sing *Soldiers of the Queen* at decent intervals and to cheer the Old Lady with domestic fervor. But
he has not yet understood the whole that he made; and he
and his compatriots overseas have missed tides on which
the world might have embarked great ventures.

* 2 *

The Third British Empire visibly emerges from the Second
in the 1870s. Canadian federation helps to fix the dates. It
begins a phase of political integration, not of the whole but
of several great blocs within the System; and it brings the
federal theme to be woven widely into the Third Pattern.

The federal union of the six separate Colonies of Quebec,
Ontario, Nova Scotia, New Brunswick, Prince Edward
Island, and British Columbia in 1867-71 [4] launched the
unique political phenomenon which we now describe in
terms of Commonwealth and Dominions; though it evaded
definition for two generations and still misses an exact
formula.

---

[4] British Columbia joined the others four years after their federation.

Canada almost at once revealed a national outlook, character, and policy which promised the early realization of full sovereign responsibility in every fact as well as in form. The Dominion of Canada was plainly something other than a colony or a dependency. The rapid appearance of clear, coherent economic policies demonstrated a community consciously master of its own destiny. Canada was in character and legal disposition now an equal of the United Kingdom. Her constitutional history for three-quarters of a century was to be the unfolding of meanings implicit in the new Federal State and Nation of 1871.

Curiously, the most vigorous opposition in Canada to federation came from those who believed that it would ultimately mean absorption in the United States. Against local federation, Joseph Howe of Nova Scotia argued for the association of the several colonies in a larger Imperial federation: the first loud plea for a proposal canvassed through the following fifty years. Some unusual premonition may have crossed his native liberalism to make John Bright oppose Canadian federation; for this new British System which it introduced was to turn away from free trade, and the several Dominions were to march in the van of economic nationalism.

Thirty-three years after Canada's, the six Australian Colonies formed their Federation. New Zealand was twelve hundred miles distant and already distinguishable in social and cultural character; and like Newfoundland in the Canadian case, it stayed out. But Australia and New Zealand in their remote seas under Asia were with the years and wars to develop a special relation of their own within the general system. Its seed was planted at Anzac [5] Cove on April 25, 1915. The soil was the common racial stock (for the Australians and New Zealanders are of English, Irish, Scots, and

[5] For "Australian New Zealand Army Corps": the combined force which first sought and found a common martial glory for the two peoples.

Welsh stock, except for a tiny percentage, and possibly more British in blood than the inhabitants of the Island itself). The climate was the common peril which appeared in 1941-2. The first fruit was the Anzac Pact of 1944. The Anzac Pact was also perhaps (to modify the figure) the stirring of what is still largely wrapt in the womb of the future: the Fourth British System, on whose difficult gestation this book attends.

* 3 *

The opening of the Suez Canal in 1869 also helps to date the coming of the Third British Empire. It turned the major course of the world's trade and shortened by thousands of miles the eastward passages to India, Malaya, China, the East Indies and Pacific. It linked the Australasian routes (theretofore via the Cape and Horn) with the great ports of Southern Asia. It made the Middle East, as it had been in ancient times, the strategic hub of world communications. It brought Palestine, Syria, Egypt, Persia and the Arab lands generally back into world politics and economics. It led the British into a new phase of imperial expansion in North Africa and on the coasts of the Red Sea. It took them into Egypt to re-organize the administration and finances of a country reduced to disorder by the extravagance and tyranny of its rulers. It brought the curious and brilliant imagination of Disraeli to the Imperial theme.

British Ministers before him had missed the significance of the Canal. They had refused to contribute to its construction or to buy shares in the Company. But perhaps some deep sense in his blood of race and place stirred the imagination of Disraeli. No Jew could be indifferent to the corner of the world between the Nile and the Persian Gulf. Here for thousands of years the traffic and ideas of three continents had met and crossed and mingled. Here had appeared three world religions. Here were the cradles of

civilized life. Here the great conquerors even to Napoleon
had come through ages beyond count.

The passage by the Cape to the Eastern world had somewhat reduced the significance of the region, but now the
opening of Suez more than restored it. Mr. Disraeli and the
Rothschilds moved at their first opportunity to seize advantage for the British System, in which their Jewish people had
found liberty and scope unprecedented since the Dispersion.

The strategic considerations were weighted by the rapid
growth of two imperial systems with evident ambitions to
compete.

During the 17th, 18th and 19th centuries, the Russians
were planting out colonies of peasants, political exiles, and
convicts across Asia: eastwards to the Pacific, southwards
about the Caspian to the marches of Persia and Turkey,
southeastwards to the frontiers of Afghanistan with its approaches to India. They had reached Tobolsk by the time
of the Armada. Two generations later they were at Irkutsk
and Baikal and above the northwest and north frontiers of
China. At the end of the 17th century they were in Kamchatka. Vitus Bering found his strait in 1728 and probably
discovered Alaska. This advance was of little consequence
to any European power of the time; but in the 19th century,
Russia began to look southwards in both the Eurasian land-
mass and the Pacific. Paul I shared Napoleon's designs on
India. In 1847, the Russians came down the Amur annexing
Chinese territory north of the river and presently founding
Vladivostok. Strong Russian squadrons appeared in the
Pacific. In the middle of the century the Russians held a
fort just north of San Francisco on the Californian coast
and were busy about Hawaii.

The Crimean War had repercussions in the remote South
Pacific when the Russians based an 80-gun battleship and

four 60-gun frigates on Valparaiso, while their North Pacific force had at least fourteen large frigates. In May 1854, a Russian squadron was operating from Manila.

Fear of the Russians gave the first impulse to the instinct for self-defense in Australia. Each of the little Colonies began to arm furiously. The Royal Naval Squadron in Australasian waters was reinforced by colonial ships. New South Wales built Australia's first home-made naval vessel. Victoria acquired a tiny navy of her own, which came to include in 1867 a fifty-three-year-old battleship,[6] at her birth the largest ever built in England. The appearance at Melbourne of the Confederacy's *Shenandoah* inspired Australia's first ironclad.

Russian "scares" recurred to alarm Australia for several decades, and to prompt conversations among the various Australian Colonies and with the Mother Country on the theme of local federation.

The Russian effort in Asia was sharpened after the Czardom's final failure in 1878 to acquire Constantinople and control of the Straits. Compensation was sought elsewhere. Though Alaska was sold to the United States in 1867, Russia collected Sakhalin from the Japanese in exchange for two of the Kuriles in 1875, and moved down to the frontiers of Chinese Turkestan and Afghanistan with the capture of Merv in 1885. Russia's pressure was strong on Turkey, Persia, and China. In 1898, she reached in the East Port Arthur and warm water. It seemed that she might play a role in China corresponding to that of the British in India.

The Germans maneuvered for position in the Far East. As the Russians moved into Port Arthur, the Germans took Kiaochow. They opened negotiations with Spain for the

---

[6] Between Trafalgar and the rise of German naval power the world was mercifully free of naval "races," and the old wooden walls served for generations until the coming of the ironclad.

purchase of the Philippines.[7] The United States was roused. The Spanish-American War carried the Americans across the Pacific to the new storm-center of world politics. Dewey sank the Spanish Pacific fleet at Manila. Manila was invested. The German Admiral von Diedrich arrived with a squadron superior to Dewey's. The situation was tense. At its crisis, Commodore Chichester of the Royal Navy moved his ship between the German and American squadrons.

The Americans took Manila and the Philippines to secure their advanced bases in the westward course of empire.

In 1898 the Philippines seemed remote, and there was lively opposition in the States to annexation; but history was digging in her hooks, and "manifest destiny" would not be denied. The Philippines might prove but an incident and a stepping-stone in America's career. But America from the day she reached her western coasts was involved in the problems of the Pacific and its contiguous lands.

The British bolstered Turkey against Russia and were active to establish effective counter-influence in Persia long before its oil intensified the problems and importance of the Middle East.

But Russia was overstretched and underdeveloped for the tasks set her from the Baltic to the Yellow Sea. She lacked the economic strength to consolidate her eastern flank.

A German-Russian coalition in the East was a possibility of the Eighties and Nineties. But for their European rivalries, it might have appeared. If the Germans had succeeded Spain in the Philippines, such a combination might have mastered China and reduced Japan. Much history swung with Dewey's guns and Chichester's maneuver in Manila

---

[7] They did buy from Spain the Carolines, the Ladrones (or Marianas) except Guam, and the Palaus, for 25,000,000 pesetas (about $4,875,000). For Alaska, the United States paid $7,200,000 or a penny an acre.

Bay; and with the Anglo-Japanese alliance to check German and Russian hegemony in the Far East.

Japan's victory against Russia exposed the weakness of the Russians eastward and of their economy and polity. It struck also a tremendous blow at white prestige. It reverberated in every bazaar from Baghdad to Batavia. It evoked in Asia the spirit of Nationalism. It raised in the Pacific and for the British Empire and the United States new political and strategic problems, still unsolved, which they will have to meet together. The tragic flaw of their histories in the Pacific was that they did not see their common interests and move together, from the day when Dewey took Manila while the Royal Navy held the ring.

But America was not ready to preview her oncoming destiny, and Britain's attention was already dominated by the German threat. Yet the German danger and the Japanese might have been diverted if the British and Americans had realized their community of interest in the Pacific and shaped on it the strategy and order which two World Wars have since demanded.

The history of British-American relations might have been (in the Pacific at least) vastly different if Australia had been in the late Nineties sufficiently mature to express and project her essential interests.

The Australians were the first to realize the trouble that could come from Japan; and long before their federation, the eastern Australian Colonies were resistant to German expansion in the Pacific. Theodore Roosevelt was the first among world statesmen to detect the strategic significance of Australia, and he sent his White Fleet to establish relations. But time did not tarry for Americans or British or Australians, and the electorates would still not have understood.

Alternatively, a British-German combination might have served. But it could have been founded only in a broad understanding of the problems raised by the expansion of populations, empires, industries, and technical resources in the 19th century: an understanding that we have not yet made effective in world-politics.

The German blunders after Bismarck's fall now seem fantastic (and many of them had roots in his *real-politik*). Even Herr Adolf Hitler who lived to repeat them thought the German errors monstrous clumsy. "No sacrifice," he wrote in *Mein Kampf,* and specified colonial ambitions and sea-power, "would have been too great in order to gain England's alliance."

The Kaiser welded the Third British Empire. With no major interest of his own at stake, he challenged the most vital of all Britain's interests, her power upon the seas, which means her power to feed her people and theirs to earn their daily bread.

Neither the colonial nor the commercial rivalries of Germany much troubled Britain. She rather welcomed the competition. It sharpened wits and stimulated the sporting instinct. The British in their sluggish, foggy airs are inclined to take things easily. As individuals and as a people they are seldom at their top in easy prosperity. They sink into comfortable routines and accustomed techniques. With the most highly developed technical sense and skill in the world, they have, for example, repeatedly fallen behind both Americans and Germans in adaptability to consumer demands. It is very good for the British, as the world will observe again, to have to stir their mental stumps.

Necessity is the mother of their inventions; but before she can conceive, the English must be prodded or persuaded from their comfortable cultivation of the quiet arts of living. The normal Englishman will seldom work like a German, a Chinese, a French peasant, an American engineer or salesman. He must be roused in his corporate loyalties and by competition.

You know much about the English if you reflect that they invented most of the team-games and polish them to something near perfection in their sort. Soccer is the fine art of all the football games. Cricket is played through the summer days with a magnificent air of leisure and at a tempo which would send Americans out of their minds. From cricket significantly has come the curious vocabulary in which the English admit to some moral sense. They play the game, keep a straight bat, and face the bowling; and they will be most gratified at the Judgment by a quiet "Well played, sir," from on High.[8]

What is and is not cricket is largely a matter of moral style, so to speak; and it is here and in the English senses of irony and humor that Englishmen and Germans, so like in many ways, most misunderstand one another. The English were initially sympathetic to the Second German Reich and even welcomed its expansion in regions overseas which had been for a century their own oyster or cup of tea. They were not hostile to the growth of a German merchant-fleet. They traveled much in German ships. But when the Kaiser went in quite unnecessarily for a first-class navy, they were deeply shocked. They were less shocked by the challenge than at the raw misinterpretation of a navy's proper *raison d'être.* A navy was not a saber to be rattled, a show-piece, or a luxury. It was not a militarist trapping, to be waggled as a fist in shining armor; for a navy's role is primarily defensive. It was not a necessity to Germany's peace or prosperity, and the Germans had never really been blue-water seamen. The British thought it damned bad form and much as if a Frenchman had worn the colors of the

---

[8] An alternative (if conceivable) could only be: "It wasn't cricket." A medieval Pope who understood these things once addressed to England a Decretal illuminated with bats and balls.

Marylebone Cricket Club. Mr. Winston Churchill in 1912 expressed their cold distaste. A navy, he said, was for Germany "something in the nature of a luxury."

For Britain her navy was a fundamental necessity, as twelve centuries had taught her; while the Kaiser's surface-fleet at least had no essential function in the German war-machine. Politically it was disastrous, for it provoked the slow anger of the British as nothing else could have done.

The Kaiser should have understood all this, because he had some sense of the British character and quality. But he was infused with the vain conceit which is almost an occupational hazard in high places, as Shakespeare noted.

The gradual degeneration of Anglo-German relations in the two decades before 1914 illustrates the play of human pettiness in great events and tragedies; for the suspicions, envies, doubts, and ambitions of William II and his familiars Tirpitz and Holstein were those of small-minded men who missed history's proportions and perspectives.

Bismarck was hardly a great man though he was a great politician of his school. But he looms tremendous beyond the little men who smashed his creation in what now seems something like a frenzy of self-conjured fears.

Bismarck was not ambitious for sea-power, which he saw as a two-edged sword in German hands. He was not especially eager for colonies. He had no place for non-Germans in his Reich of blood and iron, and he excluded Austria from his plans because of the various non-Germanic peoples within the Hapsburgs' realm. He encouraged France after 1871 to enterprises in Africa and Asia which might take her mind from Alsace-Lorraine; and he thought it excellent that Russia's imperial ambitions should be worked off in the remotest parts of Asia. Bismarck (with his Reich constructed) developed a passion for peace; and his eyes were always fearfully on Germany's long and exposed eastern frontiers. He wanted at first nothing less than to raise difficulties in the west by clutching for colonies or at Britain's Trident. Moreover, being a man of much practical sense, he knew that German industry might acquire by peaceful trade within the open British System the profits of empire without its troubles and expense.

The British were ready to do business with his Reich, though they sometimes disliked his manners, and Queen Victoria saw in her penetrating way through the veils of the man to the new Germany which had found its first (but unhappily not last) formidable expression in him. "Bismarck is a terrible man, and he makes Germany greatly disliked ——*no one* will tolerate any Power wishing to dictate to all Europe." [9]

Their interest in Europe declined as the Third Empire grew upon the British. They were (a Canadian statesman first said it) "splendidly isolated." The Germans might then with their skill and industry have achieved in peace what they were to seek in war. Germany might have been the first or second industrial power of the world by the second quarter of the 20th century if she had been content to exploit in peace the possibilities of an expanding world-economy.

British trade suffered a little from German competition in the first phases of German expansion. But the German pressure pushed the British into new efforts and markets, and Germany herself became a major customer. The War of 1914-18 did not come from British fear of Germany's economic power, however much the Marxists declaim this thesis. The German Ambassador in London reported to his Government in 1908: "If the relations between the two countries depended merely upon the commercial interests, and all the representatives of these interests, our mutual relations would be excellent." The notion that the City

---

[9] From a letter to her daughter, the Crown Princess, while Bismarck was contemplating in 1875 a second and "preventive war" against France.

wanted war was to him "absurd." American competition was
actually more severe than German in the opening years of
this century [10] but it did not lead to war or thoughts of war.
Free competition is much less dangerous to peace than
tariff-walls and economic autarchies and monopolies, as we
should have understood from the Elizabethan quarrel with
Spain.

Yet the Germans brooded and hatched their dragons.
Bismarck, prodded by the German Colonial Society and
ready to make mischief between France and Britain, began
in 1884-5 to press demands in East and West Africa. Mr.
Gladstone's response was in his highest style: "If Germany
is to become a colonizing power, all I can say is, God speed
her! She becomes our ally and partner in the execution of
the great purposes of Providence for the advantage of mankind."

But William II disposed otherwise. The colonial difficulties were soluble. The obsession of the Kaiser with naval
power was not.

As the hammers drove the rivets of his ships, their strokes
were felt throughout the British System, and each blow
helped to weld it. The Germans raised much heat and
energy for the making of the Third British Empire.

Its new form begins to be visible at the first of the Imperial Conferences which were to be a notable feature of it.

The Imperial Conferences and their scant machinery
were improvisations like much else in the British System.
When federated Canada to most people's surprise did not
depart from the imperial connection she set a problem.
How did this phenomenon of independent sovereign states,
each insistent on a common allegiance to one Crown, operate? What sort of political system could represent this
paradox? Races gifted in logic would have tried to rational-

---

[10] As Maurice Bruce has pointed out in *British Foreign Policy:* Thomas
Nelson and Sons, London and New York. 1939.

ize the irrational. The British at first did nothing. They merely noted another of the oddities which grew in the course of Empire.

. But then the Queen came to a Jubilee for the fiftieth year of her tremendous reign. Her people at home planned a celebration. Mayors composed loyal addresses. London costers polished up their pearlies. County towns raised Jubilee funds for local hospitals. A daring few thought of statues: prim statues, superbly corseted and topped by ridiculous small crowns (ten years later at the second Jubilee they were to multiply in bronze and marble across five continents, from Adelaide to Aberdeen). Suddenly, the whole affair was transformed. The costers and the vicars and Her Majesty discovered that this was not to be a mere domestic jollification. Bearded Australian miners laden with legendary nuggets, fur-trappers from the Canadian tundras, Indian Princes dripping with pearls and diamonds, people of most various habits, customs, clothes and conventions (some exceedingly un-Victorian) came to the party; and they seemed to think of it as a family affair. The British suddenly realized with the Jubilees what they had been up to all about the world.

EIGHT

THE THIRD EMPIRE: METHODS

AND MORALS

THE Third British Empire saw a constantly accelerating expansion of technical and industrial resources.

In the age of the First Empire, the chief motive-power was still animal, from man and his domestic beasts, with some aid from wind and water.

With the Second Empire came steam-power to transform man's life and his relations with the earth and to create for the first time in history an urban as the dominant human type.

In the age of the Third Empire have come the internal-combustion engine, the oil-fuels, the automobile and air-craft. Railways multiplied after the invention by Bessemer of cheap steel. Steamships and cold storage [1] had enormous

---

[1] Cold storage for seaborne meat was introduced by the New Zealand Shipping Company in 1882.

consequences in the world's agronomy. With cheaper transport, trade quickened and called for more goods from factories which demanded more raw materials. Cheap transport also opened the deep hinterlands of Australia, Africa, and the Americas to production of materials for the machines and food for the factory workers. Industry went forward with lengthening leaps and bounds. Machinery moved into the open spaces newly brought to plow to increase their harvests (and to help ruin their soils, but that was not yet much observed). It released farm-workers for the maws of the factories. The peasants poured into the cities. The cities sent migrants overseas to drive the agricultural machinery. The scientists beat down the worst of tropical pests; for the first time in history it became possible for white men to work in the tropic sun and survive and father children on white wives, who now could follow their men to Middle Africa and Malaya.

The limited liability company came to finance the new expansions, and London seemed to have money for every enterprise. People moved in tens of millions across the oceans. The railways moved them on across the continents.[2] The aircraft presently moved them over both. Cables and radio solved the political and economic difficulties which had hung on the time-lags in communication; and swamped men's powers of discernment, selection, and intelligent attention in a daily flood of news and gossip.

A string of new Chartered Companies appeared to renew the role of the Companies in empire-building: the British North Borneo, the Royal Niger, the Imperial East Africa, and the British South Africa Companies all came in the Eighties and all have brought wide regions into the British System.

[2] The Canadian Pacific was opened in 1886 to play its part in the imperial story.

The economic advance was unprecedented in Africa, Australia, Canada, New Zealand and all the regions where British money spread or percolated, from Illinois to the Persian Gulf. The world was rapidly becoming (or so it seemed in the Nineties) one great economic community. If some nations were difficult, the British System was, Mr. Chamberlain insisted, big and rich and great enough to keep the peace and give example; with the Royal Navy to preside over the general security and to police the seas for honest merchantmen and their argosies of Empire.

But there were snags which the Third Empire did not at first perceive. The largest hardly seemed to be noticed at all except by a handful of poet-prophets, Ruskin, Morris, and their sort. Their contemporaries thought them admirable fellows in their own literary fields, among Queen's Gardens and Wild Olives, but often wrong-headed on large matters of State and Trade. Mr. Ruskin did not care for industrialism. He had doubts of the magnificence of the new cities, like old Cobbett who had shouted against the Wen.

But to us Ruskin and Cobbett seem not altogether without cause. For we too begin to see what the movement of the masses from the countrysides to the cities has implied.

It has detached man from the natural rhythms in which his organism moved through the procession of the seasons with their varying tasks. His working years are now fixed in a mechanical pattern and lived out to the beat of the machines or in the routines which follow from them in shops, offices, and factories.

He now in Megalopolis spends many hours of each week crowded into buses, street-cars, and suburban railways which grind at him in what would be intolerable noise and tedium if he did not seal his mind and senses against the clatter and the crush and the appalling waste of his brief time between the earth and sky.

He lives now in an environment almost wholly artificial. The typical city-dwellers seldom have grass and earth beneath their feet. They eat little food straight from the earth and their sun is blanketed. They have little exercise in the open air unless by the device of organized sports, which lack the peculiar stimulation of creative work.

The herded crowds have little real community. Though men surge all about them, they have few close acquaintances, normally fewer than the peoples of villages and small towns who are acquainted with all their neighbors. Their typical group activities are within the administrative pattern of an office or factory, and at leisure as elements of excited mobs about an arena where they contribute nothing except their money and presence to the spectacle promoted. The typical city-dweller provides less and less for himself either at work, where he merely sells so much of his time and energy to others' tasks, or at leisure. He is at the receiving end of the cinema and radio. His own creative activity is almost nil, though he would seldom recognize this; but his restlessness, unease, and ennui reveal the lack.

His wife, more fortunate, at least cooks and cares for her home, expressing herself and developing in some degree positive tastes and preferences, as the industrialist who designs his car for her eye, the salesmen and the advertisers know. She spends most of the family's money, and her preferences cultivated or injected govern the retail markets. In the middle and upper brackets she has acquired new leisure from her household duties with the multiplication of household gadgets and prepared foods and in the shrinking of the family. To fill her new leisure, enormous resources of time, energy, capital and creative imagination have been diverted into films, fashions, fiction, games, clubs, the "beauty" industry, tourism.

The machines should on the face of things have enormously increased the average leisure-time of men. In fact, the working-time over all the year has probably for the majority increased since the Middle Ages, when in Western Europe the working-man spent from 120 to 180 Sundays and holy-days each year at leisure. The increment of the machines has been absorbed in part by the handful of masters, but more by industries and services which meet the new human demands, mostly unproductive. The distribution of resources is aptly illustrated by the cost-of-living index adopted in Britain in June 1947. In the earlier indices, food accounted for 60 per cent of the basic budget. The new index assumed food at 35 per cent, and added to it were charges for radio licenses, cinemas, football, postage, medicine, laundry, hairdressing, canned fruit, alcohol, perambulators, bicycles. Thus, even at the basic standard of living, we make enormous demands on mass-industries and enterprises unknown to our forefathers. But only the exceptional budget can range widely and firmly over the vast and various range of consumer-goods which now excite desire. The modern man confronted with this cornucopia is more conscious of what he wants than of what he has. He does not feel richer than his ancestor of simpler tastes. He may own a second-hand car and be armed with mobility that Caesars could not imagine; but confronted by a Rolls-Royce, he may feel frustrated and "underprivileged" and nurse grievances and nervous irritations that his peasant forebears never knew.

The typical urban is in temper excessively susceptible to mob-appeals, mob-satisfactions, emotions. Crowds have for him an hypnotic effect. The exceptional individual may assert himself in the crowd, but most men become its victims. They sway like a reed in the wind of fashion. The urban is often lonely, and responds to the appeal of mass-movements which give him the brief comfort of marching with his fellows, even if only in a brown-shirted squad. Mass movements and military organizations refresh his starved social sense and his human need for a vigorous physical life. If many modern men seem to enjoy their wars, we need not be much surprised. War may release the clerk or the factory-hand from his narrow and ugly routines to adventures, sexual and otherwise, and relieve him of personal responsibilities he has come to find oppressive.

Voluntary associations for creative purposes become more and more rare in the vast city, and the State with its organized and disciplined activities moves into the social vacuums.

The Churches and the Family are the chief surviving resorts of voluntary creative social action. A few vocations still demand individual expression and responsibility: as art, letters, medicine, and the higher executive posts of the economy and public services. But the decline of the Churches and the Family reflects men's increasing reluctance to accept the considerable personal responsibilities and the burden of self-knowledge, the examination of the personal conscience and consciousness which both Religion and the Family require.

The effects of this immense change in human affairs are, of course, immeasurable.

Our cities are of another kind than those ganglia of the classical and medieval cultures which were organic developments and expressions of their surrounding countrysides. Major administrative centers like Rome or Byzantium might climb towards a million in population; but the typical city of the old cultures could seldom grow beyond perhaps one-tenth of the rural population on which it rested. Its life remained integrated with the life about it. But the modern city dangles dangerously in a wide net of communications. It came into being and lives by the power-fuels, which govern its life.

The rapidity of its development must have added to its impact on the human organism.

There is little doubt that urbanism has increased the incidence of nervous and mental disorders. It demonstrably promotes sterility. Birth-prevention may be a major instrument of sterility, but it is only an instrument. Whatever the reasons, the modern industrial and commercial city is a parasite on its countrysides. Its population must be completely renewed in four or five generations. In the United States 100 infants of one urban generation are succeeded by about 75 in the next. The gross reproduction rate for the County of London in 1931 was 0.805. The rural populations have until now fed the man-eating monsters. But with the decline of rural populations and the increasingly sedentary habits of working-populations even in the countrysides, we face the extraordinarily complex and varied problems of aging and decreasing populations: problems quite different from those of static populations.

The speed of urban development has also transformed political and social structures, theories, and methods. The State has had to provide substitutes for the social framework of the old communities. It also has had to meet the innumerable new problems of concentrated multitudes dependent on distant fields for their food, drink, clothes, and all the materials of their industries and homes.

The huge cities, with their inflated land and rental values, taxes, rates, and living costs, with their immensely expensive and non-productive transport, drainage, and road systems, would prove bankrupt if time stood suddenly still. They keep functioning only because of a constant flow to them from the economic surplus of the countrysides and the smaller communities.

The new cities are delivered as hostages to economic groups. They can be held to ransom by the organized action of any of the many responsible for their transport, water, drainage, light, or food. The bases of power have shifted within the urban communities, though the organized groups themselves have not yet fully sensed the change. But we can see in the demands for preferential treatment by special groups, as the miners in Britain, the first signs of an awakening to power.

The life of the cities hangs between hand and mouth or freight-yard and retail store, and the complex structure which sustains them can be easily dislocated at innumerable points. The modern cities grew in an era of exceptional social order. They depend on it for their survival. If pressure-groups press too far they may overthrow it altogether, or they may provoke in populations already jittery desperate demands for extended State controls and disciplines. We have lately seen in several countries traditional liberties threatened by labor legislation and the like. Labor could easily tip over the urban structure. It would find itself buried in the wreck.

Megalopolitan civilization can continue only if the special groups who control its essential services use power with more wisdom than men commonly reveal or if they are brought under authoritarian disciplines, which would mean the end of many liberties which we have known and cherished in the West.

But if we survive the next few years the present urban situation may pass in changes as remarkable as those which produced it. The automobile is re-establishing in a fashion the city-dwellers' relations with the countrysides. The development of electricity grids makes possible the dispersal of industry. The character of modern war makes this more than desirable. In town-planning (notably in Britain) opinion is on many social grounds substantially for city-communities of not more than 50-100,000 people. The concentration of huge aggregates of individuals within a cage of bricks and steel is now accepted as dangerous, stupid, and unnecessary to the economic mode.

The big cities have probably passed their peak. If we have war, they will be smashed. If we have a progressive peace, populations will move less towards them and more towards smaller cities designed for healthier living.

But meanwhile this urban dweller is the stuff of modern politics, the medium in which statecraft must work. It is hardly surprising if both the science and the art of politics seem to fall behind the changes which have come upon us. Politics are quite unable to pace them. Yet at this moment in our history great masses of mankind have chosen to throw on the State all the responsibilities belonging to the religious, ethical, social, intellectual and economic life. The State has in fact become the universal scapegoat, and Socialism a flight from reality. But the load is too heavy for the State; and war, we should remember is its escape.

* 2 *

The Colonial politicians who came to London for the Jubilee of 1887 sat down with British Ministers in general conference for the first time. They at once produced ideas, startling to the Home Government, for bracing the imperial structure. Griffith of Queensland and Hofmeyr of South Africa wanted a system of Imperial preferences. The British Government shied like a startled mare. The Australians were aggressive. They insisted that the United Kingdom give serious attention to the business of Empire, especially in the Pacific. They were angry, because the Germans had lately ignored that dispensation natural and divine which reserved to Australia and New Zealand the Southern Hemisphere from 120° West to 60° East. The British Government, somewhat dazed, found itself committed to a powerful naval force in the western Pacific (Australia making an annual contribution to its cost), to a new naval base at Simon's Town on the southern tip of Africa, and to the strengthening of a whole string of ports and forts. The Colonies also demanded a share in shaping foreign policy; and while Whitehall flinched at the strange notions of the wild colonial boys, their eldest statesman [3] hinted broadly that he saw in their meeting "what may perhaps be called the rudimentary elements of a parliament."

The United Kingdom could probably have led the way to Imperial federation from this conference if she had wished it. But she let ten years pass to the Diamond Jubilee before she even called another conference, although Canada convoked at Ottawa in 1894 a meeting on matters of trade and communications (it made the first gestures toward Imperial preferences).

The Conference of 1897 was marked by initiatives at last from a Minister of the Home Government. Joseph Chamberlain as Colonial Secretary came out strongly for a *Zollverein* on the Bismarckian model. He saw a customs union leading inevitably, as in Germany, to a Council of Empire and (in fact if not form) a Federal System. The Colonies were as eager as the Secretary of State for a program of Imperial preferences. Canada had already offered Britain a preferential tariff. But many of the British Ministers including the Chancellor of the Exchequer were dubious or hostile, and the plan made little head before the South African War intervened.

The third Conference met in 1902. Wilfrid Laurier, the Canadian Prime Minister, called for a full partnership: "If you want our aid, call us to your councils." Chamberlain seized on the words to invite participation in the general responsibilities of Empire. He suggested a "real Council of the Empire" for "all questions of Imperial interest." He invited a more equitable distribution of the burdens of

[3] Griffith of Queensland.

defense. He promised to consult on foreign policy. He and the Colonial Ministers again agreed to work for a preferential-tariff system. But when he tried to force this on the country, he split his party to the bottom; and in 1906, it was overwhelmed at the polls.

Chamberlain went on fighting. But the British electorate was loth to move much from the fundamentals of free trade. It still waited patiently for the Enlightenment to spread and for the benign growth of a world community in trade.

The British, who had come first of modern States to Nationalism, had long since lived through its more aggressive moods. They forgot that others had tasted only now the first heady draught. The 19th century had been prolific of new National States in the Americas, Australasia, and Europe. Argentina, Belgium, Bolivia, Brazil, Bulgaria, Chile, Colombia, Costa Rica, Cuba, the Dominican Republic, Ecuador, Egypt, Greece, Guatemala, Haiti, Honduras, Liberia, Mexico, Nicaragua, Norway, Paraguay, Peru, Rumania, Salvador, Uruguay, Venezuela, Serbia, Australia, Canada, New Zealand, Newfoundland are all as sovereign self-governing States creations of the 19th century.[4] Germany and Italy as unitary States appeared only in its second half.

The young are commonly eager to assert themselves, to try their muscles, physical and mental, to achieve self-confidence. The brood born of the 19th century gave recruitment to the spirit of Nationalism which had already worked its disputatious way with the elders.

In the United States and the Dominions, in Japan, Germany, Italy and a score of other States, it prompted tariff-

[4] States born to the 19th and 20th centuries are a majority of existing States: an interesting commentary on the transience of political arrangements. The U.S.A. is a veteran among national sovereignties; and its Constitution, the oldest written Constitution now in force.

walls, as if each nation would monopolize its inheritance and haul itself to full estate by its own boot-straps. The British had envisaged a large mansion of the world with an orderly distribution of tasks according to the various talents and resources of its inhabitants. Now it was converted into self-contained apartments with a workshop in every pantry and each tenant his own plumber, yet passionate to possess all modern conveniences, even if they cluttered the carpets and choked the passageways to a larger world. In our time some States are become so morbidly self-centered that they refuse to take in the newspaper. They keep their children behind locked doors and shutters, secluded from the vanities and snares of unaccustomed fleshpots and ideas.

The British were sympathetic to the reasonable development of local resources, enterprises, and activities. But though notoriously mad themselves, they could not believe until the last that the world would go to the extremes of what were in British eyes dangerous and profligate delusions. Their opinion was naturally influenced by their own commanding lead in manufactures. But they did see free trade or a convenient approximation to it as an essential character of world-community. Doubtless they were right.

Without social and economic collaboration, Leagues of Nations and United Nations become mere instruments for political negotiations; and political machinery is of little use in the face of fundamental economic conflicts, as wise Americans had learnt from the War between the States.

No Federal Union would survive tariff-walls between its states, and none has dared admit them. Yet they are now accepted (almost as if they were facts of nature) between the several sovereignties, not one of which has proved entirely self-supporting although some have kept their peoples poor in the attempt.

Chamberlain understood all this. He had been an ardent free-trader in his youth. When he saw that universal free trade was not to be achieved, he tried still to keep its general character within the British System. But this now meant a ring about it. "You cannot weld the Empire together except by some form of commercial union." The free traders were not persuaded. They held still to their universal idyll.

If peoples as close to one another in blood, sympathies, and values as the British Dominions could not form a commercial union, the prospect seems remote for the diverse constituents of the United Nations, unless the moral and intellectual humors which inform mankind are much modified. But men are very slow to read what is written large, even when it is written on the wall.

If Marxism grows throughout our world, it will be among the ruins of closed national economies gone down in collision. No nation now has power to compel peace. The alternative is to meet the proper needs of men and to knit them in common interests: to make peaceful commerce a necessary condition of their daily lives and to emphasize the interdependence of peoples. But this is feasible only where commerce in goods and ideas is sufficiently free.

For a thousand years, the German States squabbled and tyrannized until they formed a customs union. The strength and unity it brought turned heads unaccustomed to them. Otherwise, Germany might have set a great example to nations still behaving like so many petty principalities.

If the Open Society is finally destroyed, the prime agents of destruction will not be dubious spies in government offices or bemused pedagogues or conspirators in cellars, but industrial and business leaders who have perverted for their local profits the fundamental characters of the Open Society: men who with one breath denounce the Monstrous State and with the other clamor for it to protect their private gains by excluding competition.

In this process they have been the prime agents also of

the growth of the State and its bureaucracies, for these had their tap-roots in the mulch of tariffs.

Big business has too often performed as Marx expected. He put its paradoxical behavior down to inevitable and pre-determined trends, perhaps because he could not believe that men would of free will destroy the liberties they loved or the goose which laid their golden eggs. But men governed only by immediate self-interests are mad enough for these murders and more.

Tariffs have, of course, a proper use to raise necessary revenues. But protective tariffs which mulct the general population may be justified only if they bring benefits to compensate their costs to the consumers and to international relationships. National defense makes the most persuasive argument for protection, and in the situation to which we have drifted it is almost indisputable. But we should as rational beings recognize that peace has been chiefly threatened by the conflicts of national economies. We are in a vicious circle: let us at least recognize that it is vicious.

The lesser arguments are seldom valid in the longest view. Australia might, perhaps, as a sound national policy for defense protect its sugar-growers to encourage the occupation of its tropics by a white working-population. There are proper balances to be found in these matters. But they are overset when peoples are impoverished to establish economic autarchies whose very character demands that they turn their butter into guns and prepare the universal desolation.

Economic autarchy was a major ambition of the Third Reich. It is now the dominant motif of a dozen States. In the Marxist interpretations, it is an inevitable cause of war. Yet the Marxist Governments most ardently practice it. Are we to assume that these Governments are seeking to exacerbate the situation which Marx foresaw? Or are some as deluded as the politicians and profiteers who have misused political authority for their private gains?

But the peoples of free societies need not succumb to either if they will take but thought enough, and remember that talents were meant to be traded.

* 3 *

With a Liberal Government in England, the Imperial Conference of 1907 [5] did not advance the Chamberlain program. But it developed the mechanics of Commonwealth relationships. It regularized the procedure of the Conferences, providing for their assembly every four years with the Prime Minister of the United Kingdom as president and the Prime Ministers of the self-governing Dominions as members.

In the next year, a Dominions Division of the Colonial Office in London was established to act as a permanent Secretariat for the Imperial Conferences.

From the Conference of 1907 flowed a number of lesser meetings: conferences on navigation, education, copyright, and the like. These have in the years multiplied. Chamberlain's notion of a High Council of Empire, Griffith's hints of a Federal Parliament have not been realized; but, in characteristic British fashion, a variety of means exists at lower levels for conference and co-operation on specific problems.

The chief concern of the 1907 Conference was with foreign policy and defense. The Australian Prime Minister attacked the indifference of United Kingdom statesmen "to British interests in the Pacific." The children were more mindful than the parent of the patrimony. The Conference proposed a General Staff for the whole Empire, to study the common military problems. Canada made provision for an auxiliary naval force and the bases at Esquimault and Halifax. New Zealand granted annual aids to the Royal Navy. Australia established its own Royal Australian Navy

---

[5] It adopted the title of Imperial Conference for its successors. It and its predecessors were known formally as Colonial Conferences.

as one element of a new plan (the German War crossed it, but the R.A.N. came into being) to provide a great Pacific fleet with divisions based on the East Indies, the China Station, and Australasia.

A Defence Conference in 1909 worked at methods to organize the forces of the Crown that they might, if the Dominions wished, be rapidly combined at an emergency "into one homogeneous Imperial Army." [6]

The Committee of Imperial Defence was taken from its cupboard and dusted. Ministers of the Dominions attended from 1911 when Canada led the way; and though it was in peace merely consultative and advisory, it became in 1914 a War Council.

The Imperial Conference of 1911 met in the shadow of Agadir. Sir Joseph Ward, the Prime Minister of New Zealand, proposed at once "an Imperial Council of State representative of all the self-governing parts of the Empire." The United Kingdom Government coldly rejected it. But the international situation compelled the Asquith Government to frank discussions on foreign policy and defense. In the cold wind from the East it took some comfort at last from the young nations gathering at its side. It agreed to give the Dominions opportunity to express their views before it entered into external conventions and agreements.

The usual reluctance of the United Kingdom to tighten links has been a strange phenomenon. The Commonwealth Relations Office (it succeeded as the Dominions Office with its own Secretary of State in 1925 to the Dominions Division of the Colonial Office) is still astonishingly shy of anything which seems to force the relationships. The Dominions have taken most of the initiatives of the Commonwealth System. Somewhere at the back of Great Britain's mind is the recollection of the American Revolution; and across the body of the Third Empire are two long weals or scars which are still

[6] Prime Minister Asquith to the House of Commons.

sensitive. They are from the troubles of South Africa and
Ireland.

* 4 *

The story in South Africa was not pretty; and although
the reconciliation after the Boer War was a rare triumph for
political sagacity, and a wise saw and instance for all who
come to make a peace, the war itself had lasting consequences in the British System and especially in the response
of the British public to the idea of Empire.

The Boer War lowered the temperature. It cut with cold
questions across the enthusiasm which had grown through
the last quarter of the 19th century. It raised in Great Britain
a host of critics ranging from Lloyd George to Chesterton.
It called up again the scruples of the Nonconformist
Conscience. It put the imperially-minded out of office at
the election of 1906. It wrecked the dreams of Joseph
Chamberlain.

The British first took the Cape Colony in the Napoleonic
Wars, while the Dutch were under a puppet-government
and their Stadtholder, a refugee in England. The British
restored it to the Netherlands at the Treaty of Amiens, but
when the war was renewed took it again. At the end of
the wars, they kept it, paying the Dutch compensation.
The long-settled Boers, already speaking Afrikaans and (like
the French in Canada) liking little that they heard of
Europe, shrugged their shoulders and accepted the new
regime. Their ambition was to be left alone with their
slaves to work the land.

At the Emancipation of 1833, the Boers were granted by
the British Parliament £1,270,000 in compensation for
their slaves. It was inadequate, and much of it was mislaid
in tangled procedures for payment.

At that moment, thousands of Kaffirs invaded the Colony
to loot and burn. D'Urban, the British Governor, swept them

back, hunted them across the border, and compelled them to cede a strip of territory up to the Kei River, useful as a moat.

The Home Government repudiated his acquisition and ordered it to be returned to the Kaffirs. The Boers were even more furious than the Governor and the handful of British settlers in Natal.[7] They had lost their slaves. They had suffered what seemed to them constant interference from missionaries and officials in their relations with the natives. Now they saw the British Government inclining to the Kaffir tribes, who were to Boer eyes a constant menace. The Boers felt much as Virginians might have felt if in 1760 the British Government had forcibly freed their slaves and at the same time left the frontiers open to scalping-parties.

The Boers in thousands loaded their wagons with tools, kitchen-pots, stools, feather-beds, wives, and children and went into the wilderness. They traveled in the Great Trek until they felt themselves free of the officious arm of Government: across the Orange, and on across the Vaal. Some went to Natal, whose British settlers had been refused political recognition by the Home Government. The Boers set up there a Boer Republic. They fought a bitter campaign against the Zulus which provoked criticism in England, and the British Government restored the British flag in Natal.

The Boers retreated in another trek to their compatriots settled in the Orange Colony and Transvaal. The British in 1851 conceded to those in the Transvaal rights to govern themselves without interference provided that slavery was not restored. In 1854, the Orange River Sovereignty between the Orange and the Vaal was acknowledged on the same condition and freed from allegiance to the British Crown.

[7] From Christmas Day, the Natal Day of 1497 when Vasco da Gama saw it first.

Thus two Boer Republics came into being while the British colonies of the Cape and Natal were growing rapidly and achieving self-government. The notion of a federation spread among both Boers and British; but Governor Grey, who encouraged it, was snubbed by the Home Government and dismissed (but restored at the insistence of Queen Victoria). Grey might have, as Reitz of the Transvaal said, created "a British Dominion extending from Table Bay to the Zambesi." [8] But British Governments of the 1850s were interested in nothing less than new Dominions. So South Africa went on in its divisions to tragedy.

In 1870, diamonds were found at Kimberley: in the Orange Free State, the Boers said; in Griqualand according to its native chief, who dished the Boers by putting his territory under the British flag. Diamonds drew to South Africa new and often disputatious prospectors and speculators.

In 1867, the Conservatives had come to power again in England after their long eclipse: a third event to mark the beginnings of the Third Empire. Flushed with the success of Canadian federation, Disraeli's Government thought to revive the old notion of a federal South Africa. At the critical moment, a queer thing happened. The Boers in the Transvaal were at war with the Zulus and the Matabele. A British Commissioner sent to inquire thought the Boers' position desperate. To cover them he took over the Transvaal, promising self-government. The British within the next two years fought brisk campaigns to bring the native *impis* to order. The Boers once relieved demanded their freedom again, with added force because they had not been given the self-government promised. They took up arms and won a snap decision at Majuba Hill in 1881. Mr. Gladstone who had just led the Liberals back to office was not a man of

[8] Quoted in Marriott: *The Evolution of the British Empire and Commonwealth.*

war. He made peace and the South African Republic came to being.

Then, in 1884, gold was struck on the Witwatersrand.

Within a few months the Boer farmers found themselves almost swamped by a flood of diggers, speculators, sharks, storekeepers and all the queer human tide which flows after gold. The clash of temperaments was instantaneous. Paul Kruger, the Boer President, rushed legislation to prevent the Uitlanders taking any part in the public affairs of the Transvaal. Tempers soared. They touched off Dr. Jameson.

Jameson was a friend of Cecil Rhodes. Rhodes is one of the strangest figures of the Imperial story. Like many of its heroes, he was the son of a country parson. His activities reveal an extraordinarily good eye for the main chance and a visionary's passion: an almost mystical sense of imperial destiny and a ruthless determination to have his way with history. The combination is not infrequent in the British empire-builders, though seldom at the pitch it reached in Rhodes, and it sometimes provokes foreign references which the British never can quite follow, to "perfidious Albion."

Rhodes went to Africa at seventeen and almost immediately made a fortune in Kimberley diamonds. He helped to create the De Beers Company and he went into local politics. In 1889 his British South Africa Company was chartered by the Crown to operate in the region between the Transvaal and the Congo. Jameson led in an expedition and sketched out what were to be the Rhodesias. And in 1895 (with Rhodes now Premier of the Cape and his friends busy on the Rand) Jameson crossed the Boer frontiers with a party of the Company's police and two Maxims. Oom Paul Kruger promptly rounded the lot up, sent them back for trial by the British Government, and laid hands on their co-conspirators in Johannesburg.

The Kaiser rushed in with offers of help for Kruger and tried to pass troops and guns to him through Lourenço

Marques. The Portuguese abruptly stopped this enterprise and thus delayed World War I by half-a-generation.

But the Uitlanders in the Transvaal now demanded British intervention to redress grievances which had some validity. Oom Paul dug in his heels. He demanded that the British should renounce an old shadowy suzerainty over the Transvaal. They refused. Kruger mobilized 40,000 men, swept into Natal, won a brilliant victory at Colenso, invested Ladysmith and Mafeking, and forced on the British their largest military effort since Napoleon was shipped to St. Helena.

The result was inevitable. The war was actually won by June 1900, when Kruger fled to Europe. The Orange Free State was annexed in May, the Transvaal in September, and Lord Roberts had his Garter from the Queen before she died in January 1901. Yet the war somehow dragged on until May 1902. The Boers had produced a leader named Louis Botha, whom some people have thought the first man of his generation; and he had in his train a young officer named Jan Smuts and two guerrilla leaders, De Wet and Delarey, who would have delighted Stonewall Jackson and Jeb Stuart. They gave General Kitchener and his Imperial Army a run for their money, and more. The British public began to think this a bad sort of war which found in the opposition such admirable shots, horsemen, and good fellows as Botha and Smuts. The mood of Mafeking rapidly declined. Many in England had throughout protested at the war. Now more and more asked whether a Great Imperial Power had any proper reason to fight a small nation of farmers. They asked also why the Great Imperial Power needed three years to bring the farmers in. The Boer War shook British confidence in the course empire had taken and in its methods and machinery.

Yet one could almost cease to regret the Boer War if its admirable aftermath were set as a model before men. To both nations belongs credit for a peace which will always argue for tolerance and generosity in peace-making, not only from the victors but (and this is much more difficult) from the defeated.

Botha and his guerrillas earned British respect and admiration and gave a new leadership to their own people. The British (Milner the High Commissioner and Kitchener the Soldier were generous, wise men) now accepted the chief enemies for what they were, the moral leaders of their people, and dealt with them as such.

The Treaty of Vereeniging brought the Boers back to the British Crown, but it granted representative government as a prelude to complete self-government; and the British spent immediately many millions to restore Boer farms. Within five years the Orange River and Transvaal were each again self-governing. Within seven years they were joined with Cape Colony and Natal in a federal union. Its first Prime Minister was Louis Botha. His greatest successor has been Jan Smuts. Of all the statesmen of the British Commonwealth these two have best expounded, developed, and defined its character; and twelve years after they laid down their arms against it, both took the field in the van of its defenders.

However the future turns, this phase in South Africa will always remain one moment whence men may catch some comfort from the operation of political intelligence.

* 5 *

Ireland is another case. The theme of Ireland crosses and confuses every normal pattern of development in the Second and Third Empire. The roots went back centuries beyond them; and the Irish problem grew in a complex of racial and religious prejudice which at the last could be cut only by the knife.

In Ireland, the good sense, competence, and tolerance which mark British policy in Canada, Australia, and New

Zealand are almost entirely missing. Ireland was the blind spot. It was also the Achilles heel.

The failure to deal successfully with Ireland has had immense consequences. Ireland, more than South Africa or India, provoked hostile criticism in the outer world. On almost any principle which the British Commonwealth came elsewhere to apply, the United Kingdom's attitude to Ireland seems indefensible to someone looking in from outside. If autonomy was wise and right for Canada, Australia, New Zealand, Newfoundland, was it not wise and right for Ireland? If the Boers came to be admired for a tenacious fight, were not the Irish admirable for efforts to recover their ancient liberties? If treaties with Indian princes were held as solemn obligations, might treaties and agreements with the Irish be repeatedly repudiated in letter and spirit? If the efforts in 1914 of Botha, Smuts, and their people for the Commonwealth were recognized with enthusiasm, did the contribution of the Irish through centuries to the strength and splendor of the Empire count nothing for them? If the British are tolerant and generous after battle (and they repeatedly have been) why did large numbers keep an unrelenting prejudice against the Irish? If the British have a practical genius for politics, why did they constantly invite the dangers spreading from the Irish trouble, the dislike and distaste which it provoked in large populations of the Americas and Australasia?

Irishmen rose to great place in all the Dominions and Colonies. An Irish Premier of New South Wales raised the first force ever sent by a self-governing Colony to aid in Great Britain's wars: [9] the precedent for immense efforts which in two World Wars have been the Commonwealth's salvation. The Irish were permitted to serve every cause but their own; although until the Revolution of 1916-20 (for it

[9] To the Sudan.

was as much a revolution as the American), they would have been content with what was freely given to the Boers. If control of Ireland was a strategic necessity which justified suppression of the national ambitions, then Hitler was justified in Austria and Czechoslovakia, Stalin in Lithuania, Estonia, and Latvia. What other cause than strategic necessity can be pleaded for the record in Ireland?

The restraint of the British Government in World War II may heal the ancient wound. But in Britain prejudice still infects the general habit of many minds. Sydney Smith's comment is still too true of too many: "The moment the very name of Ireland is mentioned, the English seem to bid adieu to common feeling, common prudence, and common sense, and to act with the barbarity of tyrants, and the fatuity of idiots."

No people's vision of the world is better for these distortions.

The grievance may still be planted deep in the Irish also. It injures both peoples in their approach to the modern world, where their common interests are immense.

It made for a century a major difficulty in Anglo-American relations. It would have soured relations with the Dominions more than it did if the Irish in the Dominions had not known a happier aspect of Britain than the Irish at home or in America could see. The threats of the North and their effects among British army officers must have been factors in the German decision to make war in 1914. The technique of Irish resistance and its success in 1922 inspired imitators elsewhere. The tactics of boycott and ambush were noted in India and recalled in Palestine. The Irish Revolution made the first breach (but not the last) in the System grown through the Second and Third Empires. It revealed weaknesses and methods which could be used against it. It sapped the political and moral grounds on which Britain dominion rested. It echoed in Rangoon and Calcutta and the chancelleries of the world. It provided precedents. The arguments for Pakistan were difficult to refute with a precedent from Northern Ireland.

The Irish issue now may seem apart from the main course: an affair finished at last and put aside.

But historic relationships cannot be shed; they can only be developed for good or ill. The two peoples have now an immense common interest in the stability of Western Europe and in world peace. The mind of the United Kingdom Government is today closer to the mind of Ireland than in three centuries. The Third British System is passing. It is almost gone. But the Fourth is emerging. It could find a happy omen and portent in a new understanding with the Irish. Some development of relations is inevitable. They should this time be approached with emphasis not on the difficulties and divisions, but on a shared pride. These are two of the few parent peoples. Their children have built together new nations. Together they must face the crisis of the West; for both are still moral powers in our world, creative peoples. Their creative energies, though both refuse to see it, have been most inspired in combination.

The Irish theme has run through every phase of the British System. It is still there. The strange relationship which twists and turns through the lives of the British and Irish in their homelands and abroad is not historic accident. Geography, economics, the general values of the western world inextricably link them; and they seem somehow to supplement one another. The British System is, in fact, the creation and expression of many peoples from Quebec to Kandahar. At its center are four races and cultures, not one: English, Irish, Scots, Welsh. Each, but especially the English, draws on other races and cultures and has within itself remarkable variety. The Irish may indignantly proclaim their political release from the British System. But it is blood of their blood, bone of their bone. When we look beyond the narrow bounds of politics to life we see that they belong to it as the Scots, Welsh, and English belong and as it belongs to them all with the new nations they begot. The Anglo-Irish quarrel was a quarrel in the family, or at least between relatives-in-law.

Beyond their political, military, and economic contributions, the Irish have brought their cultural values to the System, as they have to English literature, art, and music. Within and beyond the political dominion of the British System, the Irish have a cultural empire; and only a man unaware of the power of ideas could ignore its influence.

In this cultural dominion, the religious fact has been of course a major matter. It has been also at the center of the quarrel. The quarrel grew and darkened at the Reformation when the Temporal asserted its supremacy over the Spiritual Arm: a claim of the English Crown which the Irish would not then accept and would still refuse even to their own State, as clearly appears in the Constitution of Eire.

In England, religion combined with the new nationalism to become in the Established Church a national cultus, a mold of form, a social habit, which gave to English life much of its style. In Ireland, religion also was intertwined with the national life, with the struggle for survival, the resistance.

The opposition of combined religions and nationalisms was bound to be intensely bitter and to score and scar the lives and memories of both peoples. Further complications appeared.

As the Protestant temper in England deepened through the 17th century and new divisions opened there, between King and Parliament, between old Gentry and new Money, the Irish were inevitably involved. The Irish never can get free of issues from across the narrow Sea. (Even in the latest of Britain's wars the Irish serving as volunteers in

the forces of Britain and the Dominions approached ten per
cent of Eire's population, the proportion usually considered
available for combat strength in modern communities.) The
Irish fought twice for English Kings rejected of their own.
They were with the King and Cavaliers against the Parliament; with James II, against Dutch William.[10] They showed
an astonishing penchant for lost causes, if great causes are
ever wholly lost.

Was Charles I wholly defeated? Are the values which he
and his sons and grandson and great-grandson symbolized
wholly dead in England? The Puritans and Whigs won in
the field and on the Parliament benches. But they could
never wholly conquer and subdue the temperament of an
older England which appears in certain graces and courtesies
and humors; and in the ironic wit which Ireland preserved
and restored to English life and letters in the long succession
from Swift to Shaw.

The Anglo-Irish quarrel reached its most bitter depths
with Cromwell, that representative, and yet queerly unrepresentative, man who remained the hero of the Liberal and
Protestant tradition though he ruled by blood and steel and
martial law and all the tricks and tools of dictatorships.

Cromwell was the sword arm of forces which would seem
now contrary and in effects conflicting. The man himself
was torn within, caught between Cross and Crown.

In the Puritans was a blazing intolerance which produced
the dictatorship in England, murder and rapine in Ireland.
It sprang from their sense of Election. Cromwell's stern
soldiery had the unity, arrogance, and *esprit de corps* of
men who feel themselves set apart by destiny, a chosen
people, a royal race. To men like these the Irish and all not

[10] The cause lost at the Boyne was larger than James': it was for the
principle of legitimate monarchy as it had been understood in Western
Europe since Alfred and Charlemagne.

Elect were as the Red Indians to their co-religionists of Massachusetts, "devilish men who serve nobody but the devil."

The Puritans in this temper left the angry injuries of Ireland to fester. They left also a curious twist in the English character. The English entertain fewer prejudices than most people. They are normally broad-minded and careful in judgment. But when they do entertain a prejudice, it seems beyond the reach of all argument and reason. It coils about its victim to crush it like a boa-constrictor. The trait derives in part from the institutionalism and arrogance of the Puritan.

But the Puritans' proud sense of justification made for the strong girders of dominion. It brought also the demand for a Rule of the Saints. This at first produced the Military Oligarchy, the Government of the Major-Generals. But England reacted swiftly; and the Restoration restored not only the Stuarts but a lively sense of liberty which seized on the claims made for the Saints and extended them to the democracy. The Puritans smashed through much tangled undergrowth. Perhaps democracy needed such a battering-ram to clear ground for its generality. The Puritans opened the way for more than they knew.

The Independents were obviously (and the terms Independent, Dissenter, Congregationalist suggest it) not of one cast. From them came Roger Williams, insisting that "soul matters" should have "no weapons but soul weapons"; and an officer of Cromwell's Army proclaimed defiantly the pure essence of democracy: "The poorest he that is in England hath a life to live as the richest he."

When the Independents' claims were broadened to embrace both Saints and sinners, the modern democratic sense was awake.

Liberalism and illiberalism were oddly crossed and mixed in the Puritan mind as they are in Socialism.[11] Both have sought to give men (in Cromwell's reputed words) "not what they want but what is good for them," a phrase which Lenin and Stalin might have daily echoed.

Puritanism and Marxian Socialism are alike in their determinism and in their conception of an Elect: the Rule of the Saints, the Party Dictatorship emerging rapidly into the personal rule of a Man. The doctrines of predestination or determinism give strength at first in the conviction of Election. But in the long run they weaken the personal response to moral obligations. Moral issues are shifted to the broad shoulders of the Lord or to the nature of things.[12] As neither normally is vocal on specific problems, the leaders must appear to give voice to the decisions: as the King and Victim, Tyrant and Scapegoat of *The Golden Bough*. They come like Macbeth's procession of blood, "with twenty mortal murders on their crowns," each at the crest of a wave of recurrent determinism: Caesar, Cromwell, Napoleon and the rest, the Men of Destiny.

Some, like Cromwell and Caesar, recognize their roles towards their ends and ease the way for salutary reaction. But even Cromwell's dictatorship, the most efficient in history, went down in haverings, confusions, doubts, and fitful brutalities.

England, however, escaped the worst consequences which may follow such a passage. When the Elect lose faith but cling to the power acquired in the strength of faith, cynical tyrannies appear and, at their heels, divisions and dissolution. Politics which perish thus are seldom born again, for cynicism rots a society to the bone and spills its seed. But

---

[11] And as they are in the Puritans' lineal descendants who proclaim the liberty of conscience but demand the intervention of the political authority to enforce prohibitions, blue laws, and the like.

[12] Or as with anti-saloon leagues and such, to the State.

England recovered its sense of humor and its sense of irony with the Restoration.

As counter to the "enthusiasm" of Puritanism, Charles II brought also in his train from France the spirit of inquiry, the spirit of Descartes. The Age of the later Stuarts is the Age of the Royal Society, Newton, Evelyn, Pepys: of the scientific mood which (we may mildly recall) grew not from the Reformation but from the French and Italian Renaissance and beyond from the Scholastic revival of Aristotelianism. But whereas the Jesuits, like Aquinas, Scotus, and Bacon, could combine the spirit of scientific inquiry with religious enthusiasm, in England the two remained divided in a curious dichotomy which Aquinas or Pasteur (seeking truth with the instruments of reason and yet confirmed in "the faith of a Breton peasant") would not have understood, for they would see no essential conflict between orders of knowledge which have truth as their common object. Religion inevitably was gravely weakened; and when revivals did come, as with Wesley and Booth, they were revivals of religious enthusiasm, not of religious science. They emphasized again experiential religion, not the rational bases in theology and moral science.

But enthusiasm without reason to prescribe its ends and the means to them merely drifts and is dissipated, or goes off into some mood of undefined and sporadic philanthropy.

* 6 *

I have returned on the religious issue because we may now usefully recall how powerful a factor in history religion is. It worked the great trouble of Ireland; and the English have been forced to recognize its energies in India. But they (with their own drift) too much forget or neglect its potency in the western world about them.

The essential struggle on the Continent is today religious;

and it must have tremendous influence on the Fourth British System.

Many groups and factions are in the anti-Communist camps for secular, materialist, or selfish reasons. But those who oppose Communism on merely political or social grounds are no longer strong enough to form in Europe anywhere one massive party. The real resistance to Communism comes from the Christians, though many oddities and splinter-groups from the old Right creep under their umbrella, often to their embarrassment.

But these would not survive except for the political force engendered by the Christian reaction to an atheistic and materialistic determinism. The mind and guts of the reaction is with men who often care as little for finance capitalism as the Communists themselves; but who are roused to defend the Christian belief in God and the liberties which have risen from the doctrine of free-will.

One can have little doubt on which side of the issue large populations within the British System will come down: French-Canadians, Boers, the majority of Irish blood, and Protestants who still believe in the Christian fundamentals. It has become a convention to regard the Christian churches as in rapid decline; but while they have lost much of their moral influence in society at large, the decline is comparative. They are still in the English-speaking world the most formidable instruments of social purpose outside the state.

What others sustain comparable social institutions: schools, hospitals, newspapers, and voluntary social services? What other voluntary organizations in the English-speaking world have such enrollments? Three in five Americans who are church members may not all go regularly to worship or faithfully hold to each article of faith and morals; but do all trades unionists attend their meetings and devoutly pursue the letter and spirit of their rules? We may regard the cinema and organized sport and trades unionism as powerful factors in the contemporary social scene. In the English-speaking world more people still go to the churches on Sunday mornings than to ball games on Saturday afternoons or theaters on Saturday nights; and the organization of the religious denominations is much more extensive and various than that of trades unions or any other social groups external to the machinery of government. This is true of Protestants as well as Catholics. Paul Douglass [13] lists the organized activities of Protestant churches in the United States. They touch almost every phase of social life (many Protestant leaders think too many for the clear expression of their primary religious function) from Dorcas and missionary societies to orchestras, libraries, youth groups, dramatic classes, day nurseries, clinics, gymnasiums, and employment offices.

As the issue with atheistic Communism becomes clearer, we may expect a tightening of the whole religious structure and a new concern for the intellectual defenses of Christian faith and morals. Many nominal Christians may fall away; but social and moral energy is not from numbers but conviction. We have seen in Germany the Christian churches meet one tremendous modern challenge.

The objective judgment of the British Control Commission in its report [14] on the religious situation in Nazi Germany summarizes thus: "Both the Catholic and Protestant churches at times lacked insight and resolution; but the fact remains that both denominations were the chief centers of opposition to National Socialism. They were far more courageous than the trades unions, the universities, the intellectuals, and the army in their determination to uphold truth, justice, and righteousness."

The core of moral resistance to Nazism in Belgium, France, Holland, Norway, was in the churches and their

[13] In *1,000 City Churches;* New York.
[14] Published in the *British Zone Review.*

organizations. The Communists, who have jumped much credit not justly theirs, were inactive or even collaborationist until 1941. The Norwegian Communist Party, for instance, was expelled from the National Front, whose two strong pillars were the Lutheran Church and the Labor party.

Those who from firm and coherent Christian convictions resisted the Black Totalitarianism will resist the Red with its explicit and acknowledged hostility to religious belief. The European Christians, moreover, have learnt much in the tactics of resistance; and the men who have come to the front in Western politics are of quite another breed and temper than the politicians of the pre-war Right.

I do not argue here for one or the other thesis. I merely insist that two world-views are in collision; and those who overlook the influence of religion in contemporary politics overlook a major fact. Communists do not miss it, though fellow-travelers may. But then the fellow-travelers miss so much.

State by state and community by community, mankind must reach its decision on the fundamental issues. God is in politics.

The comfortable and tolerant society of the Third British System, sent God (so to say) to the House of Lords to be respectfully forgotten among the other Lords Spiritual. He was regarded, when regarded at all, as something like the apotheosis of the familiar English gentleman who could be taken much for granted.

In Latin countries, men believed or pungently denied. The issue pervaded politics and all social life to make the political and social struggle in the Latin lands intense. The English did not in large numbers deliberately deny or reject God. They mostly forgot Him or thought Him irrelevant to life as it is daily lived. You might know an Englishman for years and not discover whether he believed in God or not. Religion was not a matter for polite discussion. Where it intruded, it was treated as a social and political gaffe of tiresome and backward peoples like the Irish or the French-Canadians, though in Ireland it might be put in useful play to sustain the established order of the North.[15] The Liberal journalism of the last half-century treated religion with contempt where it treated it at all. But it cannot longer be ignored except by idle or malicious minds. As the Fourth British System emerges into history, the fundamental religious question emerges with it. It arises for every community of the Commonwealth, and it cleaves all Europe. It will divide before the issues are resolved every people of what was Christendom. Men will have to settle which values will prevail in their societies, polities, economies. Obviously a community which rejects God and sees all life in terms only of a materialist dialectic must approach the problems of life and politics on different premises and to different purposes from one which still accepts the concepts of a spiritual and moral order.

At its crisis this issue has no room for compromise.[16]

It is unlike all other crises which Christendom has met in its thousand years. The great religious quarrels have not before gone to the final depths. The major heresies and schisms, the conflict with Islam, the rifts between Byzantium and Rome, Rome and the Reformers did not bring into question the existence of God or the reality of the spiritual order. In all history, we have not seen until now an atheistic materialism armed and militant and in control of great states

[15] The extent to which Protestant workers in Northern Ireland have been moved by religious feeling to sustain a regime obviously unfavorable to their economic interests is an interesting example of the power religious passion can still generate.

[16] The religious sentiment of recent times has been inclined to neglect the grim realism of Christ: *He that is not with me is against me;* and again: *I came not to send peace, but a sword.*

and many peoples. This is a new sort of challenge and it strikes at the heart of all religion.

The major conflict is, of course, crossed and confused by others; and there is some excuse for belated, ill-read journalists, and undergraduates, and even for Mr. Henry Wallace if they see it only as a collision between the Capitalist and Communist ambitions; between the 19th and the 20th centuries. But this is no longer the main quarrel. It lies between the secularist materialism of one century and the twenty centuries of Christian faith and experience.

Christianity must be antipathetic to a dominant materialism anywhere; and Communism and Capitalism both are native of the secularist materialistic world in which they have grown and flourished. But Christianity in its full implications propounds a moral revolution. It can have with the modern utilitarian secular culture only an alliance of convenience against a common enemy; and some may think even a temporary combination gravely weakens and compromises the Christian position. Christianity, however, has had tolerance (even if only in indifference or contempt) from the Western World of the last century and has, consequently, been able to preserve within it what is now the West's chief buttress.

The West, impoverished and menaced, must now decide whether it will turn again or not to the source of its strength and restore its moral and spiritual community. The situation most resembles that of the 6th and 7th centuries when another great threat came in arms out of the East. Christendom then had to renew itself or die. It did not die.

As it is revealed in history Christianity is under constant attack. It seems always to stand in the moral breach. Caesars of Rome and Byzantium, the Tatars, Goths, and Islam, its own schisms and divisions repeatedly threaten it. But at each attack, the dog it was that died.

Nevertheless, though the essential Christianity survives,

we may see the society of Christendom disintegrate, and with it the Fourth British System.

The Communist challenge has already become the most urgent matter in its domestic and international politics; and the Communist drive is hostile to the concepts of the Commonwealth and Empire and of Christendom, and everywhere works furiously against them.

But beyond the immediate struggle is a larger need. Communism and much else which works against our traditional culture have grown in our moral and intellectual confusion.

The moral drift must somehow be checked. Communities cannot yaw and veer indefinitely in all the winds and tides of chance and pointless skepticism. The British System and the Western World have survived until now because they were well-founded and their helmsmen retained the drills and habits of an older discipline to which they in crisis still somehow clung. But the heritage is not inexhaustible. We need to renew our anchor-gear and our studies in navigation. We must again discover where our pole-star lies: for it is foolish to make sail until we know where we are bound.

We might also again look earnestly at the beliefs which formed and informed our fathers. Perhaps they were wrong, but we should in decency give the opinion of a hundred generations some diligent attention. Men and societies must decide whether they believe in God or not, for on that issue must wait our whole interpretation of life and the intelligent direction of our conduct. If God is not, we are committed to some quite illogical positions. But if God is, the world is in His Hand.

* 7 *

The urban and industrial development of the Third Empire called into being the Labour parties and first established trades unions as powerful factors in the political economy. The legal recognition in Great Britain of trades unions during the 1870s might be taken as another sign at the birth of the Third British System.

The Labour parties of the British countries were and are primarily political wings of the trades unions. They have had their doctrinaires, in England notably from the Fabian Socialists, the school of the Webbs, Shaw and Wells. But trades unions in the British countries began, and for the most part have continued, as protective organizations chiefly concerned with pragmatic issues of wages, hours, and working conditions.

In Britain and the Dominions, the rise of the unions has been the most striking politico-economic feature of the Third British System; and the trades unionist in power has proved in many ways a staid and sober ruler. In all the Labour parties of the British Commonwealth, the radical wing has been recruited from black-coated Socialists more than from the unions; but effective power has remained with the unionists who normally fill most of the Ministerial posts and Parliamentary seats.

In recent years, Communists have penetrated many unions and captured some key positions, notably in Australia. Labour movements in Great Britain, Australia, and New Zealand were forced in the depressions of the 1930s farther toward the Left. But their general line has been by "the inevitability of gradualness"; and the main body of Labour throughout the Commonwealth remains stubbornly resistant to Communism even if sometimes confused and bemused by its tacticians.

The struggle between Labour and Communism for control of the trades unions is now one of the fundamental issues. In Britain, the Communists have made some progress in the unions but little in the minds of the workers as a whole; even though the British at home have more class-consciousness than any other people in the Western world. As Christopher Hollis once said: "What is the use of trying for a classless society in England, when nobody wants it?" The British can perhaps afford class-distinction more because they have kept as balance and against the disintegrative influences of the modern situation a stronger corporate sense than most other peoples. There is still a deep, intense attachment to the Idea of England. The basic Saxon stock is also slow to anger.

Moreover, England always has been a comparatively comfortable place. Famines have been few and war hardly touched the land for a thousand years, if we except "the ruins that Cromwell knocked about a bit." Even when the English came to feed largely on imported foods they kept until lately a comparatively generous larder.

Again, the old privileged classes had social functions in the State which they accepted faithfully, on the whole. The French Monarchy fatally denied to its aristocracy a proper part in administration. The English upper-classes gave their sons to the services, military and civil; to the professions and to Parliament and to the tasks of empire. They gave them also to the sports and games which the English love. The English workman would find it difficult to detest a young gentleman from Eton who had just scored a hundred for England against Australia in a Test Match.

The British System did not put up impassable barriers, legal or social, to those born of lowly station. The upper rungs were difficult to reach, but careers were open to the talents. The British Empire is largely the creation of men from humble walks. Cook was a shop-boy until he went as ordinary seaman to an East Coast collier; Raffles began as an office-boy. Disraeli became Prime Minister; a Jew has yet to reach the White House. The House of Lords consists only in a minor measure of an ancient nobility: of the Viscounts, for instance, more than half are creations of the

20th century. Of the five Prime Ministers between the World Wars, three were poor men's sons. In the Dominions the majority of Prime Ministers have come from the working classes; and the accession of the Labour parties to power is convincing evidence of the broad democratic character of the System.

The System has had sufficient play to prevent any considerable growth of unrelenting bitterness, and the party conflicts have seldom generated malice or socially disruptive feuds. The status given to "His Majesty's Opposition" in the Parliaments of the Commonwealth and the special privileges and aids belonging to the Leaders of the Oppositions (whose duty is to oppose His Majesty's Governments) suggest the quaint calm in which the British have come to conduct their affairs.

The British "lower" classes have retained their own sturdy dignity and self-respect. A stranger in an East End or rural pub will find it has its own *mores* and style; and he will not decently presume any more than he would in a West End Club.

This temper has been a powerful factor in the persisting cohesion of the System. Violence and anger (beyond the permitted limits of party debate) are gauche, raw, and ineffective in its atmosphere. If a "wild man" appears in one or other Parliament, he is tamed or rejected or converted into a Parliamentary "character" and reduced by affectionate tolerance: as one or two Communists who reached the House of Commons have found to their frustration.

The relations of the different Governments of the Commonwealth have been conducted in this prevailing atmosphere. Strains have sometimes appeared when Radical or Labour politicians from the Dominions dealt with excessive Tories in Britain. Australian Labour at times grows suspicious of leaders who linger overlong in London: "falling for the Duchesses" is the phrase applied. But with the appearance of Labour Governments in the United Kingdom this suspicion becomes mere superstition; and in practice Labour Governments have maintained the ties of the Commonwealth with determination.

In 1914, an Australian Labour Prime Minister pledged his people "to the last man and the last shilling" in the Imperial cause. The Labour Parties of the Dominions went with little or no hesitation into both World Wars: and these were, of course, the prime tests of the System in idea and reality.

It proved in both superior to the narrow nationalism which had grown in its own members as in the outer world.

Its effective loyalty to a community larger than the national State is in our present troubles the major lesson for the world of the Third British System.

NINE

THE SULLEN INTERVAL OF WAR

THE world before the Great Wars appears in retrospect to have been rich with almost illimitable hopes and possibilities. It seems that a new, glittering, and perhaps golden age might have been bought with the wealth, energies, and lives wasted in the two wars. But the era before the World Wars was actually their seed-bed. The hopes were illusions. The doctrine of Progress had no strong roots in reality. The elements making for a better order were crossed and confused. The Wars reveal the failure of the 19th century to master the problems raised by its unprecedented changes in the organization of life.

The First War failed to solve the major issues which provoked it. It lopped off one head of the monster. A dozen grew in its place.

The simplest human act is informed by countless antecedents through space and time. The rubber heel on my shoe has in its history empire on the Amazon and in Asia:

the East India Company, Raffles, the growth of industrial science and a world-economy. We can in human history observe the trends and emphases. But we should not assume that any one interpretation has the whole account, for we cannot abstract causes from the whole complex and context of history. Yet, we should have the courage to fix moral responsibility on human acts and individual contributions to the turns of history. It does flow through the minds and wills of men; and the thrust of one man's stick may start a welling spring and the slash of a furrow grow to a ravine.

Among the causes of the First and Second Wars, Nationalism expressed itself in countless ways: from the economic pressures it engendered, to the morbid sublimations of Hitler's ego.

We fought the First War to check the gross ambitions of German Nationalism. They were obscure and confused ambitions. A German seeking with clear head the growth and greatness of the German Empire would have seen that these were already appearing about him in the power and extension of Germany's economic influence. She had already a place in the sun, from which she will now be long absent.

The German drive was defeated. But as if the shock had scattered the seeds Nationalism everywhere in the world made new head between the Wars.

The confusion is evident even in Woodrow Wilson's program. The League of Nations was designed to curb Nationalism, but the notion of self-determination for all peoples was a sharp spur.

While Wilson was striving for a supra-national authority and law, he and his colleagues were bringing to birth new, jealous, and aggressively nationalist States.

For the supra-national conception, Wilson drew on scores of European statesmen and philosophers who had for centuries known the need for some security of nations. The

Church of Rome had sought it in conjuring the Holy Roman Empire from the ruins of Caesar's dominion. William Penn had plotted out "a general diet, estates, a parliament" wherein might be framed "rules of justice for sovereign princes to observe one to another," with their joint strength in arms as sanction.

Wilson could not have been unaware of the dangers. No American could, recalling the Civil War. Then the Union had denied the claim even of founding members to a self-determination against the general weal. Wilson perhaps hoped that the conflict of principles would in time be resolved, as it had twice in America, by growth of a federal character. Perhaps he thought that federation might creep on a world almost unawares, by the development at different levels of co-operative instruments to which powers might severally but progressively be delegated; that we should all awake one day to find the League not an occasional assembly of States but a sovereign authority.

Yet Wilson and his Allies destroyed the one great State in Europe whose form approached the federal: the Austro-Hungarian Empire. The dual system of Austria and Hungary, each with its Crown and Legislature, might have in time extended to the other peoples of the Empire. This was precisely the purpose of the Archduke Francis Ferdinand, and the motive for his murder at Sarajevo in the bright June weather of 1914. Francis Ferdinand had conceived a system of home rule for Serbs, Croats, Czechs, Slovaks, Austro-Germans and Hungarians under a Federal Parliament and Monarchy. A Serb's nationalist passion killed him and his idea. But was Francis Ferdinand wrong? If he was, then all who have sought a United States of Europe have gone further in error. But if he was right, why did the victorious Allies proceed in the Treaty of St. Germain to tear the whole structure of Austria-Hungary to pieces? Was it revenge? Then why did they not tear the major enemy apart? Why did they leave Prussia relatively strengthened in its hegemony of the German States? Austria-Hungary notoriously was "the ramshackle Empire"; but the phrase first came from a man who believed in the authoritarian and centralized State, not in the ordered distribution of sovereign power and liberties which allows for local responsibility in a federal system.

The Austrian Monarchy was to Liberal eyes backward, reactionary, incompetent. Have the succession States all spread enlightenment about them? Were Vienna and Budapest rude cities, less in light and life and learning than Belgrade or Bucharest?

The decisions of St. Germain were in curious contrast with the terms given to the Germans at Versailles. Versailles left the Germans strength enough to fight again in twenty years. But St. Germain Balkanized all Southeastern Europe and broke a regime which had established a reign of comparative order. The propaganda made against the Austrians by Czechs and Serbs in 1917-19 is (even at its most vicious) mild reading beside news we have since had of those parts.

The Treaty of St. Germain was made by authentic nationalist and democratic impulses for which some provision (if not this) had to be made. But it was made also by sinister ambitions, by old hatreds, by envy of a superior culture; and by the ignorance of Woodrow Wilson, Lloyd George, and their delegations.[1] (Clemenceau probably knew better than the others and therefore did worse.)

One might argue that there was no alternative in the collapse of the Hapsburgs but to give Czechs, Croats, Serbs and the rest their demands and more. But some measure of confederate authority was needed, as it still is, in the Danu-

[1] "One of the most striking features of the Conference was the appalling ignorance of every nation as to the affairs of every other nation—its geographical, racial, historical conditions, or traditions."—Right Hon. W. M. Hughes, P.C., Prime Minister of Australia, in the House of Representatives: Commonwealth Parliamentary Debates, 87.

bian lands, and the Great Allies might have demanded it. Justice did not require the crass and unnatural boundaries which left Vienna a trunkless head: Vienna, since its dim origins the fortress of Europe in the East. Did Clemenceau and Wilson and Lloyd George think that passion was all spent beyond the Carpathians, that the new regime of Lenin would come to nothing formidable? Did they think that a Soviet Russia would put aside ambitions which have always moved the East since Attila watered his horses at the Rhine? Did they think that facts of geography which had shaped Czarist foreign policies were changed with the new regime; that the Straits and the Carpathian Gaps no longer existed for Lenin and his earnest assistants?

The Balkanization of central and southeastern Europe left no State strong enough to balance Germany, to check a renewed *Drang nach Osten,* though it had just been the immediate occasion of the bloodiest of wars. When the Germans rose again, there was no Great Power between them and the Black Sea; and when they fell back, the Russian tide flowed in over a continent where no dams or dykes survived east of the Rhine, except the armies of America and Britain. The 1919 treaties and Hitler between them swept away the traditional system of Central Europe and opened it to Russian hegemony. The East had not advanced so far for fifteen centuries. At the last phase of the Napoleonic Wars, Russians had ridden with their allies beyond the Rhine. But the Western statesmen had firmly re-established the European Balance by meeting at its center to make the Peace of Vienna.

It was a wise, shrewd settlement, which restored France to the comity of nations while it drew once and for all the sting in her flesh which for two centuries had set her marching over Europe.

The men who met at Versailles lacked the political and

human insight, the accumulated experience and skill of Castlereagh, Metternich, and Talleyrand, the heirs and agents of the old governing classes. An immeasurable opportunity was lost. In 1919, all Europe was at the disposition of the Big Four, not merely in terms of power and geography but in the minds and hearts of its peoples. Wilson had from them honors almost divine because of the values which he seemed to represent and which, in fact, he did represent to the best of his knowledge and capacities.

We can gauge the opportunity by the speed and smoothness with which the peace was made, grandiose as was its pattern. The squabbles and conflicts at Paris in 1919 have resounded through memoirs since. They seem very small beside the difficulties of peace-making in the dragging conferences of 1945, 1946, and 1947; and to Byrnes, Bevin, Marshall, and Bidault the Conference at Versailles must appear a miracle of conciliation. The statesmen there were all (in voice at least) ardent Liberals and Democrats. No ideological conflict divided them. Lenin was not among them nor any of his aides; his reign seemed from Versailles but a brief and awkward prologue to the rise in Russia of a parliamentary democracy. The world of the delegates at Paris was made safe for democracy. Whatever doubts Mr. Wilson felt, whatever cynicisms were coined about Clemenceau, neither seriously doubted the future of the Liberal order. Yet Mussolini, Hitler, and Stalin were already mature men, and two of them were well launched on their careers.

As one tries to pierce, for instruction in our times, to the causes of the catastrophic failure which followed Versailles, the figure of Wilson more and more becomes symbolic.

Wilson was a great Liberal, distinguished in mind, in character, in quality of conviction. He, more than his colleagues at Paris, embodied the Liberal Idea. Perhaps he represented it better than any other American since Lincoln, any European since Gladstone. Why did he fail and Liberalism with him?

His essential failure was, I believe, at Paris. The men who broke him and his cause at home were not the prime authors of his defeat. Even combined, they were not big enough for that; unless the time and circumstances had served, they would hardly have attempted it. They won because the climate had changed about Wilson. It had grown cold. The popular warmth declined. Men's devotion fell away, their fires went out. They went out because deep in the minds and hearts of common men crept a slow doubt: a doubt of Versailles, a doubt of St. Germain, a doubt of their morality, a doubt of the honesty of the whole Liberal view.

The people are fooled some of the time and some of them all the time as the great realist and seer of democracy knew. But as he also knew, there comes sometimes in history a movement from the depths of common men: a judgment, a doubt, a decision, which is beyond all political manipulation, and to which statesmen and history must bend. It is a movement (or so, I think, it seemed to Lincoln) of the natural conscience; of a deep response in men to some universal order, some law or rhythm of the creation. It may not often move them as a commonalty; and when it does, it may hardly reach the surface of their minds except in distorting rationalizations. But when "Man's dominion has broken Nature's social union," as Burns remarked to the mouse, "the best-laid schemes" have strange upsets.

A profound unease of the spirit came on all the world. It reacted against the peace (how many could be found to defend Versailles twelve years later, though clause by clause it was not the worst of treaties?). It spread through the post-war world, destroying the confidence of the victors and corrupting the defeated. It made the psychological and moral milieu in which Hitlerism grew.

It was reflected in the moral disorders, in the intellectual and social phantasies and frenzies (no age was more prolific of social and political wild-cats) of the world between the wars: in the contemptuous distaste for old loyalties, the cynical refusal of new.

The cult of the debunker, who had no alternative to the babbittries which he despised but shared, was characteristic. A vicious journalism appeared from men who could no longer examine their own consciences, but pursued their neighbors with whips and scorpions. Images and catch-calls created in malice or prejudice came to dominate the public mind and feed ignorant passions and party hatreds and nationalist resentments. A pacifism appeared which had no devotion to the tranquillity of order, but was nursed in skepticism, doubts, fears, and confusion. This was the agony of the Liberal world, the death of its doctrine of Progress: it produced its last great figure in Woodrow Wilson and he was still its symbol as he lay paralyzed, a President still vested with powers his palsied mind and hands could not use.

We did not read his riddle, and in the failure we came inevitably to the Second War.

We had better read it now and quickly or the Third will be upon us; and we must seek the answer first in ourselves, in our Western world which has already seen its greatest opportunity pass into its greatest tragedy: of which the climax and *dénouement* are yet to come, of which we have not yet known the catharsis.

* 2 *

The Third British System was with the rest of the Western world invested by the mood of doubt, skepticism, and cynicism. The British countries suffered less than some others, but more than enough to produce the weariness, the reluctance for new responsibilities. The British lost a million dead. Wounds, sickness, and the strains of trench warfare sucked the best energies of millions more.[2]

The missing generation left a black gap in Britain's public life, which in part explains the vacillating and dreary leadership of the years between the wars. Human affairs are best conducted where there is a proper balance between energy and experience, imagination and judgment, enterprise and order. This normally is provided by the men of middle years, and in their presence age and youth may best contribute their special virtues. The weakness of the middle generation in the post-war world threw an unnatural and unhealthy strain on its seniors and juniors. Youth ran beyond its proper responsibilities, lacking the massive hand and presence of the elder brother. The demagogues traded on its brashness, violence, inexperience, and lack of real self-confidence. The old had to hang on too long and carry burdens which should have gone to men in the prime. The old and young were in collision, for they lacked the middle generation to interpret. Experience was not passed smoothly on; there was a rift in the continuity of consciousness.

The natural conservatism of the old, which usually is tempered in society by the influence of their successors, had unnatural weight. It proved stiff and recalcitrant. The Right suffered from hardening of the arteries; and with the weariness of the aged, Conservatism was exploited and discredited in many countries by political confidence men. Youth's natural impetuosity was equally a victim. Its enthusiasms unchastened by experience were easy meat for social agitators. The twenty years between the wars were filled with nuisances which a normal middle-generation would not have tolerated if it had been properly in the European saddle.

Even the British Dominions felt the losses of that genera-

---

[2] Approximately 10,000,000 men were enlisted by the British Empire in World War I: 3,284,000 from the Empire overseas.

tion. The American losses were in proportion to population of much less consequence, and the United States advanced much more rapidly in the post-war decade than its Allies.

Australia's case is extraordinarily interesting. The first years of the 20th century were there a period of promise. Hopes ran high, the national pulse was strong, migrants were flowing in, the young men were charged with energy and a passionate determination to make a Great Power in the South Seas. They dreamed of twenty millions of people by 1950. They launched a national capital which was to have 50,000 inhabitants by 1930.[3]

The First War fell like a hammer on the neck. It did not cut the cord of national life, but it slowed and numbed it. The change of temper was marked. Australia at the moment when she most needed young men lost nearly 70,000 dead, and twice as many were in some way disabled, from a total population of about 4,500,000. Moreover, her losses came from the most adventurous and energetic of her young males, for she had raised her forces by voluntary enlistment.

The pioneering temper flagged almost immediately and when it was most needed to people the North and West. Although many thousands of ex-soldiers were placed on sub-divided settled lands, the mass of tired servicemen, and of their more careful contemporaries who had stayed at home, preferred the comforts of the cities and jobs which called for few personal responsibilities and risks. These came more and more to look beyond themselves for security, to the Arbitration System and the Social Service State. The instruments created by the State to serve ex-soldiers and their dependents gave in their turn an impetus to social controls and regulation and to the habit of dependence on the State.

The soldiers had fallen years behind their contemporaries.

---

[3] Australia had in 1947 about 7½ millions; the national capital at Canberra, about 15,000 people.

The volunteers of the Australian Imperial Force and Royal Australian Navy never recovered their full part in the community. In politics, for instance, men of their generation had come to high places in the time of the Second War, but only one of five Prime Ministers between 1940 and 1945 was a veteran, and he was Prime Minister for only a few days.

Nevertheless, the Dominions emerged from the First War into world-politics on a note of aggressive self-confidence. Their political leaders seized the cue for the world stage. Their electorates may not have always understood what they were up to, but they had support from the rising national pride of the peoples. The Dominion troops had shown the mettle of their pastures. Their countrymen now wore their laurels proudly.

Nationalism had a sharp fillip also in the economic field. The war had boosted in the Dominions local industries, profits, and wages. Its enormous expenditures suggested to the less instructed (and few were much instructed in difficult economic matters) that their several communities were much wealthier than in fact they were. If there was money to fight wars on this scale, there surely must be money to feed new social services, raise wages, and provide a new social deal. So the curious delusions grew that the more wealth is wasted, the more wealth there must be: that the more money borrowed, the more money there must be to borrow. The delusions and confusions about money and real wealth were a characteristic sample of the general confusion of mind between the wars.

Whole peoples began to live largely on their "credit"; though to a cosmic eye their collateral security must have seemed meager. The rise in nominal profits and wages was met in many countries partly by increased production, but also by money borrowed, usually from London. Borrowed money was an inflationary factor. Tariffs and other economic oddities sent prices soaring beyond all proper relation to the basic costs of free production. With rising wages, the workers seemed to think that they benefited from the queer bonanza, that they were better off than their parents.

Workers are slow to compare lifts in their wages with rising prices. The wages are in their pay-envelopes; the prices are diffused. There is some time-lag usually, and the worker has less general acquaintance with prices than his wife who spends the household budget. If the workers sometimes in the 1920s had doubts of their new prosperity, these could be diverted by the succession of novel gadgets: radio, talkies, automobiles in mass-production, and their like.

The cost of the war in real wealth had, in fact, been colossal. The British peoples came out of it less punch-drunk than the other Powers heavily engaged; but their whole system had unquestionably been loosened, and Britain's economic position was grievously weakened.

A loss of authority and competence appeared at once in Ireland, India, and Egypt. There was also sharp reaction from the pre-war and wartime inclination to strengthen the Commonwealth ties.

During the war, the Dominions earned and demanded responsibility in the shaping of great policies. "The protected colony was rightly voiceless," as a Canadian Minister said; "the participating nation cannot continue so."

In this sense, the Imperial War Cabinet appeared in 1917 and 1918, with nicely balanced representation from the United Kingdom and each of the Dominions. It provided an effective instrument for the co-ordination of the military and diplomatic efforts. It seemed to promise a new political entity: one of those *ad hoc* creations in which the political genius of the British peoples has been best expressed. The Dominion representatives, said Lord Curzon, "are not coming as members of an Imperial Conference of the old style. They are coming as members for the time being of the sovereign body of the British Empire. This seems to me the greatest step ever taken in recognizing the relations of the Dominions and ourselves as on a basis of equality."

The Prime Ministers resolved that the procedure should be continued beyond the war: that an Imperial Cabinet should meet annually and become, they hoped, "an accepted convention of the British Constitution." [4]

The Prime Ministers went farther. They resolved to call, at the war's end, a special Imperial Conference to consider "the readjustment of the constitutional relations of the component parts of the Empire"; and they recorded their views that "any such readjustment, while thoroughly preserving all existing powers of self-government and complete control of domestic affairs, should be based upon a full recognition of the Dominions as autonomous nations of an Imperial Commonwealth, and of India as an important portion of the same, should recognize the right of the Dominions and India to an adequate voice in foreign policy and in foreign relations, and should provide effective arrangements for continuous consultation in all important matters of common Imperial concern, and for such necessary concerted action, founded on consultation, as the several Governments may determine."

It sounded like integration. Actually, as Smuts saw and said, it "negatived by implication the idea of a future Imperial Parliament and a future Imperial Executive."

The emphasis was to be on autonomy rather than "continuous consultation." This appeared immediately at the Peace Conference. The Dominions demanded and won representation distinct from their part in the general delegation of the British Empire. Hughes of Australia flatly declared, "Look at it geographically, industrially, or how you will, and it will be seen that no one can speak for Australia but those who speak as representatives of Australia herself." The "vastness of the Empire and the diversity of interests,"

---

[4] Quoted by Marriott: *The Evolution of the British Empire and Commonwealth.*

as well as the war-efforts of its constituents argued for him.

At Versailles, the British Commonwealth appeared before the world not with a central Government but as "a league of free States, free, equal, and working together for the great ideals of human government." [5] The world could not quite believe in this curious hydra. It required an act of faith to accept the political phenomenon of six sovereign states in one entity: and M. Clemenceau had long, one gathered, dismissed the Trinity. But whatever the theory of the thing, neither M. Clemenceau nor Mr. Wilson could ignore the bouncing and peppery presence of Mr. Hughes. He was determined to impress the fact of Australia on the world, and by reverberation to tingle Australia's own slower ears. He went at the Conference in furious tackles; and Mr. Wilson found himself in unexpected scrimmage. Scrimmage was not Mr. Wilson's forte. He preferred to carry the ball. Mr. Hughes' technique was not neglected by Dr. Evatt, his successor, in our later day.

Smuts and the Canadians, with less bravura, had perhaps as much effect in both post-war passages.

In the League of Nations the British Empire held a permanent seat on the Council, but each Dominion, except Newfoundland, had also its own representation, with right of election as a temporary member of the Council. The Dominions had thus in a sense a double representation denied even to the United Kingdom. The precedent was exploited by the U.S.S.R. and its constituents, the Ukraine and Byelo-Russia, in the United Nations.

South Africa, Australia, and New Zealand confirmed their status before the world by assuming mandates over ex-German territories. Australia was denied absolute possession of the Pacific properties by President Wilson, who was supported by protests from Japan.

[5] Smuts.

At Versailles, then, the first clear clash between the British System and the Japanese appeared. The bone was Australia's insistence that her mandates should be ordered to her interests: her security and her economic, industrial, and general welfare; in other words, her "White Australia" policy and her protective-tariffs system.

She thus threw down a glove to Asia and to history, and, first of the Dominions, took an initiative before the world in an issue of the highest policy, on which her destiny would unquestionably turn. She set the whole British Commonwealth in a new position vis-à-vis the Asian peoples, and emphasized an element of potential loud discord. The "White Australia" policy in effect raised a color-bar even against His Majesty's subjects of the Indo-European race.

The policy itself is justifiable, I believe, though the proper arguments for it have not been well publicized abroad. But it did make great demands on the tolerance of the British Government, which foresaw, perhaps better than most Australians, the problems it would raise. These began obviously with the defenses of the whole System in the Pacific.

Britain nevertheless went along, maybe a little in the mood of a parent who feels that the young must have their fling. New Zealand contributed to the cost of a base at Singapore, but Australia and New Zealand both proceeded promptly to reduce their own naval and military establishments. The majesty and might of the Royal Navy and the enduring patience of the British tax-payer were still taken much for granted throughout the British System. [6]

[6] One little classic of Governmental economy deserves to be preserved for the edification of all democracies. After War I, the Royal Australian Navy joined in the Royal Navy's great task of hydrographic survey, one of its major contributions to the world. The Australians were, when the depression came in 1929, working in the waters between New Guinea and Australia which were to be of primary importance in the operations of 1942-3. The Australian Government axed the survey in an economy drive; and work which might have been comfortably completed before War II began had then to be undertaken in the teeth of the enemy.

The Commonwealth and the Japanese mandates faced one another across the Equator. The Japanese at once began to develop theirs in a strategic frame which would serve as springboard. The three British Governments concerned in the Southwest Pacific (the United Kingdom, Australia, and New Zealand) took no serious defensive measures whatsoever, although Australia had repeatedly insisted at Versailles and afterward that the mandated areas were essential in her pattern of defense. Defense expenditures had become exceedingly unpopular throughout the British System. The majorities, especially their Liberal and Labour elements, in the British countries seemed convinced that the era of wars was gone forever. The curious "Peace Ballot," which undoubtedly checked the inclination of the Baldwin Government to resume reasonable military precautions, was taken when the Italians had already won the Abyssinian War, Dollfuss was dead, Hitler had recovered the Saar and ordered conscription; and while all too obviously the British Commonwealth, the United States, and the Western Democracies had not a shred of policy to cover their nakedness.

The British Commonwealth was in the middle Thirties defenseless but for the much diminished Royal Navy, a miniature air force, and small regular armies in the United Kingdom and India, barely sufficient for their roles as garrison and depot troops and for the policing of frontiers and protected areas.

If the Naval Disarmament Treaties had taken full effect (the Japanese fortunately repudiated them), the Royal Navy would probably have come to 1939 with hardly any of the battleships which actually held the seas for three years. The five of the *Royal Sovereign* class and the five *Queen Elizabeths* would have gone. *Repulse, Renown, Hood, Nelson, Rodney* were also marked for salvage. Perhaps they would have had sufficient successors, if the Peace

Balloteers, the Opposition, the public purse, time, and the enemy had all permitted.

The psychology of disarmament concerns us again in the West. The British Commonwealth and the United States are essentially "civilian" polities. Their social structures are brought to war purposes only with tremendous tensions, strains, and distortions.

In peace, their populations have always grown restive at military budgets. Standing armies were a grievance against the Stuart Kings; and the prick remains in the British consciousness. Regular troops still have for the Americans a remote suggestion of the Red Coats.

But European peoples have long accepted heavy military establishments as a normal burden; and since Napoleon their young men have served for trifling pay in large standing armies, mostly based on national conscription. The British never had peace-time conscription until the eve of World War II, and popular opinion still mistrusts and mislikes it.[7] The British have always relied on their naval power to give time to mobilize their other resources for war; and the United States (though Americans have been slow to acknowledge it) also presumed for a century and more on the Royal Navy to hold their ocean moats. The United States has at least four times created powerful fleets for war: in 1861-5, in the Spanish War, and in the World Wars. Three times it let its Navy rapidly decline when the immediate task was done. Despite its brilliant tradition, the United States Navy has lacked strong stays in public opinion. The Americans, with their continental bias, have lacked (until War II at least) the Englishman's understanding of the needs and nature of sea-power.

The great American fleets, consequently, have been mostly

[7] Though Australia and New Zealand had compulsory part-time training before and after World War I for "cadets" between 14 and 18 years, and "Citizen Forces" of men from 18 to 26 years.

created for the occasion. This gives an immediate advantage.[8] But it also leads to the discarding of ships and complements when their special purpose is achieved; and it has always been difficult in peace to persuade Congress to provide substantially for a general-purpose navy.

Yet in the new situation of America, she clearly must maintain her naval power. In another war, she is unlikely to have the years of grace needed to create a navy; and a navy in one form or another will continue essential in a war of guided missiles.

The warship has been essentially a gun-platform. If it becomes primarily a rocket-launching platform, its mobility will give it marked advantage over static sites ashore which will presumably with developments in radar be rapidly "fixed" by the enemy. Mobile platforms of great weight are not feasible ashore: the buoyant element is still of first importance.

Fleets cannot be quickly improvised; and the psychology of disarmament is a prime study for those who must get popular assent for defense policies. The gradual decline and disruption of defenses in the Democracies between the wars should be reviewed with the closest attention.

* 3 *

The political course of the British Commonwealth paralleled the popular illusions. With the end of War I, the politicians turned sharply from the large concepts of Commonwealth co-operation to domestic concerns.

War was done and the urgencies were passed which had prompted the British peoples to combine their strengths.

[8] As in the Pacific War, where U.S.N. ships were admirably designed for the tropical and sub-tropical areas and for archipelagic war. British naval design normally is more for general purposes and all contingencies. The British Pacific Fleet was not as well equipped for the war against Japan as the U.S.N., but the old Clyde-built cruiser *Australia* survived a record number of suicide-bomber attacks—five in two days.

At the moment when Nationalism was rising in the Dominions, the military need for a larger view and system seemed to disappear. The pressure in politics now (as always in the first years of a confident peace) was from local social groups and issues; and from the economic unrest which the dislocations of war leave as a secondary disease.

Though Mr. Winston Churchill [9] announced the Imperial Conference of 1921 as "the first peace meeting of the Imperial Cabinet," each of the Dominions refused it that character; and it decided against the Constitutional Conference earlier proposed. It was disposed to leave relations much as they were or as the Prime Ministers from time to time might choose to conduct them. "The general feeling," said Lloyd George, "was that it would be a mistake to lay down any rules or to embark upon definition as to what the British Empire meant." This Welsh twilight also spread from Australia's Mr. Hughes: "Any attempt to set out in writing what are or should be the constitutional relations between the Dominions and the Mother Country would be fraught with very great dangers to the Empire." Their general sense continued to prevail until and through World War II, dominating the attitudes of the elder statesmen and especially of Mr. Mackenzie King. Nevertheless, an effort to define the relations in writing was made at subsequent Conferences, but not with integration in mind.

Emphasis in the post-war years was shifting, in fact, from political to economic relations. The Imperial Economic Conference of 1923 was of much more consequence than the accompanying Imperial Conference. The Economic Conference tackled problems of communications, currency, exchange, and scores of associated matters; and the Dominions had from the Conservative Government a promise

---

[9] He was Secretary of State for the Colonies.

of tariff-preferences for a long list of trade items. The first Labour Government under MacDonald crossed this plan; but when Baldwin came back to power, he launched the Imperial Economic Committee and the Empire Marketing Board, restored the preferences Labour had canceled, and created more.

The Imperial Conference of 1926 set out to "investigate" inter-Imperial relations. It rejected any notion of an Imperial Constitution; but defined in writing plain enough the sense afterwards given legal sanction in the Statute of Westminster. Enumerating the Dominions, it declared them "autonomous Communities within the British Empire, equal in status . . . united by a common allegiance to the Crown and freely associated as members of the British Commonwealth of Nations." [10]

The Conference saw that equality and similarity in status might still leave special responsibilities in functions. The Commonwealth had diversities of gifts, and no Dominion wished to challenge the pre-eminence of the British taxpayer in providing for defense. The Conference recognized that for both defense and foreign policy "the major share of responsibility rests now, and must for some time to come continue to rest, with His Majesty's Government in Great Britain."

The Conference of 1930 met under a Labour Prime Minister in Britain and with a Chancellor of the Exchequer unsympathetic to Imperial preferences. Mr. Snowden would have liked to sweep out tariffs altogether. He was an unreconstructed free trader. But the economic gale of 1929

---

[10] The text and sense of the 1926 charter were largely from Arthur Balfour: a man who (as John Buchan said of him) saw the world as a bridge to pass over, not to build upon; and who wrote that a philosopher must possess "the instinct which tells him where, along the line of contemporary speculation, that point is to be found from which the next advance may best be made."

was rising to a blizzard; and the Canadian Prime Minister [11] insisted that the day was now or never for the Empire to find its welfare in closer economic union. Mr. Snowden shook his stubborn head. But the Labour Government was blown away in the storm. The MacDonald group joined with Baldwin's Conservatives as the National Government, wherein Snowden made way at the Exchequer for Neville Chamberlain.

Chamberlain enacted his father's policy though it did not realize his father's furthest purposes. Ninety years before, Peel had brought in free trade. Now Chamberlain pitched it out, neck and crop, with his Import Duties Act of February 1931. This imposed a general tariff but exempted Empire goods until a preferential method could be settled: the task set at Ottawa in 1932.

Ottawa produced not a comprehensive harmony, but a long string of agreements between Great Britain, the Dominions, India, and the Colonies, one with another. These naturally irritated many outsiders. Yet the course was forced on the British countries by the policies of other Governments. Preferential tariffs were not outrageous novelties as some publicists and politicians south of the border seemed to suggest. An Australian Prime Minister [12] pointed out years before its Smoot-Hawley Tariff Act that the United States gave preferences to its possessions against foreigners amounting to about 100 per cent. Japan gave her empire 100 per cent; Spain gave 50, France 50-80, Portugal and Italy 50-90 per cent.

Ottawa's provisions were mild beside the tariff arrangements of most non-British States. Nevertheless, they made a profound impression on the world. Nations which had gam-

[11] Mr. R. B. Bennett: Mr. Mackenzie King (strange as it may have seemed to latter-day Canadians) had not an uninterrupted course from remote antiquity.

[12] Mr. S. M. Bruce (later Viscount Bruce).

boled freely in British pastures while keeping their own preserved felt, with intimate knowledge, that one tariff breeds another and that their appetites grow by eating in the fashion of Gargantua's.

The British Dominions had as individual States long been passionate Protectionists. Americans, Germans, Argentinians and the rest now feared that if they carried the Mother Country all the way with them, they might produce a vast closed system which would shut off competitors from their choicest feeding. Most peoples still felt obscurely that free trade had been a counsel of perfection. Now as Great Britain went over to protection they were shocked.

Yet Britain remained by far the world's best customer. In 1938, she bought raw materials, food, beverages, tobacco, machinery and manufactured goods worth £923,000,000 or $67 per head of population, taking 21 per cent of all the world's exports. She was the best customer of 31 countries including most of the chief exporting countries, led by the United States. She would apparently be in a formidable position if she wished to get really tough (and a number of export economies will in our latter day fall distinctly sick if she relapses).

In 1938, the British spent by head of population nearly ten dollars in the United States. The Americans each bought from Britain less than one dollar's worth of goods. If each American now bought as much as normally each Australian, Canadian, Argentinian or even Dutchman, Dane or Norwegian buys from Britain, her chief economic trouble would be ended.

In 1913, Britain had imported merchandise and bullion in excess of exports to the tune of £158,000,000; but her invisible imports (the net income from shipping, investments, financial services and so on) gave a total credit balance of £181,000,000. By 1928, although her exports were short of her imports by £358,000,000, on total balance she was still £137,000,000 ahead of the game; in 1932-3, £113,000,000. But she was clearly on a slide which might become a dangerous skid if either her shipping income or her return from investments was seriously affected. The tariff and financial policies of the United States, Italy, Germany, and Japan all joined with the world depression to produce threatening jolts in the early 1930s. British exports were halved between 1929 and 1932 and imports nearly halved. Ottawa steadied the machine and helped to pull the Dominions out of the slump. But it made no provision which could counter the liquidation of Britain's overseas investments in the event of war.

The time was long gone, if it had ever been, for a unitary economic system; and the Dominions and the United Kingdom were already in some markets and measures competitive. Nevertheless, the economic co-operation achieved at Ottawa was the major move between the wars towards strengthening the Imperial System; and in marked contrast with the drift politically.

Yet the political drift was in a sense a surface drift. Strong centripetal currents still flowed below. While the Dominions were increasingly asserting their autonomy in the field of high politics and international relations, they were also weaving at more pragmatic levels a strong web of new associations, and the realities of the British System, we should remember, are more in low-life affairs, the groceries and such, than in the flourish of tuckets or the roll of after-dinner speeches. The British may not be a nation of shop-keepers, but most would like to be. The seamen and the soldiers and the poets (consider Shakespeare) dream of buying against old age "a nice little business round the corner," preferably from a pub. Few of them may achieve it; but wise Government in Britain will not take from too many their vision of a cozy competence, redolent with smells of cheese and spices, adjoining a snug parlor with its kettle on the hob and bloater-paste on toast for tea.

One looks below high politics to discover what the British are really doing. Between the wars they were busy together in scores of deals not much advertised.[13] Here—in the exchange of scientific and technical information, in similarities of the military and civil services, and in regard for the English Common Law, for example—more than in the shapes and phrases and prejudices of politics are the realities of the British System: here and in its commerce and in the strong bonds of culture and sentiment of which the Royal House is the chief symbol.

The Kingship, moreover, achieved tremendous influence in the last years of George V. It gave a center of loyalties which the bitter party controversies could not touch. It helped to knit up the ravell'd sleave of care in the Depression and the international political crisis which grew on it. The prestige of the Crown has not stood higher than at the Jubilee and about the death-bed of King George V. His reign had increasingly revealed his and his Queen's steadiness of mind and temper and craftsmanship, qualities always immensely admired in Britain and especially comforting as the skies darkened over Europe.

At the first shock, the abdication of Edward VIII seemed likely to dissipate the prestige gathered by three careful reigns through a century. In retrospect, the position of the Crown seems to have been strengthened. The peoples and Governments of the Commonwealth were forced to look closely at the institution and to review its part and character.[14] They each sharply recognized that the Crown was indispensable to their System and community.

[13] For details of the growth of co-operative machinery in the British Commonwealth between the wars, see Appendix, Note 3, page 392.

[14] Each Dominion under the Statute of Westminster had to assent to the Bill of Abdication before it could be enacted; any change in the Succession or of the Royal Style and Titles requires their agreement.

Edward VIII's personal popularity eased the situation. He had much sympathy from Labour, especially in the Dominions: members of the Australian Party spoke vigorously for him in the House of Representatives. His successor had general sympathy in an unhappy personal situation, and the prestige of the Queen Mother was like a strong bridge across the crevasse.

The Imperial Conference which assembled at the Coronation knew that here was the seal of the fellowship, whose strength was presently to be once more tested.

From the Coronation and Conference several Commonwealth Ministers tried to talk sense to the Germans. But sense of their sort was not much in demand, and Hitler was convinced that, though the Kaiser had mistaken the strength of the British System, Germany now could count on its dissolution at the stroke of war.

TEN

THE SECOND WAR

THE War still lies too heavily on the human mind and will for clear perspectives. We can, however, grasp some meanings, rawly evident.

It clearly was one act or canto of a developing tragedy. War I is intimately related with it and passed into it through an uneasy interlude, packed in Shakespearian fashion with ironic phrases and strange humors, humanity's ears straining for the knocking at the door. Then we seemed subject to every conceivable political and social aberration. We were walking as if in a gallery of distorting mirrors, except that the figures in the mirrors were our reality.

The first decade was the heyday of ballyhoo, of a glib materialism when the conventions of morals, manners, and intellectual integrity exploded with a bang. The lid blew off the Victorian convention and the sides blew out, and we could see that it had long been hollow.

The optimists thought that society was merely shedding like a snake its old skin. The poet saw dried bones in a wasteland.

The second decade came not with a bang but a whimper, as all humanity writhed to the diminuendo of the New York Stock Exchange. The boom and crash of 1929 was of course only one feature of the world depression; but it summarized it in the curious panic quality, the sense of frustration, futility, and hopelessness which swept over the multitudes. Men were the victims of their spending money. Piles of paper profits broke the backs of vast industries, stopped the machines, threw tens of millions into the gutters. No one seemed to know precisely why the world was suddenly bankrupt or even whether it in fact was. The economists flourished their explanations and interpretations, but only economists understood them and they were mostly in dispute. Man, who had produced the London Underground, the Model T Ford, the aeroplane, now stood confounded and confused before his own economic machinery to confess that he did not know how to work it, that he did not really know how it worked. You can still hear the echoes like distant wails after Walpurgis: ". . . wheat into the sea . . . burning coffee in Brazil . . . the gold buried at Fort Knox." These were riddles; but what Sphinx had the answer? Mr. Coolidge did not choose to run or rede: and where were Mr. Smoot and Mr. Hawley?

The economists may have had the rights of it, but the man in the street did not establish communication with them. He still does not know what struck him. He whored instead after strange economic and political superstitions. Any sort of lucky charm or amulet would serve. He went in considerably for bone-pointing, at the bankers and the bulls and bears and usurers and such. The most impressive feature of the whole crisis is the pervading air of ignorance and helplessness. Man did not know what to do with his own inventions of money, credit, rates of exchange, and the instruments of distribution. His self-confidence was swept away. He seemed lost in drifting sands. The notion of security floated like the mirage of an oasis before his agonized eyes. He cried out for it, and his cries reverberated through all the legislative halls and smoke-filled hotel rooms. Security became the main theme of politics: social security, collective security, personal security. The world cried for security as if there was any minute, in all the days of all our lives from the beginning, when any man was secure. But the world needed comfort. It had just discovered, perhaps, that it no longer believed in God. So it rushed towards the image of the Social Service State or (where it was of a more romantic and susceptible turn) towards the Fuehrer and the Duce and the Man of Steel in the Kremlin. As Voltaire had said, if God did not exist, it would be necessary to invent him. Unhappily, men do not seem particularly good at making gods. Their home-made varieties fall asleep, or go on journeys, or eat young girls, or get into wars.

The Depression was, in fact, a psychological and moral crisis: the economists could explain only the blackboard facts and figures which expressed its consequences in the way of goods and services. The world did not "recover" from the Depression. It began to buy and sell again because it had to eat and to find raiment. Mr. Roosevelt's economists had no panaceas. But they could produce a shift in psychological emphases, they were shrewd propagandists and they could catch the turn of the tide and ride the wave, looking much as if they owned it. Their agility was fascinating though they did not answer the real questions. But as hardly anyone was asking them, this scarcely mattered.

Mr. Roosevelt's career was largely an affair of impromptus and *ad hoc* decisions which, if not always inspired, were sufficiently inspiring for great political success. He kept attention on the political performance and sufficiently distracted from the questions which searched far beyond any answers that politics could give. Mr. Roosevelt perhaps saw that this was in fact his highest use: for the history of the 1930s was essentially in the way of an *entr'acte*. It could have been otherwise only if it had known a spiritual and moral revolution. It did certainly offer conscience a thou-, sand tongues, and every tongue brought in a different tale; but the voices were lost in the din which man raised to keep from thinking. The moral decline was headlong through the twenty years. The moral philosophers saw what was happening as their best had seen for two generations. Some foretold accurately the next phase. They dreaded less the collapse of the socio-economic façade than the moral ruin it would reveal. Some were (so to say) war-correspondents before the time. They were already at the moral front, and all men's other campaigns are after all only its sideshows.

Intellectual and moral confusion was evident from the beginning of the War. In the First War, when the intellectual and moral heritage was still considerable, Governments had put out war aims which had some claims to intellectual and moral respect. But in War II, the Governments found it easier to declare what they were fighting against than what they were fighting for, and observers noted that the GI, the Tommy, and the *poilu* often were vague about the meaning of the whole affair.

Even Mr. Churchill, a master of public utterance, could only say as he took up his great role: "You ask what is our aim? I can answer in one word: Victory."

But victory itself is a flickering *ignis fatuus*. Mr. Churchill knew that the blood, toil, sweat, and tears would deserve something more than a Mafeking night. He knew that if victory was all that Britain sought, she might have remembered that peace also hath victories and that they come much cheaper. Mr. Churchill meant by *victory* that we should save the values of our way of life. He was not prepared to promise more, being a man of great experience and candor; and the values had for common use been much debased in the currency of fools and hollow men and cynics.

But when Mr. Churchill came together with Mr. Roosevelt, they found it necessary to put out some proclamation of their purposes. They produced the Atlantic Charter. It did not much clarify our aims.

For example, what precisely does it mean by "freedom from fear"? Christian Scientists might disagree, but most of us would think we had a positive need to be afraid on salutary occasion. My right under the Charter to freedom from fear will not, I fear, much console me if I meet a tiger face to face. A child who does not acquire some fear of the fire might end by falling into it; but will its parents rejoice in their little torch of liberty?

Mr. Churchill is alive to words and logic. He perhaps will yet give us a gloss to the Atlantic Charter.

To mean anything real, papers of the kind need to be couched in clear, specific terms with unambiguous reference. If we are to have charters of human rights and such, let us look again at Magna Charta. The men who drafted it left no room for doubts:

"No sheriff or bailiff of ours, or any other person, shall take the horses or carts of any freeman, to perform carriages, without the consent of the said freeman.

"No freeman shall be taken, or imprisoned, or disseised, or outlawed, or banished, or any ways destroyed, nor will we pass upon him, nor will we send upon him, unless by the lawful judgment of his peers, or by the law of the land.

"We will sell to no man, we will not deny to any man, either justice or right."

These like the Ten Commandments mean something. As Coke pointed out here is in proper progression assurance against loss of liberty, loss of property, loss of citizen rights. The men who framed them understood the meaning of law and the meaning of words and the meaning of the possible far better than their successors in our time.

The Seventh Article of the Atlantic Charter piously hopes that the peace "should enable all men to traverse the high seas and oceans without hindrance," which is the merest nonsense in a world where pirates have not lacked progeny, and card-sharpers still abound, and gun-running, opium-smuggling, and the slave-traffic are not unknown.

Compare the clarity of Magna Charta (and reflect on the education of the editors who accept "medieval" as a synonym for "lawlessness"):

"All merchants shall have safe and secure conduct, to go out of, and to come into England, and to stay there, and to pass as well by land as by water, for buying and selling by the ancient and allowed customs, without any evil tolls; except in time of war, or when they are of any nation at war with us. And if there be found any such in our land, in the beginning of the war, they shall be attached, without damage to their bodies or goods, until it be known unto us, or our chief justiciary, how our merchants be treated in the nation at war with us; and if ours be safe there, the others shall be safe in our dominions."

There with superb clarity and decision and brevity is notice to foreign merchants of their rights under the Law; and notice to foreign States of English intentions. Clarity in the Law is a prime mark of civilization. The language of the Great Charter may be profitably compared with the turbid stuff of the semi-literates who now write most of the world's laws and regulations.

The Atlantic Charter was confused in its expression and rapidly confused in its application. Consider an instance. The specific occasion of Britain's declaration of war was her solemn guarantee to Poland. If we were fighting for one clear definable cause it was for the integrity of Poland against aggression. Here we had specific obligations signed and declared.[1] Moreover, the cases of Poland, Lithuania, Latvia, Estonia were clearly covered by six of the eight clauses of the Atlantic Charter. They went overboard at Yalta. From Yalta, victory alone became the war aim. The expressed desires, hopes, and beliefs of the Atlantic Charter were shrugged off in a few days of horse-trading.

Mr. Ernest Bevin, that remarkably honest man (to whose "characteristic faithfulness" Mr. Churchill has paid tribute), once said: "I make a solemn confession. I was a party, in the Coalition Government, to the Atlantic Charter, and one of my first experiences [2] was to find myself deciding whether I could accede to the new Polish frontiers, which I have never yet been able to reconcile with the Atlantic Charter, but to which the very necessities of war at that time compelled me to agree.

"The first day I was in office, when I went to Potsdam, I had to face the demand for the new Polish frontier on the Oder, by which thirteen million people had up to that time been driven westward.

"In the end I agreed, because I felt there was nothing else to do, in the light of the circumstances that war had created. It was inevitable that such enforced, large-scale emigration of people should provoke the deepest reaction in Germany, and I fear that we have not seen the last result of the Polish *affaire*."

Of course we have not. The Russians pushed Poland west-

[1] Some consider that our guarantee was actually fatal to Poland by provoking general war. But the Baltic States and Finland were laid low without benefit of our promises. Those who feel or felt that Britain should in consistency have supported Finland and the Baltic States against Russian aggression miss this point. Morally, the cases have much common ground, but Britain was not specifically engaged to defend these other States. She had no obligations (unless as a member of the League of Nations) more than the United States: which had initiated the Kellogg Pact, we may remotely remember. But Poland's claims were clear.

[2] On taking office as Foreign Secretary in 1945 and succeeding Mr. Eden at the Potsdam Conference.

ward, to breed fear and hatred between the Poles and the Germans, who were thrust out of their fields and homes to make room. The Polish Government in exile foresaw this maneuver in 1943, and Mikolajczyk protested to Roosevelt in 1944. They did not want a Germany and Poland at deadly feud. For their resistance to Yalta the Poles became "the stubborn Poles."

One can question whether the circumstances of war which Mr. Bevin found irresistible really cast light on anything. But his viewpoint is understandable and human.

There is reason to believe that Mr. Churchill went to Yalta convinced that the honor of Britain was involved in the Polish issue and that he plainly said so to the others, confident that Mr. Roosevelt would take and support his points. The frontiers of Poland were a problem proper to the peace settlement, not to a war conference; and Mr. Churchill said so.

But Mr. Roosevelt was a tired man with the hand of death on his forehead, whether he felt it there or not. He was desperately anxious to be done with the war, and desperately afraid of a revival of the German-Russian Pact (which would have called for no more cynicism in the parties than the deal of 1939). When Stalin demanded Eastern Poland and promised compensation for Poland in Germany, the President entered the trap. Perhaps he saw no alternative. But Yalta sowed dragon's teeth once more in Central Europe; and the authors of the Atlantic Charter looking at their spring sowing must have wondered whether the fall would be free from fear.[3]

Nothing is more conducive to the spread of cynicism from high places to the cots of the humble than large-sounding proclamations lacking moral content and unfulfilled in pol-

[3] An able account by Mr. Werner Knop of this phase and of the curious case of the Neisse-Oder line appeared in *The Saturday Evening Post* of 12 April, 1947.

icy. The failure to sustain the Atlantic Charter reveals the bankruptcy of the Liberal tradition which produced it: as its verbiage reveals intellectual confusion.

The lack of clear aims and principles let in the mood of expediency, of compromise, of concession to Russia which the Russians very naturally exploited. They fooled the Western Allies to the top of their bent. If Mr. Elliott Roosevelt's book is a just record, it would seem that the Russians knew all his father's stops, plucked out the heart of his mystery, sounded him from the lowest note to the top of his compass. Victory became the end which justified all means. But in any right order of thinking, victory could not be an end. It could only be a means to peace.[4] Here is the typical and terrible confusion in the modern mind of ends and means. Unless we can straighten our thinking in at least the measure of elementary logic, we are doomed and probably damned. We must learn to act not from "the light of the circumstances that war had created" (whatever Mr. Bevin meant by that) but from the authentic light of reason. After all, we assume that it distinguishes us from the apes; and we have all the history of such progress as we have made in the world to suggest that it is an essential defense against the ape in man. A peace founded on the Atlantic Charter was lost at Yalta. We had instead an armistice which, founded on Yalta, could only be a series of shifting accommodations characterized by cynicism and squeeze-plays.

The moral and intellectual confusion is more ominous than all the physical destruction: for where it persists, we can have no valid hopes for recovery and reconstruction.

---

[4] We must in a modicum of charity assume that Mr. Roosevelt was a desperately tired and sick man: that Mr. Churchill was overborne by the others and the staggering burdens of Britain's effort. Otherwise, how did two politicians of their caliber discard the strong cards (Lend-Lease, for instance) in their hands?

* 2 *

The material loss of the War may be calculated in various ways.

The Brady Report, which omits China, set the cost of war materials at $1,154,000,000,000 and the damage to property at $230,900,000,000, a very conservative estimate. The Vatican estimate to November 1945 of military and civilian dead was 22,060,000 with 34,000,000 wounded. Many millions more have died from the secondary effects of war and the hunger and disease which come in its train.[5]

No statistics can record the loss from production of human life and energies and time or of capital potentials perverted and destroyed. We begin to see that the world has been horribly impoverished; and its economic organization distorted in fantastic fashion.

Our largest effort has gone to destruction and to the production of its instruments. The mirror of our world reflects a terrible disorder. The German War was only one phase and expression of ruin which will spread and deepen until it engulfs mankind if we do not find the remedy. The resources of the world have been perverted to destruction. All the world is involved.

If ruin spreads, the world economy must smash; and with it, because inextricably involved, the economies of States large and small. Already one may doubt whether the economies of Central Europe can recover in a measurable time. The peoples of the Rhine and Elbe and Danube would have already died in millions and their survivors would have reverted to a primitive subsistence economy if the United States and three or four other countries had not been able to provide food, tools, and materials sufficient to keep at least a few sparks burning and a few wheels turning.

[5] For what such figures are worth, the First World War is said to have taken nearly 38,000,000 lives and cost approximately $222,000,000,000.

But in another cataclysm the United States may itself be a major victim. Gary, Indiana, may be smashed as
Ham was smashed. Chicago, Detroit and St. Louis may become rubble like Cologne, Warsaw, and Düsseldorf. The
steel plants of Pennsylvania may be pounded fifty feet into
the earth. The bridges may be broken on the Mississippi,
Missouri, Ohio; and the United States be chopped into local
regions. Some of its regions isolated might feed themselves.
Others would starve before communications could be restored. New York City could not be fed if all the bridges
were down in the Hudson Valley. The bridges could not
be rebuilt in time if the steel plants were tossed and twisted
piles of scrap.

If the American economy suffers a major blow within this
generation, the world we still call civilized will go down in
a complete social, economic, and political debacle.

The Roman Empire broke under barbarian onslaught but
only because it was already rotted from within. Its lessons
are now worth acute attention.

Six centuries were needed to renew in Europe the frame
of order. But a collapse of the sort now threatened would
reach far further and bring down much more. It would
involve the Eskimo and Hottentot. It would uproot the
whole structure of social life. In the 5th and 6th centuries it
was largely a superstructure which collapsed. The immemorial peasant still pursued his immemorial crafts. But in
our world, peasant and pastoralist have been knit into the
vast mercantile, industrial, and financial systems which have
caught up and transformed every social pattern. The farmer
depends for implements, for seeds, for markets, for the
wider range of his daily needs on the skills of other men
at distances and on an elaborate system of communications.
He is in much of his life as exposed as the city clerk to economic catastrophe. He has his land, but he could hardly

acquire in a lifetime the skills and habits of the self-sub-
sisting peasant if he were reduced to his own and local
resources.

Much of Europe would already be thus reduced if it had
not been propped in the frame imposed by the Occupying
Powers.

The world is immeasurably poorer than in 1939.

On a November day of 1945, as I walked in woods near
Berlin, I met a group of old men and women. They were
gathering twigs to store against the winter. They bound
them with tendrils, because they had no string, to drag
them in little bundles back by the high roads and the miles
of broken streets to their cellars under the rubble. I asked
one old man and his wife why they took only twigs, why
they did not take a bough or two for their fires. He said,
"Where in all Berlin would we get an ax? And if we had an
ax, where would we get strength to use it? And if we could
cut the boughs how would the woman and I bring them
home?"

They lacked even the tools and skills of primitive men.
They remain in my mind the image of what the survivors of
civilized man must come to everywhere if we continue in
our courses.

The ruin and disorder are the visible effects, the expression, the artifacts of moral and intellectual disorder. The
wars are not accidents. They are expressions of human passions, ambitions and disorders. The wars of this century
have been only the more dramatic passages, the more violent symptoms of a process which embraces now the des-
tinies of all mankind. It has other effects and symptoms
more sinister, if less dramatic, than the wars and we need
to look at the case whole.

But this evil is insidious. It works our destruction from
within us because it dims and dulls our intellectual and

moral faculties. Those it would destroy it first makes blind. The modern is in the habits of his life distracted from the intellectual effort which our problem requires; and he lacks moral energy. He confuses ends and means; and "no Winde makes for him that hath no intended porte to sail unto."

ELEVEN

"HOW IS THE EMPIRE?" [1]

THE War has left a raw gash which generations of peace and hard work may heal if the health of the whole Body is sufficiently restored. Local plasters, however, will provide no cure, as General Marshall saw and said in June 1947.

The world economy must be sufficiently restored before we can repair the waste and destruction. Its dislocation was represented dramatically by the symptoms which flared in the United Kingdom during 1946-7.

The United Kingdom is less likely to mortify than many other elements if the world economy as we have known it fails; for she has sufficient resources to make a new life of sorts for herself. But she is the most sensitive point of the world economy which grew about her. She reveals the trouble in it more readily than parts remote or numbed.

A healthy world economy can be restored only by the

[1] The last words of King George V.

vigorous co-operation of all the parts, but especially of the United States and other major primary-producers. If the historic task prescribed for the United States is fulfilled there will, of course, be a great shift of responsibilities within the System: the United States will become its financial backbone. If the United States refuses the role, it will revert into an isolationism this time defined by the resentment of the world, while the British will have to build a bloc with those of like mind to their own. We must then expect the struggle of several competitive systems in a scene of general disorder, with the weaker brethren attached as politico-economic vassals to one or other of the chief rivals.

The British have tried earnestly to avert this return to the economic jungle. But if it comes they may command the most formidable group. The British Commonwealth and Empire have still tremendous resources to be developed; and in a battle of wits the British can mobilize unique experience and skills. If the British System is re-established in sufficient strength to give reasonable protection, many smaller Powers would adhere to it rather than to an economic autarchy.

Americans should understand that if they are to lead the world it must be as captain of a team. They must deploy their resources and seek intelligent co-operation. One is reminded constantly of the parable of the talents. The greatest danger to the United States is of isolation (from whatever cause) in the oncoming world.

The American economy is increasingly dependent on its world relations for materials and markets. It is urgently dependent on the co-operation of others for the political and military defense of its vital interests. Americans may find the new necessities of their situation difficult to grasp, at a moment when they seem the one great prosperous nation and when most of the world may seem to wait on their bounty; but no Power now can live alone or of its own in the world.

Prosperity, if it is not wisely used, is provocative of envy and hatred. America cannot afford to be the only "have" in a world of "have-nots." Her prosperity would be brief if the rest of the world had to rebuild without her, for it would build against her. The suggestion advanced by General Marshall in mid-1947 was extraordinarily enlightened. It was essential to the restoration of ordered liberty in Europe. It was necessary also to America's own peace.

Unless we assume a universal and final catastrophe, the world must restore its general economy. The ideal is that it should come from the vigorous co-operation of all the Powers and pre-eminently of the United States, the British Commonwealth, and the U.S.S.R.

If one or other Power refuses to co-operate, the job will have to be tackled without it; and inevitably at odds with it. The Geneva Trade Conference of 1947 was but a beginning which must be developed.

The United States is not strong enough alone to create, restore or impose a world economy. The Americans are the most formidable single Power, but they are only 140,000,-000 people in a world of 2,200,000,000 people, and their rate of growth is now in the lower levels; and while their material and technical resources are enormous, they are a fraction only of the resources active or potential of the world at large.

The essential matter is to shape a system to include all who will work with and for it.

Here the future of the British Commonwealth becomes of prime importance. If the Commonwealth disintegrated, the American position would be desperately difficult.

The break-up of the Commonwealth would leave much of the world's social economy and its machinery of business and administration in wreck. It would provoke a wild scramble for the positions vacated. The United States might have some immediate gains in the Western Hemisphere by a closing of the ranks of the American peoples, North and South. But even this would be a probable rather than assured result.

Canada would for all practical purposes combine with the United States. But little would be gained, for in essentials the two already have complete accord. Moreover, Canada as a powerful member of the British Commonwealth is a link between its members and the United States. She brings to the relation more than her own strength while the Commonwealth survives.

If the Commonwealth disintegrated, Great Britain might have to join with a European bloc in which (without the Dominions and Colonies) her influence would be much reduced.

Australia and New Zealand might try still to go with her or they might seek an alliance with the United States. But they could commit themselves to this only if the United States were ready to build across half the world a massive system of defenses. Otherwise, in the dissolution of the British System, Australia and New Zealand would be in desperate case. They might be forced to make such deals as they could with forces dominant in Asia. Their survival as communities of the European stock would be unlikely.

Again, they would as isolated peoples bring less to an American alliance than they would as members of a worldwide Commonwealth. The remarkable war-efforts of the Dominions were partly due to their associations in the British System, which extended their resources in material, ships, training and facilities of every sort. The United States also was much dependent on the British System for material and shipping; and in Europe, Africa, Southeast Asia, and the South and Southwest Pacific theaters, the American Forces operated largely on British bases, lines-of-communications, and social economies. If the British System had collapsed in 1940, the United States could hardly have kept a toehold west of the Hawaiis and east of Newfoundland. If the British System should now disintegrate, its system of bases, which make a world strategy possible, would go with it. Asia probably would pass under regimes hostile to the West and dominated by the vast land Power which already straddles it from the Caspian to the Pacific. Africa would probably become an annex of the Powers dominant in Europe and the Middle East. The United States would have no effective outpost or *point d'appui* anywhere on the land mass of Europe, Asia, Africa.

The solidarity of the Americas might be maintained. But some American countries would be attracted economically towards a European orbit unless the United States were prepared to absorb their exports. A friendly Britain has been a powerful factor in the Good Neighbor program, which its considerable influence in Latin America has by and large supported. But a Britain forced to compromise with facts and forces hostile to the United States would set new problems for Latin America. For instance, Argentina would be, to say the least, in a strong bargaining position.

Britain must, of course, work in and with a European System; but Britain should represent in it not only her own strained resources but the strength and energies of the whole British System.

In short, the British Commonwealth is essential to the World Order which is the alternative to a world of hostile blocs. It was essential to the world economy as this developed in the two centuries before 1939; and the framework on which new order must be built is still largely British. Only on it can be developed a world strategy for the peaceful growth or the defense of a World System.

The British System will survive in some shape or another. It may be as much transformed as it was between 1763 and

1783. The Third Empire is passing. The Fourth is still unfolding. No man can foretell its character, and there is still
much confusion in its own councils.

Within it and outside are groups and forces working for
its Balkanization. Here and there some will probably succeed. But the forces of cohesion are at many points also
very strong.

We can recover some sense of its power and possibilities
by looking again at its tremendous effort since 1939, by
reviewing its main elements as they have emerged from war,
and by distinguishing the factors which make for and
against their cohesion.

* 2 *

Through the first half of 1947, the imminent demise of the
British System was extensively canvassed. Most unexpected
people appeared in the trappings and suits of woe, and
with extensive speculations on how the old girl would cut
up. But many (especially among American publicists) mis-
took Great Britain for the whole British System; and then
imagined that it all was wrecked because she was shaken.
If Britain and the Commonwealth are dying, they are an
unconscionable long time about it.

With all her woes upon her, Britain with or without the
Commonwealth and Empire is hardly subject for a funeral
notice. She is in a difficult situation. It can be put simply.
In 1938, she had an estimated nominal capital investment
overseas of about £3,725,000,000. The interest on this and
the proceeds of services she rendered in banking, shipping
and the like were nearly half of her overseas income. On
her overseas income she depended for much of the food
and raw materials she needs as well as for tobacco, films,
and other items she uses but could do without.

By the War's end, a large part of her investment had been

liquidated.[2] She had also incurred debts to the tune of about £3,500,000,000 in fighting her own and other people's battles.[3] Britain's losses in the war exceeded 30 billion dollars; or approximately one-quarter of her national wealth.

This means that she must now make up in goods sold and services rendered the income lost with her liquidated investments.

If she is to buy abroad as she did before the War, she must sell between 50 per cent and 75 per cent more than she then did. If she does not buy on the old scale her own people must go short of some luxuries and comforts and perhaps even of what they have thought necessities; but many people and many industries in many other countries will also be badly hit.

Briefly, she must do with less than she was accustomed to or she must work harder than was her custom. If she works harder, she must also sell the increasing products of her work unless they are to pile up in her warehouses as German goods piled up in the middle 1930s. This part of her problem is perhaps the most difficult, because its answer depends less on her own energy and competence than on the common sense of customers who have not in the past shown much intelligence about the operation of an international economic order. Their notion has been to sell as much and buy as little as they could. But the world's best customer must now demand something more in the way of fair trade, and something more in the way of intelligence, the rarest commodity in human intercourse.

All this represents a crisis in her affairs, and these are so extensive that the whole world is involved. Her difficulties

[2] She spent £1,500,000,000 in the United States before Lend-Lease; and helped by her orders to tool up American industry for war.

[3] If she could have devoted the rump of her external investments to her debt she would still have been about £1,000,000,000 short. Her Allies of World War I owed her considerably more than that, but she has long since ceased even to whistle for the money.

may shake the world into some sense of what her part
has been and of what is now necessary.

She must concentrate her resources where they may be
most usefully employed. She will employ them with shrewdness, acumen, and toughness: for under pressure she can
call up incomparable experience and skill. She will be found
to have reserves and resources which she with the world
had much neglected. She grew, in opulence, excessively
casual about her affairs. She must now settle which are of
real importance to her and which not. She can then assess
her proper responsibilities, which may compel other people
to acknowledge theirs.

She is in process of one of her transformations. Over a
century ago a great American observed her in another passage of this sort and was much more sensible than some of
his compatriots just now:

"So I feel in regard to this aged England," said Emerson
in 1847, "—pressed upon by transitions of trade and . . .
competing populations—I see her not dispirited, not weak,
but well remembering that she has seen dark days before;
—indeed, with a kind of instinct that she sees a little better
in a cloudy day, and that, in storm of battle and calamity,
she has a secret vigor and a pulse like a cannon."

* 3 *

Money is a mighty fact in human affairs, and it has become an essential instrument of our economies; but it should
not blind us to other realities. Money, dominion and the
rest are with peoples, as with individuals, the fruits of
moral and intellectual qualities: of energy, industry, intelligence, skill, thrift, the acquisitive instinct, organization, and
so on. In none of these do the British appear bankrupt. The
British System will not die for lack of dollars though it may
suffer acute embarrassment. It will die only if it loses the
energies and will to live.

It had, we may recall, ten million men under arms the other day as demonstration of its will to live; and in the years between 1939 and 1942, it worked economic miracles from the Great Lakes to the Ganges, by Clyde and Thames and Yarra. In the proportion of their populations and resources, the greatest efforts in the War against the Axis were from the United Kingdom, Canada, Australia, and New Zealand.[4]

Great Britain came out of the War still the second industrial power in the world, and the Dominions at the War's end were grown astonishingly. Canada and Australia are two of the four great exporting countries of the world in food and primary products; but they were also in 1945 fourth and seventh or eighth among the industrial powers, and India was somewhere between them.

They may not hold their positions as other powers grow or recover. But before we dismiss the British System with or without tears, we should remind ourselves that such strength is not dissipated overnight or in a temporary embarrassment for lack of dollars.

The Fourth British System presumably will not count on India as could the Third. The cords which fed the strength of the whole System may be even further loosed. But these ties are not so slack or few as they would appear at the political level; and as politicians would sometimes have us think. This book has insisted (doubtless to tedium) that a strong mesh of economic, social, traditional, and military interests is the real strength of the System. No people lightly casts off its main economic and military associations, however the politicians may toss in the straw.

The real test of a system of the British sort is in its response to crisis, when its necessities must govern it. As strong winds clear the drift, the ribs of rock appear. Within one

[4] For details of the war-effort of the British Commonwealth in World War II, see Appendix, Note 4, page 393.

lifetime we have twice seen great military empires go to pieces on those rocks.

We have seen three Systems built and change on them. There are constant demolition, repair, and reconstruction. Much of the familiar structure may have been blown down in the late storms. But the artisans are on the job again, and they are skillful builders.

* 4 *

The chief psychological and moral strain on the British System in World War II came with the Japanese attack and its swift success in Southeast Asia and the Western Pacific. The successes of the Japanese were brief, as great wars go. They reached the farthest points of their advance in most theaters in the first thirteen weeks. They actually went too far and fast. Every Japanese soldier overseas hung at the end of a line of ships; and the communications stretched so far that insufficient ships could be spared to exploit the areas overrun, though their raw materials were needed desperately for Japan's war industries. The long, exposed lines of shipping frayed rapidly under submarine and air attack. At sea, the United States Navy checked the Japanese advance with its brilliant victories in the Coral Sea and at Midway. On land, the Australians stopped the Japanese at Milne Bay in New Guinea and at Eoribaiwi above Moresby. By the end of 1942, the Australians were pushing them back across the island and showing how they could be beaten at their own games of jungle-war and infiltration. Fifteen months after Pearl Harbor an intelligent Japanese Staff Officer or economist should have known that the bolt was shot.

But the political effects of the Japanese excursion will work in Asia to the last syllable of recorded time.

It broke the prevailing pattern of the British and Dutch Systems in Southern and Southeastern Asia. It fed the appetite of a dozen nationalisms. During the War I was much concerned with affairs in Japanese-occupied territory. By the end of 1943, we began to suspect that some at least in high places among the Japanese knew that their reign in the Indies and Southeast Asia would be brief; and that they were less concerned to maintain the economies than to leave behind all the mischief they could raise. In this, they have notably succeeded, with post-war assistance from some among their enemies. Neither the American nor Australian authorities (and these were most concerned, for the British in the Indies were extremely sensitive to their opinions) understood the problem. General MacArthur with remarkable discretion succeeded in shedding it by an adjustment of the boundaries of his command. He went on to the Philippines and Japan and left the problems of his wake to the Southeast Asia and Australian Commands.

Neither was properly equipped to meet them; and a world in desperate need of the products of the area had to go short of them for years while a political fantasia was performed in the Indies. The Japanese in their effort to rouse Asia against the European order did not there strive in vain. Throughout Asia, their successes and the calculated degradation of their white prisoners have had immense effect. Every Asian peasant has drawn his conclusions. From our viewpoint, they may seem unreal conclusions. But all Asia lives in an infinite and intricate web of social values; of prestige, "face," and acquired "virtues." The fact that Japan lost the War is of less significance than the fact that the Europeans (and this emphatically includes Americans and Australians) lost their moral standing, their place in the accepted pattern.

The handfuls of Asiatics who speak the language of liberalism and nationalism have been able to exploit this movement in the minds of the masses with great skill. The Liberal vocabulary means little to a peasant of the Java Sultanates or to a Batak of Sumatra; but it is often persuasive to a young Australian diplomat from Canberra or an American correspondent.

The problems set in Asia, however, will not be resolved in the forms of parliamentary democracy. Asia presents a twofold confusion. The ancient patterns of its life have been loosened by the impact of the West. But they have not been wholly destroyed. The silver cord may have been shaken off, but the golden bowl is not broken. The Nationalist struggle may have the general assent of those who are touched by it; the traditional forces may briefly combine with the Westernized politician. But in the internal struggle for the social and cultural controls, the antagonism of prince, priest and hadji to the Westernized Liberals will be intense. The Westernized Asian is frequently agnostic or atheist, though he may discreetly conceal his opinions; but he is smelt out in such societies as India and Indonesia. In their revolt against Western controls, the Eastern Liberals are cutting away the bough on which they sit.

Hinduism is a culture of prestige. Its caste structure expresses this in forms which have endured two thousand years and which are still the dominant facts of every Hindu village, crossing even the appalling problems of poverty and land usage and peasant debt.

One great strength of the British in India was that they stood outside caste. They could operate at all levels, so to speak. But they nevertheless acquired their own peculiar aura. They carried the prestige of a supra-caste community. They were out of another world. They did not come within the range of a popular critique. They were somewhat like acts or accidents of God. It was the genius of Gandhi to fight them with religious weapons: with a mystique, with fasts, prayers, moral resolutions. He brought the political struggle within the terms of India's metaphysic. But the use of religious values and loyalties for a political end is desperately dangerous. It weakens the religious matrix and it provokes active hostility in religious rivals.

The British had governed India with a handful of men. They had given it unity and order and (desperate though the lot of the Indian peasant remained) raised the standard of living to an unprecedented level. Gandhi ate at the moral bases of their power. The Japanese attack was thus able to rock the whole edifice. The Japanese struck at what had been its peculiar virtue in Asiatic eyes. The European is not admired for his moral or cultural or religious qualities. Even the Malay thinks little of him as a metaphysician or moralist. But his power to control the physical universe was recognized. He could build bridges, make dams, roads, and railways, fight disease, impose order. His were peculiar techniques, and outside the functional organization of the castes (except that he inherited the prerogatives of the politico-military castes and indeed associated them with him). These gave him his prestige. They were his mystery. But the Japanese demonstrated that they were not exclusively a European mystery. The Japanese demonstrated that an Asiatic could fight the West with its own "mortal engines," and the Western Othello found his occupation gone.

One noticed among the peasantry in Southeast Asia before the War a certain suspicion of their own people who had learned the European techniques. In the Netherlands East Indies, nine in ten of the civil servants were Indonesians. Although in this predominantly Moslem area the caste system had gone, its bent remained from a thousand years of Hindu influence (the Boroboedoer is a Buddhist, not a Moslem, memorial; and beneath Islam, Hinduism, and Buddhism is still Animism). The man who acquired skills in engineering or medicine or contemporary economics was not at ease with his people. They felt him in a degree out-caste or out of caste. He felt the conflict between his

traditional place or part and his new tricks. Soekarno, the
engineer, dealt or tried to deal as an equal with both Japanese and Dutch. But when he wished to rally his own people
he retreated from the modern cities to the traditional center
of Javanese loyalties at Jogjakarta to demonstrate the legit-
imacy of his movement. The Nationalisms of Asia are in
fact only at the surface forward-looking. For their real
strength they must return into the secret and sacred places.
If southern Asia were tomorrow isolated it would not go
on in the courses of Western Liberalism or Socialism. It
would recoil into itself. The Asian "progressives" have been
representative figures only within the frameworks of political economies which grew from the European. They
understand the machinery. But only a persistent measure
of European influence will preserve political, social and
economic machinery of a European sort in India or Indonesia. The break-down of the irrigation system established
by the Dutch in Java when the Javanese were left to manage it themselves is a case in point.

The problem facing Mr. Nehru and the Congress leaders,
the great industrialists of India, the Ph.D.'s and B.A.'s, in
1947, was to preserve enough of the machinery to support
them and their purposes while freeing its controls from
European hands. As they came to the crisis in India, with
the British Government anxious to transfer power to them,
it became apparent that the structure of British India could
not stand without the British. Congress could not, as it had
dreamed, take over British India as a going concern. Moslems, out-castes, Princes who had accepted the British
hegemony would not accept the hegemony of the native
majority or the group controlling it.

Yet this group, though not able to replace the British,
was strong enough to force the British out because the moral
bases of the British reign were sapped in the Hindu majority. They were not sapped fatally, I believe, with the

Moslems, for the Moslem has a more pragmatic view of history and politics than the Hindu. He is more the soldier, the man of the world, and he understood that the greatest Powers have their days of defeat and periods of depression. He had not the Hindu peasant's mystical awe of power, the sense on which Japan impinged. He could have reached a new accommodation with the Raj. For the Princes, the Raj was a condition of their state. But the Raj could not survive when it had lost its moral authority in the Hindu peasants' strange pattern of life and values; and there was no heart in Britain to re-assert the sanctions of its rule in India. The British had lost their moral base not only in the Hindu peasantry but in themselves.

India has been held for fifty years against the sentiment of English Radicalism. The idea of the Indian Empire was abhorrent to many of the men who came to power in England in 1945. Pethick-Lawrence, who became Secretary of State for India, had been through his political life what he would have called "a friend of Indian Freedom." Stafford Cripps was of the same school. I saw both a few hours before they left India on their momentous mission in 1946. Pethick-Lawrence was an old, tired, shaky man. His very presence in the Government as Secretary of State for India was a declaration that this Government was determined to settle the Indian issue in his sense . . . if it could.

The Labour Government had sincere convictions. It believed on its own principles that India should have complete self-government. But now the country as a whole agreed. The British people no longer took the Empire of India for granted and as a thing to be thought of only at odd and spectacular moments. It was unusually on their minds; and when the British get something tedious or ticklish on their minds, they like to shake it off. The British had acquired their empires without, in general, thinking much about them at all. Earlier Englishmen might sometimes have

thought of empire as a special dispensation by which
Providence singled out the English. But by World War
II, the English had mostly mislaid their Providence and
their confidence in the Imperial Mission. They had actually
moved in political and social mood considerably towards
the Left: not the Left in the rational and definable Continental sense, but in their own way of reaction against their
own Toryism.

The Conservative Party had been a depressing, dull affair
between the wars. It failed especially in its proposed purpose of conserving, and a Conservative Party which fails to
conserve is certain sooner or later to be recogized as mere
encumbrance. If electoral returns meant anything, the majority in Britain between the wars was inclined to conservation. But in domestic and external politics the Conservatives slithered hither and yon in ridiculously inconse-
quential fashion. The people gradually sensed this. They
had not grasped it clearly at the election of 1935. But they
had in 1939; and when they came to the polls again in 1945,
what they threw out was not Mr. Churchill's war-time
Government but the Party and the mentality they had
elected in 1935.

Tory stupidity was brilliantly exploited by the propaganda
of the Left. Few people now could name half a dozen titles
of Mr. Gollancz's Left-Book Club, but it had enormous influence, especially in the suburbs. The white-collar workers
and the petit intelligentsia were especially influenced. These
were the class most threatened by war or social change:
they lived usually about the target areas of the great cities,
and on salaries and minor investments at low or fixed interests. They had normally supported Conservatism or (if the
more daring sort) the Liberal Party. Now the Conservative
Party by sheer ineptitude alienated them. It did nothing to
protect their interests in the Depression or in the inflationary periods before and after: it left them without assurances

in foreign relations, and it stripped down even the naval defenses which the electorates had always readily recognized as a prime national interest.

In this disquiet, the Left-Book Club ate its way through the suburbs, swallowing whole streets of villas and semi-detatcheds. It was a protest, but it did not go too far for the peaceful office-workers. And most ingeniously, Mr. Gollancz and his authors caught the snob complex of the suburbans. It was smart to be intellectual and to be intellectual was to be Left; and Mr. Gollancz provided the intellectuals with their intellectual fare at a price within their means. You could be intellectual with the Left-Book Club at bargain-counter rates; and the books were mostly brief, pointed, and highly pre-digested. You were in the intellectual swim without much cost either to your pocket or in mental effort.

I take Mr. David Low to be a power of at least equal consequence in the English suburbs of the late 1930s. Mr. Low came from Australia and New Zealand to be the first political caricaturist of the day. In line, image, and invention he combined extraordinary wit, broad humor, and malice. Even those who might think his sketches sometimes unfair, ill-informed, or dangerous (and there were such curious people) could not resist his energy and humor. Moreover, Mr. Low had ideas and moral courage. In neither were the Conservatives extravagantly endowed. His war on them was devastating.

His Colonel Blimp became an image at least as familiar as the old-school tie. (Mr. Churchill was often regarded in the suburbs during the late 1930s as the acme and epitome of old-school-tieism.) With Blimp and the Tories were glibly pilloried a whole range representative of the established orders in Britain and the Empire.

The professional soldiers, seamen and airmen who came to command in the Second War, Dudley Pound, the Cunninghams, Alan Brooke, Portal, Harris, Wavell, Alexander,

Montgomery, Platt, Slim and the rest were as remote from Blimpdom as men could be. But Low fixed the image of Blimp on the popular mind as a symbol of the Regular Officer.

Figures like Blimp and figures of speech like "the old-school tie" have extraordinary currency. They slide slickly across the mind and titillate it; and the idle add them for their brightness to their mental currency without any effort to assay them. But the world has always been susceptible to the easy symbol, and we must recognize the influence in history of the Colonel Blimps and their creators.

For all these and other reasons, the British entered World War II mistrustful of their leaders and, I think, uncertain of themselves. Dunkirk and the desperate dangers of 1940 healed the rifts and closed the ranks of Britain, but some of the old trouble still lingered in the back of the mind.

The Japanese successes again touched them off. As the Malayan campaign was extensively reported (but not as the best journalists like Ian Morrison of *The Times* reported), it seemed on the British side a piece of typical Blimpdom. The British people were very busy in 1941. They had little time or energy to attend to the situation developing through the year in the Far East. The disaster hit them like a sudden thunder-clap. And with it came from other countries a gale of criticism which chilled them. The British had been warmed a little through eighteen months by the aid and admiration of their allies and friends. Now suddenly they found themselves attacked while they could have no clear sense of what had really brought the catastrophe in Malaya. They were especially impressed by the reaction in Australia (as a Dominion fighting at their side) and America. They felt perhaps that their own desperate situation might be better understood by their critics, but they were inclined to accept the criticism.

I do not propose to argue here the responsibilities of the

Command and Administration in Malaya or how they met them. But it is a modicum of justice to the British people and Government to point out that, although they were engaged thousands of miles westward in a most desperate struggle for existence, they took more precautions to divert the Japanese attack than any other Power. They kept in Malaya, or sent there, troops who proved their fighting quality through two terrible months. At a moment when the Royal Navy was appallingly short of capital ships fit for sea, two of the finest were sent eastward in the hope that their presence would prompt the Japanese to think again. The Admiralty knew that the *Prince of Wales* and *Repulse* should have an aircraft-carrier with them. When the carrier intended was delayed by a piece of abominable luck, the battleship and battle-cruiser were ordered to proceed. It was an heroic gamble in the circumstances. It did not come off. But before we cast the stone again, we may remember that the United States, although at peace with its Navy intact, sent no such force to the Philippines; and that Australia, which subsequently mobilized over 900,000 men, had provided for Malaya before the blow fell less than one division.

In the middle of 1941, I went from Malaya to Sydney. I there made personal but urgent representations which seemed to me sound to men of both political parties. I found a terrifying ignorance of the problems and even of the elementary facts. Some time in 1941 I heard an Australian politician of consequence say to a Dutch official: "Now how many people have you in the N.E.I.? About seven millions?"

This is not the place or occasion to canvass old confusions, but it was rank injustice to fix on Britain the major blame for Japan's early success, as some fearful people and some unscrupulous tried to do. My point here is that the disaster and the criticism it evoked in Britain and abroad seriously reduced what was left of popular confidence in Imperial administrations and Imperial courses. Empire had a sour taste in the common Englishman's mouth after Malaya and the first campaign in Burma.

It weakened confidence also among the Australians or sections of them: much less among the soldiers than with some politicians and public servants and the more nervous civilians. Australia went on to a great war effort. But elements of her population were not in pretty shape during early 1942.

This was natural enough. To Australians who had stayed home from the wars and who had suffered no personal losses, the dangers until now had seemed remote and even somewhat unreal. The swift and sudden advance of a grim enemy caught the morale of these people between wind and water.

The shifts of opinion in Britain and the Commonwealth have had effect. The immediate post-war attitude to Empire was predominantly: "Let's get out if we're not wanted."

This was reinforced by American opinion. Indian agitation notably has had much aid and solace from the United States. British public opinion at the War's end valued American good-will highly. Moreover, it was already half-convinced of the case against the Imperial System. It came then readily to the tremendous decisions on India. India was to go her way, wherever it would take her and at whatever cost to good order and the effort to restore a world community. There was no politically feasible alternative perhaps; but even India's best friends might have thought as the situation developed that the thing went too fast for the good of India or the world.

This was the evident opinion of Mr. Jinnah and his Moslem League. For an educated Moslem learns to think in terms of world systems. Islam believes that it has a strong lien on the future of all the middle parts of the world from the Pillars of Hercules to Mindanao. Its ideas do not include a Government of Mr. Nehru's persuasion reigning over all India.

Throughout Islam is a marked quickening of the pulse. Before the Japanese War, I noted the vigorous revival in the Indies: [5] the appearance of youth movements, male and female; the spread of popular literature; the re-knitting of the old Moslem links from North Africa to Java.

Islam has a sturdy personalism which produces its own democratic temper, but it is not the temper of a parliamentary democracy.

Islam has also a mission. It is, like Christianity, a religion on the march and a supra-national society. It overrides the Nationalist impulse and the local polity. It did breed within it, as did Christendom, States which warred with one another; but it bred also a community not only of the Faith but of a socio-economic character. Islam has been a mercantile and military community as well as a religion. The hadji schools educate not only in religion and Arab letters and literature, but in bookkeeping and commercial practice. The student after graduation and the Pilgrimage returns to teach or trade. The teachers, the craftsmen, the merchants moving from mosque to mosque are the nervous system of Islam.

The unity of that great international was weakened by the European excursion eastward. The Portuguese first cut its main lines of communication; the English and the Dutch organized the local Moslem communities within the regimes they imposed, which took more and more the outward forms of National States.

International trade largely passed from the hands of the Moslem to the European; European ships even carried the pilgrims to the Port of Mecca.

[5] In *Westward the Course:* William Morrow, New York, 1942. William Heinemann, London, 1942.

Islam in a remarkable degree accepted the British System. Within its immense frame Islam was able to preserve its cultural entity, and the British System was a supranational affair of the sort the Moslem understands. British administrations have been on the whole sympathetic to Moslem interests. The British in their dominion are alive to religious and traditional values and to style. Islam has these. It has, in fact, something of a school-tie attitude. The imperialists from country parsonages and public schools understood the Moslem; and he understood their virtues. His military tradition is also sympathetic to the British. Both see the proper occasion for arms in an extension of Law. Furthermore, the British in their curious regard for an enemy worthy of their steel remember Saladin with Richard Coeur de Lion; while the Christian culture from the Scholastics shares with Islam the tradition of Aristotle. It is characteristic of the relationship that the Moslems of India seeking Pakistan thought much more than the Hindus in terms of a British Dominion, even after the shock of the Japanese attack.

Those who see the contemporary issue as between Russia and the United States with the rest of the world as pawns or on the sidelines grossly oversimplify the infinite complexities of life and politics. The issues are everywhere crossed by religious, economic, cultural, nationalist, class, caste distinctions and divisions and ambitions. If the Americans are to understand the realities of their own situation they must make some effort to understand the other great forces at work. America's prime interest is in the preservation of the World System which Britain largely created; of which the Americans may, if they rise to it, consider themselves the principal heir. But they cannot begin to understand it until they understand its complexities: the complexity of the specifically British element (the Commonwealth and Empire) and of the relations which it established and maintained in the shaping of the larger Order. Of these, the relations with the Islamic world are extraordinarily extensive, various, and subtle; but they have been a principal influence in weaving the peoples of the Middle East and India into the general pattern of order.

Since 1914, the Moslem peoples have been increasingly persuaded that the long dominance of the Europeans in the world is ending. They have seen the peoples of what was Christendom hacking one another down and their economies thrown into fantastic convulsions. They read the symptoms of moral and social disintegration. They quietly renew the bonds of Islam and prepare for the succession.

The U.S.S.R. has a considerable Moslem population. It has worked skillfully in Moslem areas. Its agents and representatives in Moslem countries are specialists in the affairs of Islam and often professed followers of the Prophet. But Islam has not been much persuaded. It still inclines more towards co-operation with the British System than with any other. But it is watching the British System intently for further signs of weakness. It is watching especially the effects of Egyptian pressure, for Egypt with its seats of Moslem learning has great prestige in Islam. The moralists of Islam are watching also the sophisticated society of Cairo. If Egypt's Government is to find support for its ambitions among Moslems generally, it must demonstrate that it is at ease in Islam. With the decline of European influence and especially of French and Italian influence in Cairo, something of a Moslem revival has appeared even among the professional and business classes (for instance, many professional women are again accepting marriage as second, third, or fourth wives) who had of late preferred the modes of the West.

If the British System further declines we must expect Islam to look more and more to its separate interests. Another fissure will widen in this racked world. The British had kept at least light bridges over it and preserved this century or more of peace between the Western world and Islam. Good relations between Islam and Britain are to the general advantage of the West; and the British Authority should be prepared to resist callow people on Park Avenue or in Canberra who believe that they hold keys to Asian politics which the British have missed.[6] The Western world must be prepared to use skill, experience, and knowledge where it possesses them. Those who have tried to hurry Britain out of Asia and the Middle East have done no service either to Asia or themselves.

* 5 *

The United Kingdom came out of the Second War mentally prepared to yield up dominion in the Eastern world. The influence of its own anti-imperialists had been powerful. The demands of Indian and Burmese politicians had their effect. Criticism in the United States had to be recognized as a political factor. The psychological effects of the Japanese impact were still working. The Australian insistence on a loud voice in all its Eastern half of the world was accepted. The British gave the Australians their head. An Australian was appointed to represent the whole Commonwealth for a time at Tokyo. The Australian effort in diplomacy was somewhat spasmodic. The wharf-laborers in Australia took policy towards the Netherlands East Indies out of the Government's hands by refusing to load Dutch ships with cargoes for the Indies.

The United Kingdom appeared to have accepted in practice the suggestions that each Dominion should have the initiatives of policy in the regions of its special interest: a doctrine in fact difficult to resist and on the whole to be

[6] I recall once talking to an Australian official charged with some responsibilities in Asian affairs. He dismissed absolutely the notion that religion could have any influence on Asian politics.

approved if the Dominions were equipped to shape adequate policies and if the machinery of information and consultation throughout the Commonwealth were sufficient. In the absence of these conditions, a Dominion might seize rope enough to hang itself. But the United Kingdom could hardly be expected to act as mentor or monitor to its children now grown large: especially as they (despite some adolescent brashness) had stood to her aid in the World Wars with magnificent devotion and a clearer perception of the issues than other heirs of the Western tradition.

All these factors made the British ready enough to withdraw their legions; and to them was added a substantial and urgent fact. The United Kingdom as she emerged from the war was no longer in a position to act as cornerstone or policeman or banker to a world system. She lacked the funds. She also lacked the inclination. Since Waterloo she had propped a great frame of order. She had fought in one generation two desperate wars to maintain it. She had wasted in the efforts her enormous reserves of wealth. She had for her pains little but kicks and criticisms. She had largely financed the growth of new nations: the United States, Argentina, Canada, Australia and the rest. She had her profits of the investment. But the profits now were thin and the investment mostly gone. It was time that the other beneficiaries of the System recognized its existence and character and needs, and made their own contributions. They might transform it. The British were prepared for a broader basis, for new centers of influence and authority. The urgent matter was that the work they had done for the general order should be not lost but enlarged. Bevin for the British Government and People repeatedly returned to this thesis in the conferences of the post-war period; and the Marshall proposals of June 1947 were the first notable evidence that the world was taking their sense.

Their circumstances have forced the British back on a

fundamental fact of their position in the world. The Commonwealth and Empire were a fruit, an expression, a symbol of the strength of the British People. The Commonwealth and Empire in turn contributed to British strength. But its sources always were and are in the British People themselves. An acute American had observed this essential truth in the crisis of the Napoleonic Wars: "The French believe that the fountains of British wealth are in India and China. They never appear to understand that the most abundant source is her agriculture, her manufactures and the foreign demand."[7]

The British now must return to their own sources, to renew the strange energies which have filled the oceans of the world with their sails and spread the law and meanings of their little islands in every continent.

Some secret sense of this is working now in the British. Their resignation of great charges has all the causes we have touched on here, and more; but the chief and central motive is in their instinctive recognition of the need to recruit their strength at its primal fountains.

[7] Mahan, II, 46: quoted by Mr. Arthur Bryant in *Years of Victory, 1802-1812*, Collins, London, 1945.

TWELVE

STATE OF THE NATION

THE British of the Island have several immense advantages in the post-war world which should now be balanced against the general gloom which rises from contemplation of their profit-and-loss accounts. In the long run the quality of a people, like the quality of a man, has more consequence than the state of their business.

The British have among the peoples of the world an extraordinary measure of social discipline. They have acquired it without excessive loss of personal initiatives and energies. History and their island situation have developed a powerful corporate strength. Loyalties held intensely need not be much proclaimed or flourished. The French with their professed devotion to *La Patrie* have seen large elements of their population succumb to other loyalties in these late years; and the interests of the nation have not held them to effective unity. German patriotism was a

256

forced and recent growth, for the Germans were until Bismarck's Reich a race much divided; and the gross mechanics of Hitler's patriotic parades and displays revealed the weaknesses they were designed to counter. Italy also came late to its national polity, and though it possessed a religious and cultural unity lacking in the Germans, Mussolini had to stimulate the nationalist pulse with his curious performances.

The United States with less flourish have also drilled the patriotic sense. The insistence on the Constitution as a symbol of the national life and purpose, the emphasis in education on a highly nationalistic version of history, and on the American Way of Life, on "American" and "Un-American" activities all indicate a necessary cultus. The Americans have had to weld many peoples into one People; and the deliberate cultivation of an ethos was essential to it. The British have their forms and modes about the Crown and the Union Jack, but their allegiances need less drilling. They use the symbols of their loyalties to call up a warm and companionable spirit, a cozy sense of common comfort. In the ships of the Royal Navy it is customary to serve each day a tot of rum to all hands. Nothing in the ship is tended with more loving care than the rum barrel; and nothing is more polished than its surround in brass, *God Bless the King*. That is a very English thing. So too is the customary salute to the quarter-deck of a King's Ship as one steps on it. The salute is for a crucifix which once hung there; and also perhaps for a people whose sense of tradition and long memories have been an abiding strength.

The British like the Spaniards have strong regional and local loyalties. But Spanish regionalism has broken every regime which flouted it. The British failed to resolve the problem of Ireland in their association; but Wales, Scotland and the notable regional differences in England itself (as between the West Country and the North for instance) have persisted now for centuries within the general consensus.[1] The variety in unity has in fact been a great strength and a useful school for races who have shaped an empire of many races, cultures, and religions.

The corporate sense is deeply rooted (as I understand it) also in the Common Law: that peculiar contribution of the English People to the whole British System and the United States which rests on a consensus of what is fair and equitable and on a recognition of usage and custom. The appreciation of custom was of great significance in British relations with the peoples of their Empire in Asia and Africa. They did not seek to impose a full-bodied system of law abstract from the local traditions and values, but worked always to a sense of the validity *prima facie* of these.

The Common Law reveals another character of the English important to their development at home and abroad: their eclecticism (it is very evident also in their language which borrows with almost excessive zest).

As a great authority on the Common Law[2] has written of Henry Bracton, one of its masters:

"Taking a text, now from the Old Testament, and now from the New Testament, anon from the writings of the Roman Civil lawyers or from the Canonists, who were the ecclesiastical lawyers of the Church; again, from a master of Jurisprudence of the Law School of Bologna, or from the precedents set by his predecessors of the English Bench, Bracton passed them all through the fires of justice and hammered out a set of legal principles which gave to the world, in the language of a famous Judge of

[1] Foreigners often miss the strength which still survives in local loyalties and cultures. But no official is now appointed to Wales unless he speaks Welsh, and Welsh literature predominates in many Welsh bookshops. Scottish Nationalism does not seem likely to have immediate political impact, for the Union is strongly grounded. But its social and cultural influence will modify in time the political and economic life of Scotland, and increasing measures of local responsibility are likely to appear.

[2] Mr. Richard O'Sullivan, K.C.; quoted here from an article by Sir Henry Slesser in *The Times* of 9 August 1946.

the United States Supreme Court, 'a far more developed, more rational, and mightier body of law than the Roman.'

"These rules and principles of the English Law were constantly being refined and polished in the law schools of the Inns of Court, and by the Clerks of the Chancery, who gave us English equity. They were carried by the King's Judges, going the Circuits, to the great towns and cities of England and to all the shires. In the course of time the Common Law was carried beyond the realm, to Ireland, to what are now the great Dominions, and to most of the Colonies; and to the plantations, and States that now form the American Union. And so the tradition of the Common Law is today a bond of Commonwealth and Empire, and a link which unites the English-speaking peoples all over the world."

The Common Law reflects yet another character of the British related to their corporate sense, and now of immeasurable importance. "The Common Law is nothing else but reason," said Coke, the great judge. Reason is usually more noticeable in the individual than the mass; but no one who has lived much in Britain during the post-war period could miss the essential reasonableness, the common sense of the British masses. This is the core of the political maturity they demonstrate: their nice sense of the possible, their recognition and acceptance of substantial facts; above all, their realization that some measure of self-discipline is necessary to the general good.

I recall from 1946 the spinster sisters Susan and Joan Vickery of Lamyatt in Somerset: one 75 years of age, one 73. They noticed before they retired one evening that a beam above their fireplace was smoldering. They did not care to trouble their neighbors at that hour. So they sat watching until dawn; and only when the beam burst into flames did they call the Fire Station. The Brigade arrived to find a lantern at the gate to guide them; tea and sandwiches set out with the best family linen. You must understand people like Miss Susan and Miss Joan to understand the English.

I came out of the Pacific to London in 1945. The chambermaid at my hotel had lost two sons in the War. The third (he had been born after his father was killed on the Somme in 1916) was then still a prisoner-of-war on the Burma Railway. Her only daughter had been in 1940 a nurse in the British Army. Her hospital was overrun by the Germans and she nursed in prison-hospitals until she was recovered in 1944. She came home to a London hospital. It was hit by a rocket. Her body was not recovered. The mother had been thrice bombed out. She had a raw scar still from burns which took the skin from her hand to her elbow. She was one of the calmest and steadiest women I have ever met; and remarkably representative of the quiet women who stood for hours patiently in the butchers' and fishmongers' queues.. She was Irish; but that also was curiously representative of this strange community of peoples we call the English. In the East End of London you may meet (if you seek good company) survivors of the old company of Thames watermen. The Thames watermen still serve six or seven years before they are accepted as knowledgeable in the ways of the river; longer than it takes to make a doctor or lawyer. Many are of Irish stock settled by Thames-side since the 17th or 18th century, but remembering well their long family lines of oarsmen. There again is the eclecticism which is in the blood, but also in the generous common sense of the Celto-Roman-Saxon-Danish-Norman-Scots-Irish-Welsh fusion which we call the English and recognize as the most distinctive race in Europe.

Only people superbly confident of themselves open wide their gates. The British raise no barriers in their hotels and restaurants, in their universities or residential areas against any alien of any color who keeps the law.[3] The British have deep roots; and the tree is not shaken by the birds which rest in its branches. Britain is, of course, not a melting-pot. It is a cross-way of the world and the world's ideas.

Yet the English can turn in crisis always back to their own deep and almost secret life. They renew themselves from roots fed in the rich humus of countless generations: a humus which has absorbed with its own the virtues of drifting alien leaves.

When I first met Ernest Bevin, I noticed a likeness which seemed not to a single man but to a whole range of men and features. It puzzled me until I remembered all the Ernest Bevins carved under the medieval misericords and about the pier-heads of Wells Cathedral and half the churches of his native Somerset. You will meet him in inns on Sedge-moor or the Quantocks or Mendips, where he once worked as a farm-boy for sixpence a day.

Generalizations about whole peoples should be taken with considerable salt, for all sorts go to make one people as they do to make the world. But characters more or less typical appear and each human group makes its own impression on history and the mind. They reflect in manners, style, social dispositions, in their literature, art, music what Freud called "the archaic heritage." You could not talk with Bevin half an hour without recognizing the quintessential Englishness of the man: the sly, cunning, broad humor which Shakespeare knew so well, the fancy at once subtle and home-spun which is in Falstaff and Pistol's crew, earthy yet elusive, local, tough, pragmatic yet poetic: the stuff you find in the English Tommy if you get to know him, a concealed ironic intelligence, a sharp and artful wit. The

---

[3] In this they are markedly unlike some of the Dominions. Australians are often hostile and jealous of newcomers even from the United Kingdom; they have a queer unease of the stranger which comes presumably from some fear or sense of insufficiency in themselves.

shrewdness and sharpness may be concealed in stolid manners and slow measured speech; though the Tommy and English townsman can prattle like a Highlander or Sam Weller on occasion. He is a deep dog, a man of passionate local loyalties and yet of errant fancies whose humor works in odd analogies and who can bring a jest from the ends of the world. Gilbert Chesterton like Chaucer, Shakespeare, and Ben Jonson had the sense of the common Englishman, whose heaven is everywhere at home, or at least via Charing Cross. He combines a passion for the local with the universal: which perhaps explains the British Empire and that other most English of accommodations, the Anglican Church.

It is much the same with his politics. The British Labour Party is a Socialist Party, but it is not interpretable in terms of Continental Socialism or of First, Second, or Third Internationals, any more than the English Liberal Party was interpretable in terms of Continental Liberalism. Affiliations are recognizable, but they are given a tremendous bent in the English character.

Labour Parties as distinct from the parties of Socialist Orthodoxy are peculiar to the British System; and their doctrinaires are usually from the white-collar classes. Dalton and Stafford Cripps and others qualified to wear old-school ties were the theoreticians of the government formed in 1945. The trades-union men in the Party generally incline more to the pragmatic, and they are often at heart far more conservative than their colleagues from the public schools and universities. Bevin remains eminently the representative man of the trades unions as they grew in Britain. His extraordinary success as wartime Minister of Labour and of National Service demonstrated his own great capacities and the confidence he had from the British workingmen. Bevin excelled among his people in qualities of mind and will; but his was excellence in degree, not difference in kind. He might draw the fire of the white-collar Mountain behind him in the post-war Parliament, for it was largely composed of journalists and doctrinaires. But he held the confidence of the trades unions. His political capacity was of course immense. In thirty-five years of trades-union leadership a man learns his politics. But Bevin's first review to the House of Commons of his tasks as Foreign Secretary [4] revealed a statesman's grasp also of the principles of British foreign policy. He insisted at once on its necessary continuity.[5] Foreign policy must in its nature conform to certain constant facts: to the facts of geography, for instance. Gibraltar still existed for Mr. Bevin as it existed for Mr. Eden and for Castlereagh. Domestic regimes may change and revolutions overturn the State; but a Stalin must remember the existence of the Straits, and the Soviets are as much concerned for warm-water ports as were the Czars.

Bevin faced immediately the consequences in foreign policy of Britain's impoverishment. From the first, he had to face its implications and to seize by moral energy such ground as he could before the domestic crisis too plainly appeared.

Bevin in private talk always seemed to me at once amazingly read and informed and broad, vigorous, blunt. He made much use of "I." But this seemed not egotism but a ready acceptance of personal responsibility.

As Bevin represented the tough country stock, Herbert Morrison had the Cockney stuff: the impish humor, the quick sardonic tongue, the physical and intellectual wiriness which the vast, dirty, shabby, and heroic town breeds in its survivors. I doubt if Herbert Morrison was ever at a loss for one moment of his life; even in his quarrels with Winston

[4] In August 1945.
[5] One would not necessarily go all the way with the French Communist newspaper *L'Humanité* which once quaintly noticed "the hand of the eternal Bevin, successor of Queen Victoria."

Churchill, which raged bitterly during the election of 1945. The two after the election were leaders of the Commons: Morrison of the Government, Churchill for the Opposition. When the House went in procession to the Lords for the opening of Parliament, they walked together at its head in a grim, cold, stony silence, rare in English political life. Yet Morrison has all the Cockney's sentiment for England's heroes. A while later he said in talk with me: "I'm sorry. I hate to be on bad terms with the Old Man. He's a great old man, is Winston."

Many were surprised when the prosaic Attlee came to the Party leadership and more surprised as he retained it year after year. Yet Attlee is a type of the Labour leaders familiar for a generation in the Dominions.

The Labour Parties cover a multitude of opinions from the conservatively-minded craftsmen and the Christian Socialists to the crypto-Communists. The Labour Parties have always had to meet vigorous internal dispute, faction, and rivalries. They have consequently had to establish (as by the Australian device of caucus control) a tight discipline. In Britain and Australia, they have come to distrust exuberant, brilliant, and personally ambitious leaders since the splits under Ramsay MacDonald and Hughes. Labour has since favored steady, restrained men who can hold a balance among contentious cliques. Scullin and Curtin in Australia were of this sort; and Attlee has been called "the perfect chairman." Ministers who served under both Churchill and Attlee remarked the change in the tempo and character of Cabinet meetings: Attlee proceeding with a precision and by time-table, in contrast to Churchill's preference for long and far-ranging discussion.

Like Scullin and Curtin, Attlee has been distinguished for a single-minded, almost a narrow-minded, devotion to the Party interest and unity. He reminds one in many ways of the earnest, dry Parliament Men who confronted

Charles I. Their evangelic bent is translated in him to a devout sense of social service.

These solemn, conscientious, balanced men of severe loyalties are often the precursors of revolutionary change. Mr. Attlee and Mr. Scullin and Mr. Curtin have something in them of "the sea-green incorruptible"; although their natural habitat is perhaps with the Gironde.

The best of the Union men brought to Government the industry and the pride in craftsmanship of the stock whence they were hewn. I never have caught its sense better than one evening in the summer of 1945 when I walked among the ruins of the workmen's suburbs above Clydeside with an old foreman from the shipyards of John Brown, where they built the *Mary;* and where at the moment the *Vanguard* was on the stocks. When the Luftwaffe attacked the great yards along the narrow waterways of Clyde, it set out not to smash the ships and stocks but to kill the men who build the ships. The yards were not much bombed but the workers' suburbs behind them were piles of rubble. The foreman spoke of it. "They houses," he said, "was jerrybuilt. An' Jerry destroyed 'em. But what old Göring forgot was that we build ships on Clyde. And men who can build ships can build shelters. You see them, man." And his thick finger led my eyes from point to point where the shelters stood like sturdy little forts among the ruins and rubble.

This man and his kind, more than the London School of Economics or the Fabian Society, made the British Labour Party: and I would not normally fear much for the future of any cause or country if they kept the controls. Nor would I fear for the survival of decent liberties. The British workingman and his trades-union leaders will not make authoritarianism in Britain. They will in their own way and time defeat, I believe, the threat and break the men who advance it. But we must admit the danger.

It does not come immediately from the overt Marxists.

At the election of 1945, the Communist Party had only a few over 100,000 votes in an electorate of nearly 33,000,000. If Britain went over to thoroughgoing Socialism, it would not be by the efforts of Mr. Pollitt and Mr. Horner and their Communist Party proper. The real threat of totalitarianism comes from the progressive extension of State controls in the hands of bureaucratic planners and the doctrinaires, the heirs of Fabianism and the pupils of the London School of Economics, and from a socio-economic situation which was certain to present plausible pretexts and pleas for the enlargement of the State machine.

It is important to remember that the British even under *laissez-faire* have been accustomed to State action in some fields where the American might resent and resist it. The State or Local Governments were active long before the First War in a number of public utilities and services which in America are still predominantly the charge of private enterprise. The State inevitably had to take large responsibilities in the Colonies once it was seen that Colonies could not be lightly shed. In many, development has had to wait on the action of the Public Authority. In Australia, for example, railways were built and operated by the various Governments because private enterprise could and would not risk the losses which most incurred. The community as a whole has had to subsidize its railways in spare lands of sparse populations where settlement had often to wait on communications; and similarly with roads, bridges, irrigation and a whole variety of social machinery.

The British devised the methods of Commission and Corporation (as the British Broadcasting Corporation) to assure great public services a measure of administrative autonomy and freedom from the caprices of party politics and politicians. They do not think the B.B.C. or the Post Office control of telephone service necessarily a symptom of totalitarianism.

When Labour came to power in 1945, it set out to nationalize coal and transport. Apart from any issues of Doctrinaire Socialism there were arguments of practical expediency for nationalizing both.

Consider coal. Coal is essential to the whole economy. But the British seams, although they still have much coal, are now often very deep, difficult to work, and expensive. Some mines can still produce cheaply but not enough. American coal could be landed in England more cheaply than English coal at an average can be brought to the surface. But Britain lacked dollars for American coal. Moreover, the interests of defense demand that her coal-mines and coal-mining population should be kept in production. Yet coal was becoming less and less profitable overall for the private coal-owner; and more and more expensive for the coal-users. As coal was a national interest of first importance there was some case for making coal a national responsibility. If coal had to be won at a loss then the community should bear and spread the loss; as the community in Australia had borne the cost of unprofitable railways necessary to the general interest.

I remember arguing this in 1945 with long-headed and level-headed miners in Durham. They pointed out that most of the power provided to the community was from publicly owned bodies; municipal light and power authorities and the like. The miners thought it reasonable that if the power was owned and sold by public bodies, the source of power might not illogically also be publicly owned.

The railways also seem to offer a reasonable case for public ownership. Railways now are subject to intense competition from road and air services. The industries of Britain urgently need the best possible transport service at the cheapest possible rates. The general interest is that they should have it even at a loss to the transport system.

The community again, it could be argued, should take the responsibility.

To my mind there were strong arguments also for releasing capital, energy, and initiative from less profitable services for the creation of the new industries which Britain desperately needs. Britain somehow must keep in the van of industrial development; and the van is the place for enterprising minds and capital.

A large body of Conservative opinion, including most of its younger leaders, accepted nationalization of coal and railways; and few Britons felt that any fundamental principles were involved.

But the extension of a nationalizing Socialism over a wide range of healthy and profitable industries is another matter altogether. The Complete Socialist sees the economy as a vast piece of social machinery. He believes that it should be organized and "rationalized" and efficiently controlled by a central authority and in terms of social "planning," of blue-prints and blue-books. His concept of the economy arises from a particular concept of life and of the nature of man. He believes that men not only can but should be marshaled and dragooned and organized: that labor should be "directed" and (with wealth) mobilized to serve the master-plans of what a great Chief Justice, Lord Hewart, called "the New Despotism."

Those who resist this mechanist concept of life and society believe that in reality the economy is moved by an application of ideas and resources at countless points: that its health ultimately depends on the play of human personality. They would recognize that the weakness and vices as well as the energy and virtues of men will be expressed; but that this is inevitable, men being what they are. They regard the disciples of planning, the mechanical perfectionists, as caught by an illusion which pursued can only bring the social economy to disaster.

Most men of much experience (including most trades-union leaders) are aware of the powerful play of personality in human affairs. I find it difficult to believe that Mr. Bevin and Mr. Morrison remained in maturity doctrinaires of the mechanist school. But in the compromises of Party and Government they have had to tolerate the planners and the pedagogues, for the school of Mr. Dalton and Sir Stafford Cripps is a most formidable wing of the Labour movement with especial influence in the suburbs.

The old tough pragmatic sense which once asked plain questions and required plain answers has been somewhat obscured in the British Commons. In the complexities and perplexities of modern life has grown a superstitious awe of the expert. Government has largely fallen into his hands; and he is of all men the last to take the broad and general view or to permit the rugged intrusion of common sense on his veiled mysteries.

The economic crisis which appeared in 1947 set a curious test for both the planners and their victims: for it was most evidently a man-made crisis. The world's supplies of food and raw materials were certainly straitened; but not in a measure which required of the British people the privations which their politicians increasingly imposed on them. British rations were reduced again and again because of dislocations in the machinery of exchange: a failure of the people in control to make the machinery work.

We have seen in war the device of Lend-Lease overcome the barriers and obstructions to free commerce which had been raised by Governments. Under Lend-Lease the economy of two-thirds of the world operated smoothly and with precision to meet the enormous and extraordinary demands of vast war-machines.

Lend-Lease was an awkward device. It would not have been needed in a world of free trade. It was actually something like a stile hurriedly erected to surmount the tariff

barriers and the economic nationalisms which had Balkanized the Western world. But it demonstrated what might
be done if the necessities of mankind could once break
through the political and economic fences which now
divide us.

The Americans allowed their politicians to commit a
crashing blunder when they abruptly cut off Lend-Lease.
If Lend-Lease had run on for several years, the Americans
might well have had a large return, as other peoples recovered enough to contribute substantially. America would
have been saved the colossal aids and loans (or gifts, as
they actually are) since required to prop tottering economies and to preserve her political front. Her own export
industries would have continued to flourish and she could
have been certain of full employment for years ahead. She
could have held or knitted closely to her every foreign
country eager for aid; and few Governments from Warsaw
westward would have dared their people's anger by casting
off Lend-Lease. Lend-Lease or some improvement on it
was the necessary economic element for a proper peace.
Without economic collaboration, the political machinery of
the United Nations could be only what it is, a grotesque
obstruction in the way to world-order. Americans must
remember that economic barriers can also be iron curtains.

If the concept of the Open Society or the American Idea
had been applied in 1946 to the world's problems, we
should by now have been making sense of our situation.
But Governments would not have it so. The State can no
longer leave the economy to solve economic problems. It
has, in fact, destroyed or perverted to its political ends the
economic instruments and institutions which might have
met our economic problems.

This was remarkably demonstrated in the affair of the
British Loan.

The Loan was prompted by the closing of Lend-Lease

and Britain's lack of dollars. If the ordinary American had seen the Loan in plain economic terms he would have readily understood the situation. He could understand that credit is sometimes required at the store: that Britain might need tick to buy wheat and meat and eggs until she could get back into business.

But this is not how the loan was put to him at all. It was presented through the distorting mirror of politics. It became a political deal between Governments. The immensity of the Loan made this perhaps inevitable. Only the public power could deal in such extravagant terms.

But here one is struck by wonder and a wild surmise. Was it really necessary to raise that credit all in one fell swoop? It was originally intended to extend over four years; might it not have been taken as a series of bites? Did the immensity of the credit contribute to the inflation of American prices which reduced its real value? If it had been taken in annual mouthfuls, would it not have been easier to plan its purchases against American price-levels? Was not the British Government perhaps a little grandiose in its notions? Did it really need to raise credits in 1946 for tobacco still ungrown and films still unmade? We might carry the fantasy further to the wild extremes of reaction, the ultimate depths of Torydom. We might wonder why the British Government needed to be concerned with tobacco and films at all. Suppose (for we may as well be hanged for a sheep as a lamb) it had told the private industries which sell tobacco and show films that Government had no dollars for them and did not propose to raise them; but that if they could get credits from American film-makers or American tobacco-growers, they were free to do so. Suppose that the British Government had taken responsibility for only those essential goods and credits which could not be acquired in what was (before Government clapped on all its controls) once the normal way of business. I have just a faint, sneaking, lurking suspicion that Mr. J. Arthur Rank might have been able to get films on his own credit or that the American bankers who own Hollywood might have been ready to take more films from Mr. Rank in exchange for their own. I have an even more contemptible notion that some American tobacco-merchants might have been willing to give Carrera's or the British Imperial Tobacco Company credit for a year or two or three rather than burn tobacco-piles. I may be entirely wrong, but I even think that some farmer interests in the United States might have made their own arguments for credits to Britain if eggs and meat and wheat were otherwise to be thrown on the American market to bear down prices.

The Loan might have seemed less formidable if it had not appeared as one mighty bite but as separate credits spread over many industries and markets for several years. Obviously the politicians and their economists did not think so. But then the politicians (and sometimes their favored economists) are more interested in sweeping political gestures than in workaday affairs: especially if the gestures persuade the innocent elector that the political authority is the one resource of man, his only refuge in time of trouble, the authentic Wizard of Oz.

I think it strange that the British public did not put these simple questions. Perhaps we could not have expected Mr. Dalton and his friends to anticipate them. But I should still like to know why it was necessary to raise funds in 1946 for crops to be grown in 1949.

There is some excuse for people who now think that the Loan was part of a large plan or plot to canalize and control under Government all Britain's traffic with the United States.

However all this may be, conclusions do appear from the strange history of the Loan. Ministers may have be-

lieved as they told the British people that the Loan in
the conditions they had proposed or accepted would last
for years. In that case, they were incompetents; and to
trust them further with control of the economy was mad-
ness. Alternatively, the Government may have known that
the Loan would not meet Britain's need. In that case, it
grossly deceived the people, and its purpose could only
be sinister.

Now most men are for most of the time rather stupid.
But it is difficult to believe that no one in the governing
clique of higher bureaucrats and politicians foresaw the
consequences and course of the Loan Agreement they entered. Someone must have known something; and in any
case the probabilities were suggested by outsiders, if the
bureaucrats are still aware of opinions not their own.

We may infer that some among the ruling group foresaw the consequences and hence probably sought them.
If they sought or welcomed them they must have intended
to use them. The use that has been made of them is to
extend the controls of the State over wider and wider
ranges of life. The economic crisis has, like the War, served
the planners' interest and purpose. It has with the control
of labor and the emergency powers delivered the British
workingman into their hands to be made over.

This has been possible because many people of good-
will still accept false views of the functions proper to Government and of the character of the economic process and
of the competence of men. We are none of us as wise or
virtuous as the planners assume themselves to be, and even
Sir Stafford falls short of the Deity in omniscience. But the
ingenious still accept the pretensions of the planners. We
can see now very clearly (and in Britain of all places!)
how a people anxious and worn and bamboozled by doctrinaires can be worried out of their liberties.

As confusion and stagnation spread from Government's

controls, the petty tyrants impose more and more controls
to distract attention and ultimately to stifle criticism. In
Britain we have seen the control of trade and investment
followed by the control of labor. Gloss it how you will,
this is the Servile State foretold with a remarkable measure
of accuracy by Mr. Belloc in 1912.

Britain has offered evidence enough for Macaulay's dic-
tum: "Three things invariably happen when a Government
touches any commodity. It becomes scarce, it becomes bad,
it becomes dear." But can people still make sense of the
evidence beneath their noses?

Lord Beveridge has hopes still of the native intelligence
of his countrymen. In a protest,[6] especially notable for its
author, at the inefficiency and restrictions imposed by Act
of Parliament he has declared: "There will be a time when
people will turn against all these absurdities and waste—
and it is urgent that they should."

One can hope that he is right. One can be certain that
the planners in power will try to check the popular reaction
by all the means at their disposal, and these in the machinery of the modern State are formidable.

The planners are constantly tightening their grip. Economic disaster has not shaken them in Russia. It has merely
brought more and more controls by the instruments of
armed force and secret police. The tribes of inspectors are
equally serviceable in other countries and their powers
steadily increase with the subversion (described by Mr.
Richard O'Sullivan and Sir Henry Slesser) of the Common
Law.

The British peoples (forgetting their Cromwell) are reluctant to believe that some familiar politician may be
bent on the reduction of their liberties. They are slow to
suspect that honest Ben or honest Clem could be a threat

[6] In an address to the University Liberal Union, 26 June 1947.

to the long traditions whose prime symbol is still the Great Charter. But modern legislation and administrative tribunals have left little of the terms or temper of the great instrument of English liberties.

I sometimes wonder if the honest Bens and Clems really know what they do. A narrow social passion may blind them to the larger implications of their deeds. Stubbornness and personal pique are not unknown in politics; and sheer ignorance has its part.

In the present British situation, many have been brought to accept totalitarian measures under pressure of the economic facts. They have seen no immediate alternative to the Government's program. But their real problem was to change the situation.

The advance of National Socialism can be checked only by the restoration in the Western world of the Open Society. It cannot be restored by any one Government alone. The whole community of Western peoples must return together to it.

But only the United States has the resources necessary to the first steps. If the Americans are not prepared for a great effort to apply in the world the American Idea and concepts of a Free Economy, the West will inevitably be driven into National Socialism and desperate attempts at economic autarchy which can only breed new conflicts.

The effort would require of the Americans a remarkable degree of insight and intelligence. But all their own interests call for the effort, because too much must be involved in a collapse of the political and economic order of the Western world.

But the proper shape of things should be allowed to emerge in right order and reasonable freedom. We want to reduce the intrusion and delusion of the Monstrous State, not to enlarge it. The digestive tract (although of the body and subject to its order and general conditions) must perform according to its own nature. So must the economy, as *laissez-faire* insisted; but within the general order of the body, as *laissez-faire* disputed.

Opposition to an open world-economy comes chiefly from two sources. The heirs of *laissez-faire* believe that the economy should be conducted like a free-for-all without reference to political and social and moral order. The Marxists and National Socialists believe that the economy should have no freedom of its own, but be subordinated utterly to the State as a mere wing and instrument of the dictatorship.

We may thus expect an occasional alliance of unreconstructed Capitalists with the Communists and Planners to resist a free world order. The jagged individualists will dislike the order: the Communists will hate the freedom. Both will call up the demon of political nationalism with all its train of prejudices and old hates and envies. We see it riding high already and on substantial broomsticks. The American and British peoples will have to resist the sound and fury of their cabals and covins, and the venom these will breed.

If we have sense enough for the effort, the political methods will not be difficult. Politics are but a tool, and man is a tool-maker. The machinery proposed for the British Commonwealth in Chapter Seventeen might be modified, adapted, and developed for larger purposes. The various regional centers of consultation are obviously desirable, where the special interests of local communities can have their proper emphasis within the general frame. This method preserves a sufficient and proper political autonomy.

Here once more the lessons of the British Commonwealth which reconciled autonomy with collaboration are apt. The National States linked in a world economy may still continue in their own political responsibilities, as Britain, Canada, and Australia have, within the British System.

There is less risk of American or Anglo-American imperialism in full-blooded co-operation than in dependence on American credits, loans, and hand-outs.

Inevitably, peoples engaged in common economic and social enterprises draw closer to one another politically.

I see no harm but only gain in that. It is the second phase of growth towards One World. It is essentially the method by which the British System grew to grandeur; and its rejection by narrow bigoted Nationalists has brought the British System to its present pass.

THIRTEEN

THE REALM OF CANADA

THE Dominions and the Colonial Empire have had great benefits from British experience by direct contributions and indirectly by their entrée to the world-wide System and their use of its facilities and resources. But a culture cannot be uprooted and transported. Although the colonists may take something of their heritage with them, it must strike and take root in the new soil and grow in the conditions of another climate. The Australians, Canadians, South Africans, and New Zealanders are already distinct peoples with their own cultures and way of life, distinguishable from those of the English, Irish, Scots, French, and Dutch who begot them. Being young, they are callow and self-assertive and not always very well instructed.

The British once thought that in the nature of things young communities would declare for their independence as young men and women are prone to do. This is much what happened, but ties survived; and the Dominions until now have closed ranks in trouble much as members of a family do.

Each has set up in its own household and business. The question now before the British Dominions is whether the natural inclination to drift apart and go their own gaits will be countered by evident common interests and the growth of partnership in a world which needs above all else to realize common interests.

For a guess at the answer one must look at each Dominion in turn; for each has its special problems, characters, and attitudes.

* 2 *

The senior is Canada; and Canada has less urgent interests in the British relationship than the other Dominions. Canada is now high among the Middle Powers with enormous resources yet to be developed. She has, moreover, an intimate relationship with the United States unique among sovereign states. Both British and Canadians were once much of the opinion that Canada's destiny would unite her with her neighbor. Many Americans still expect it. But as Canada led the way to a new sort of international relationship within the British Commonwealth, so now she is evidently developing with the United States a new sort of relationship between sovereign nations distinct and separate in their political organization.

English-speaking Canadians and Americans may go to and fro across their frontier and be indistinguishable from one another. Their economies may be very closely linked. They will, it seems, develop together a system of defense for all North America. They have countless common interests. Yet, as communities, they have each their own strong characters and courses, and the courses do not by any means all run in one groove. In 1914 and again in 1939, Canada went into war immediately as a member of the British Commonwealth. Public sentiment in Toronto in September 1939 was very far from public sentiment in Milwaukee; and no one could cross from Detroit into Windsor in the early years of the War and think himself still in the same country. The differences are marked, in fact. Americans often refuse to look at them, as if they implied some criticism of their own way of life; and this leads them into childish misinterpretations of their neighbor.

Thus some Americans explain decisions like Canada's in 1939 by trying to persuade themselves that Canada is a sort of colonial dependency which must do what London tells it to do. They think of Canada as in a situation more servile than their own thirteen colonies ever were; and though they know with one part of their mind that this is nonsense, they cling stubbornly to it with another part as all men cling to prejudices which involve their self-esteem.

Although English-speaking Canada is largely the foundation of Loyalists emigrated from the south at the Revolution, conceivably it might have joined with its neighbor seventy years ago if it had been only English-speaking. But French Canada would not have assented; and at no time since has it shown any real inclination towards a larger union.

Through all Canada the inclination to union is now less than it was fifty years ago. Canadians can conceive that circumstances might one day compel a union. They have no profound dislike for the notion. In general they have an affection for the United States very rare among close neighbors. But few see need for union. They have grown a strong nationalist sense. They are all Canadians as the French for two centuries have been *Canadien*.

The effort in World War II has intensified their pride as Canadians. They have felt their muscles and tested their mettle. They have developed an extraordinarily vigorous economy. They have been reminded of their vast lands still unused. The Canada which lived within a hundred miles or two of the American border has always felt the strong tug southward. But young Canadians begin to turn towards the west and north. Not many yet are on the move, but new directions have appeared to the Canadian mind. The needle has come round a few points. The bent of the older generation and the majority may still be towards the south. A people's course is shaped, however, not by its comfortable multitudes, but by the few who watch the swinging needle and seek the new directions.

In 1945, I talked to scores of Canadian soldiers in Europe. In 1946, I crossed the Atlantic with several thousands of them. I kept some tally of their views. I asked eighty-four if they believed that Canada would join the Commonwealth in war again. Seventy answered, "Yes," most with conditions and reasons. These were more interesting than the flat "Yes" of a handful (all the No's were flat). The general sense was that the United Kingdom was unlikely to fight except in a cause sufficient for Canada; and that the British link was worth preserving as a useful counterbalance to the influence of the United States. Only a few objected to American influence or thought that it might become aggressive. But as several said in much these words, they felt that they could and should draw on the best in both their worlds. One instanced the legal system. "I think the British legal system is better than the American. I like the tenure of judgeships during good behavior. I want to see Canada follow the methods and traditions of the British Courts rather than the American."

Another argued for the British, and Canadian, method of Parliamentary Government with executive responsibility to the Legislature. Several held that the British social system and social services represented an attitude towards the common man which they preferred. (The Labour program in the United Kingdom had strong appeal in all the Dominions to elements of their populations not sympathetic with much else in English life.)

These men were anything but hostile to the United States. But they also saw in Britain values they wanted for Canadian life. Though they were inclined to regard "the bridge of understanding" notion as high-falutin', it was much their sense.

* 3 *

The French Canadian still turns an edge towards both worlds. He has been much an isolationist. The reasons are very obvious. First, Quebec was a British conquest. The French, to preserve their liberties and identity, had to remain a solid bloc capable of political and social resistance to what rapidly became after the American Revolution an English-speaking majority. Secondly, the French were for a century a Catholic island in a Protestant sea; and the waves hammered at their coasts. Until the Irish poured into Massachusetts to make Boston a predominantly Irish city, the nearest considerable Catholic community was in Maryland; and the French had as neighbors in New England and Upper Canada the most rigorous of Protestant communities.

The religious opposition was accompanied by the clash of cultures. The tradition of the French was hostile to the Puritan view of life. In Britain, the cultivated classes and many elements in Anglicanism retained some sympathetic relations with French culture and religion. But in the English Colonies the Protestant culture grew (as James Truslow Adams emphasized in *The Epic of America*) more harsh and narrow in "the down drag of the wilderness." The rise of frontier sects whose preachers lacked the old stern disciplines of Presbyterianism and Anglicanism reduced the intellectual content of Protestantism. On the frontiers of the forests, the scattered populations were seldom able to come together regularly as organized congregations. The "revival" at irregular intervals became the typical religious assembly. Revivals brought the settlers together from their scattered, solitary holdings. They had few other occasions to meet; and the astounding outbursts of emotionalism came not only from the starved religious sense but from the release of social instincts long unexercised. Revival meetings at times ended in something like orgies, and one is not surprised remembering the lonely and dangerous lives of desperate hard work from which they were almost the only reliefs and escapes. But all their conditions combined to whip up fervors, prejudices, and emotions rather than to inform with cool wisdom. Here the old object of protest took on all the shapes of evil that inflamed imaginations could propose. The Pope of Rome and his minions became the fantastic figures which still haunt the dark places of some American minds; so that otherwise sensible men gave credence to the ridiculous calumnies in which the underworld of Protestantism still deals. The Ku Klux Klan in its several revivals fed on stuff of the sort; and on the frontiers of the 18th and early 19th centuries notions of the kind ran even wilder. The French Canadian was seen as a limb of the Great Beast. Even today, the Orange movement is stronger in Ontario than elsewhere outside Belfast and its immediate environs.

The French, for their part, saw the Protestants about them as heretics and schismatics given over to unnatural vices and to such fearful doctrines as the Albigenses knew. They closed their ranks about the faith and customs of their Norman peasant stock, and deliberately resisted every wind of change and opinion which blew from the south or west. The *habitants* on their thin soils became the most conservative of all Western peoples. The *voyageurs* and missionaries as they sought for furs and souls and opened the great interior waterways from Quebec to the Gulf of Mexico carefully avoided, unless in battle, the spreading points of infection.

After the capture of Quebec and the French Revolution, the French Canadians were largely isolated from their political, racial, and cultural origins. Their distaste for the performances of Revolutionary France was confirmed in subsequent proceedings and especially by the anti-clerical and anti-religious bent of the Third Republic. The French Canadians detested French Freemasonry and all its works. A government which banished the religious orders was to them Satanic. Their attitude in the World Wars was influenced by their view of French politics as well as by their relations with the English-speaking world. The growth of Catholic populations in the United States and non-French Canada gave them new associations in North America; the increasing materialist and secular influences gave them, however, new causes for suspicion and hostility. But as their populations overflowed from the farms they began to move not only into Montreal or the outer reaches (they are making new settlements north and west) but into New England, where the French population now is formidable.

French Canada between the wars was thus opening cautiously to the world. Its relations with its mother-country quickened from the Catholic Revival in France. The French Neo-Scholastics (Maritain, Gilson, and their fellows) evoked a warm response in French-Canadian seminaries and universities. The Youth Organizations of French Catholic Action (the *Jeunesse Ouvrière Chrétienne*, the *Jeunesse Étudiante Chrétienne*, the *Jeunesse Agricole Chrétienne*) have been reproduced with enormous memberships in French Canada; and the Christian Social Program to which the French *Mouvement Populaire Famille* (an adult movement of the family) adheres and to which the political party *Mouvement Républicain Populaire* presumably subscribes has the general sympathy of the French Canadians.

Increasing intercourse with the world has touched the reservoir of intellectual energy in French Canada. It is producing new and vigorous literature and art. Several Paris publishers appeared in Quebec and Montreal after the fall of France and put out a flood of books: reprints of French classic and contemporary authors, but also new works by Canadians. The movement of creative life in the French-Canadian culture is very evident.

With new horizons, the attitude of the French-Canadian Catholics to international affairs is changing markedly. I have been told by eminent Canadians that the attitude of French Canada was less in doubt in 1939 than that of other racial groups from northern and eastern Europe in the Prairie Provinces. In the post-war situation, the beliefs and sentiments of French Canadians have been caught up by the struggle in France, Italy, and Central Europe against Communism. They have warmed to both Britain and the United States as bulwarks of the West. The principal spokesmen for Canada at the post-war Conferences and the first sessions of the United Nations were Mr. Louis St. Laurent and Mr. Paul Martin, both of French stock. St. Laurent was leader of the Quebec Bar until Mr. Mackenzie King persuaded him to join the wartime Cabinet. He had none of the tricks or apparently the ambitions of the professional politician, but by the end of 1946 he clearly could have had, if he wished, the succession to Mr. Mackenzie King in the Liberal leadership. Four times in three weeks I heard Mr. St. Laurent described as "a great gentleman": once by a British diplomat, once by a French-Canadian railwayman, once by a Canadian-Scots lawyer, and once by the Canadian Prime Minister. Those of us who sat through the long, dreary first meetings of the United Nations in London (when it was already evident that diplomatic style and manners were not to recover their pre-Nazi decorum) will always remember one gesture of Mr. St. Laurent's for its grace and ease as well as for its import.

Australia and Canada were in competition for the last non-permanent seat in the Security Council. Both let it go to ballot several times; and then St. Laurent walked to the rostrum and smilingly withdrew Canada's nomination. In a few quiet words he spoke the full sense of the British Commonwealth, suggesting that Canada would be as happy in Australia's presence on the Council as she could be in her own. His meaning and his manner produced in the Assembly a sudden quiet, before the public galleries and all but a few delegations rose in applause. I think that most people felt the sudden presence of guests until then unentertained in the assembly of the nations: sweet reasonableness and a high civility.

St. Laurent's clear but careful expositions of world politics have had notable influence with French Canadians. They had accepted the British System because it left them at peace in their own ways. Their inclination henceforward will be, I think, more positive. The interests of Catholicism and the British System today are closer than at any moment since the Reformation. The creation of three Cardinals from the British Commonwealth at one Consistory was evidence enough of the Vatican's attitude. It was not missed by the French Canadians.

* 4 *

Mr. Mackenzie King has sometimes been regarded as hostile to the development of Commonwealth relations. He came to office with the mantle of Sir Wilfrid Laurier looped to his own spreading toga; and Laurier had steadily resisted centralizing notions. Mr. Mackenzie King resisted the proposals for an Imperial War Cabinet in 1940. In 1944, when Mr. Curtin, the Australian Labour Prime Minister, went to London with suggestions for a Central Imperial Secretariat, Mr. King killed them. In April 1946, when the Commonwealth Prime Ministers assembled in London, Mr. King delayed his arrival to avoid the appearance of a full-dress Imperial Conference of the old sort. He persistently and consistently opposed formal political developments which might seem to tighten the Imperial bonds. His attitude probably represented a fair average of Canadian sentiments; for Mr. Mackenzie King's prolonged reign as Prime Minister (exceeding even Walpole's in Britain, and the longest in the whole history of Britain and the Dominions) suggests that he caught in most major matters the medium of Canadian opinion.

No one could talk with him without some sense of his careful judgment and his immense experience. He has been described as cold, reserved, taciturn. I found him frank, forthcoming, vigorous; and I came to suspect that he had grasped the problems of the British System as clearly as any man of his generation. Of all with whom I have discussed these problems, he and Ernest Bevin seemed to have the clearest sense of their complexities; and of the need always for coolness and caution.

The British Commonwealth is too multifarious a thing to be driven or ridden. Each element has its own special conditions, attitudes, and difficulties. The whole must grow with events, because events must have made clear their necessities before the variety of peoples and interests will perceive the overriding needs and combine to meet them.

In British Commonwealth relations, everything has to be done by general assent (except, of course, for specific matters between individual members which need not concern the rest). The politician must gain his points by persuasion of his peers. He cannot as in domestic politics rush his rash judgments into legislation with the bludgeon of a party majority.

One effect of the expansion of the political interest in modern communities has been a surging mass of bad legislation. In a good society, laws should be few and at their best should win not merely a majority's but the general assent. Our passion for legislative action is rather like a morbid craving for patent medicines and magic salves. We are always plopping local plasters on local symptoms.

In the relations of the British Commonwealth this taste for panaceas has been resisted. Few propositions get far which have not from the first general assent. The Commonwealth has perhaps been excessively resistant to proposals for extended collaboration. It has gone step by step and only on the firmest ground. This is how Mackenzie King and Laurier wanted it. Both have seen the Commonwealth as a new sort of politico-social system. Both, I believe, wished it to grow, not to diminish. But both felt that the growth must not be forced; that it must spread from deep roots in the lives of the peoples according to their wishes and needs, and always waiting on these. Neither Laurier nor Mackenzie King belongs to the confident tribe of planners. They have seen politics in terms of growth, not of mechanical construction.

Efforts to force Commonwealth relations inevitably would raise unseasonable doubts and difficulties. Mackenzie King has been a quietist in politics where quietism was possible. His long tenure suggests that this was Canada's inclination. But in every issue vital to the Commonwealth, the Canada of Mackenzie King has stood with the team. Canada's war effort from 1939, its aids and loans to Britain, its constant and careful contributions to Anglo-American understanding are the great facts for a judgment of Canada's relations with the Commonwealth.

Politicians of the Laurier-King school will do nothing at

all to provoke hasty suspicions in the United States; for they know that the chances of world order primarily come from developing relations between the United States and the British Commonwealth. If these cannot work together, what Great Powers can? Canada is sure of the Commonwealth ties. She sees no need to flaunt them. She wants to see them grow with the United States in the normal and natural courses of good neighborliness.

But Canada can afford to wait on time's changes and developments more than can other Dominions. Australia, New Zealand, the United Kingdom have to solve urgent and threatening problems. If the Commonwealth is to survive as the first external frame of their lives, it will have to be braced and developed. They may have to go farther than Canada needs or wishes to go.

I expect that the Fourth British System will reveal new variations in its form of relationship; but variety has never yet been fatal to its unity.

* 5 *

Like the United States, Canada emerged from the War with little of the dreadful weariness which was on Europe and which came as much from fear of the future as from the ruin and strains of war. Canada had found her strength in the War, and the promise of a great creative period. She had been fourth of the United Nations in war-production, third in naval power, fourth in air power, and her contribution in Mutual Aid exceeded by head of population the United States' in Lend-Lease. She had the material equipment of a Great Power and needed only population to become one.

The population passed 12,000,000 in 1945. Her demographic situation is among the best of the white peoples. Only the Russians, Rumanians, and Yugoslavs of European peoples have a higher rate of growth.

But more than natural increase is needed to make Canada a Great Power. She will need immigrants in large numbers. Immigration raises domestic and external difficulties sufficient to have checked federal action. If the Federal Government had sponsored large migrations from the United Kingdom, the French Canadians would have suspected an effort to build the English-speaking population against them and the increasing influence which they hope their heroic birth-rate will bring them. Immigration, consequently, was usually left to the Provincial Governments and they left it mostly to natural attraction.

Canada, in comparison with Australia and New Zealand, has the advantage of proximity to Europe. The steamship fare for migrants and the seasonal labor which used to flow from the United Kingdom stood for years at £10; and Canada has normally assumed that the immigrant who came on his own initiative and resources was a more likely prospect than invited guests nursed by Governments to selected jobs.

None the less, the Canadians have been alert in the post-war situation to the need for recruitment. While the Australian Government was proclaiming its large schemes, Mr. Mackenzie King with no proclamation at all was importing Polish troops for work in the primary industries.

In the immediate post-war years, millions of agricultural workers stood idle in a starving Europe, while farm-lands in the New Worlds were unused or fell far below their levels of potential production for lack of labor. The Canadian Government was the first of the Dominions to seek the laborers in the market-place.

In July 1947, some 26,500 immigrants, most of them from the British Isles, entered Canada.

The growth of Canadian population was always a lively interest of the United States because of the constant movement to and fro across the border, and the privileges which the United States grants Canadian citizens. Now it has become more important because Canada holds the main frontier of continental defense.

* 6 *

Defense arrangements between Canada and the United States have massive implications for the two peoples and for the whole British Commonwealth.

The joint strategy will be determined by what the General Staffs call the Polar Concept. Their strategic problems in the Arctic and sub-Arctic area can be solved by Canada and the U.S.A. only in co-operation. Both require the adequate protection of the coasts which curve for 5,000 miles beneath the North Pole. The United States has only a narrow segment of the Arctic area (under the Sector Principle only 28 degrees from Alaska, as against Canada's 81 degrees). Moreover, the United States itself lies wholly under Canada. Attacks on its major industrial districts almost certainly would come across Canadian territory and through Canadian skies.

The alternative to co-operation is a political and psychological breach almost inconceivable. It would demand the militarization by the U.S.A. of the Canadian frontier from end to end. Canada would be caught in a squeeze-play between its giant neighbors; and its great cities, all within a hundred miles of the American frontier, would become at once hostage to American fortunes.

The vast North was until just now an undefended march; for what moat or Maginot could have seemed yesterday as sure a defense as the frozen zones of silence? An occasional air reconnaissance and lonely patrols of the Royal Mounted Police crawling slowly over immense distances were the only watch. The region of icebound seas and icelocked islands between the continental coasts and the North Pole is still largely uncharted and unobserved. A hostile working party might be making airfields in those wastes for months without report. Yet across the ice-cap is the one serious threat to their safety that Americans and Canadians now conceive.

The post-war interest and activity in the Arctic (and Antarctic) recalls the competition in 19th century Africa, which led to crisis after crisis, all contributing to the collision of 1914. Again large unexplored and unexploited areas have suddenly become of prime strategic consequence. The new military techniques make of the Arctic a strategic area comparable with the Mediterranean, that perennial battle-pit. The Arctic is cupped between the long shores of Russia and North America as the Mediterranean is cupped between its continents: and the Arctic will become also a major traffic zone with a network of air bases and of cross-routes between the Americas, Asia, and Europe. From Moscow to Chicago is 4,620 miles; from Murmansk to New York, 4,400. The two giants have counted carefully those miles. Both now are staking claims and laying out their lines and bases.

In 1932, a Russian icebreaker pounded through from ports in European Russia to the Pacific gate, opening a Northeast Passage. In 1946, Russian ships and aircraft began to put down laboratories and weather posts from Archangel to Bering Strait, as part of a Five-Year Plan employing hundreds of expeditions to establish lighthouses, radar stations, and weather posts. At Petropavlosk in Kamchatka, Russia began to build a huge military base, 500 miles from American posts in the Aleutians and within a modern bomber's range of Chicago, St. Louis and Detroit. Roads spread in Kamchatka. Its Avancha Bay was dredged for heavy ships. The Russians were busy at Paramushiro in the Kuriles, once Japan's northern naval base. Across from the Kuriles and the Komandorskis is Alaska.

The Americans are busy also in the North, eastward and

westward of the continent. The U. S. Navy's "Operation Frostbite" with the aircraft-carrier *Midway* began flying tests deep into Davis Strait between Greenland and Labrador. In 1947, U.S.N. submarines began in "Operation Iceberg" to chart Bering Strait. The U. S. Army with "Operation Frigid" in Alaska and "Operation Williwaw" in the Aleutians tested vehicles, including armor, and other equipment.

The United States by late 1947 had more than thirty bases from Attu to Greenland. Dutch Harbor was still the major base of the North Pacific, but Kodiak off the south coast of Alaska was rising to rival it. A complex of lesser bases was growing on the frame of Chericof, Caton, Great Sitkin, Hog, San Bay, Fort Randall, and Ketchikan in Alaska. At Point Barrow, the Navy was drilling for oil. Oil does not lessen Alaska's strategic significance.

From bases at Elmendorf near Anchorage or from about Fairbanks almost any point in Europe or Asia could be bombed by aircraft already in service.

The Civil Aeronautics Authority was building in 1947 over thirty non-army airfields, radio, radar, and weather stations.

Eastward in Greenland, the U. S. Army had airfields at Ikateg, Narsarsvak, and Sondestron Fiord with outlying weather and radio-radar stations. From these Greenland fields, Moscow is little more than 2,000 miles. It is less from Iceland. The Danes may declare that Greenland is not on the market. Iceland may still hug its independence. But both are now caught in the main tide of history.

Canada's first considerable contribution to these activities was "Operation Musk-Ox," when snowmobiles were taken up west of Hudson Bay and across the tundra to Port Radium (where uranium is a major interest) and down to Edmonton. The snowmobiles without heavy equipment averaged only 38 miles a day for 3,100 miles. Ground operations would obviously be too slow to counter an attack from across the ice-cap if they rested on bases in the South. Hence permanent posts with adequate lines of communication are needed in the North through the vast area from Alaska to Baffin Bay. Here is the impelling motive for Canadian-American co-operation. Canada did not propose to give bases on Canadian territory to the United States. But obviously American and Canadian defenses northward would be planned in one pattern, for which Canada would provide lines of communication and staging-points across her vasts.

In 1935, a prophet of remarkable perception, General Billy Mitchell, said to the U. S. House of Representatives Military Affairs Committee: "Alaska is the most central place in the world for aircraft and that is true for Europe, Asia, or North America. I believe that in the future he who holds Alaska will hold the world."

His opinion, then neglected, now succinctly sums up a proposition of world strategy.

The U.S.S.R. must remember bitterly that Alaska was once Russian territory. But even without Alaska, most strategists would give to Russia the balance of immediate advantage through the North. Her Arctic coastline extends across nearly half the world. Most direct air-routes from America to eastern Europe and Asia must cross Russian territory. Russia has already settled 2,000,000 people in her north. She has deployed there whole armies of forced labor. She has been ready to pay for her experience with men. On the Sector Principle, by which the Powers about the Arctic would claim everything solid from their own coasts to the Pole, Russia commands almost half of the whole Arctic area. The United States was naturally reluctant to recognize a principle which would give it (for its Alaskan territories) only 28 degrees; and these at the far west of the long line to be defended. The United States must look also to Canada's sector of 81 degrees, and the 69 degrees which Denmark has in Greenland but could hardly defend.

Russia makes claim to 159 degrees, and her neighbors Norway and Finland to 21 and 2 degrees, under the Sector Principle. Whether this is recognized or not, the facts of geography must be. Alaska could be made untenable for the United States if it lacked Canadian co-operation; for example, the Alcan Highway is the one route overland (it was to have been closed after the War, but it is now being maintained). The whole arc from Bering Strait to Greenland's icy mountains must become a shield if America's great cities are to sleep at ease.

The problem set the United States and Canada could have only one answer. The first step towards it was the United States-Canada Joint Board on Defense. The two countries have in a sense one frontier to the north. Its defenses cannot be improvised, as "Operation Musk-Ox" crawling its few miles a day through the vast solitudes of snow has demonstrated. Bases and lines of communication will need much time and effort to develop. Neither Americans nor Canadians are disposed to dally.

Common programs of defense require in corresponding measure common foreign policies. At a time when Canadians have come to feel themselves more than ever before in their history their own men, Canadian policy will inevitably draw closer to American.

Neither people can escape the axiom that the needs of defense are properly the first determinants of foreign policy; because the first object of foreign policy is the safety of the State and people. Nations may profess adherence to the United Nations as a first principle of policy. They are right to do so only if and while they are certain that the United Nations can secure their safety.

This raises new possibilities for politicians throughout the British Commonwealth. As Canada reaches new meas-

ures of agreement with the U.S.A., is she to move farther
from the Commonwealth? Or is this new nexus through
Canada to draw closer the whole Commonwealth and the
U.S.A.?

In many specific matters consultation has much increased
of late within the Commonwealth. But a grave neglect of
the broad political frame continues. The political pattern of
Commonwealth relationships needs to be re-examined. The
Canadian-American necessities could be an appropriate
occasion and a prod if the American people would make
serious effort to understand the uses of the whole Commonwealth in their situation; and see that Canada is something more and greater than a National State when she
appears as the representative of a supra-national community
of free peoples.

FOURTEEN

PACIFIC DOMINIONS

AUSTRALIA and New Zealand are in quite other case than Canada. Their situation is more exposed. They are the only white communities of consequence between Chile and South Africa; and they are inevitably involved in the tremendous problems of the Asian complex above them.

Both peoples were born and bred under the protection of the Royal Navy and the British System, which in the 19th century was the one Power of consequence from Cape Town to Cape Horn and from the Himalayas and Hong Kong to the South Pole. Australia and New Zealand lived a singularly sheltered existence, and like excessively protected children they missed a sufficient sense of the conditions of their peace and being. These are still not widely understood in spite of two wars.

The decline of the British System in the eastern hemisphere has already gravely weakened their frame of security.

They urgently need for survival a rapid development of their populations and resources.

These necessities begin to be seen, but as in a glass darkly; they have yet had little influence on political and economic programs or on prevailing social habits, and the lessons of War II have not been generally absorbed even by the politicians and the bureaucrats.

They were perhaps obscured by the swiftness and strength with which the United States moved in the Pacific. Too many Australians and New Zealanders imagine that the United States would move as rapidly again.

But the United States has no imperative interest in their security, as it has in the security of Canada. If the Japanese had attacked only British and Dutch territories in 1941, would public opinion in the United States have been ready for war to protect these remote communities? The United Kingdom was much more obviously a bastion of America's defenses; but the United States did not declare war when the Kingdom was dangerously threatened in 1940. The peculiar mechanics make a declaration of war by the United States unlikely if the Congress and the electorate are not over-whelmingly for it; and the *casus belli* must come close home before the vote can be got out. The Australians and New Zealanders who think of the United States as their sure and certain shield are very naïve.

They assume that the only danger to their solitary possession of vast territories is in some dramatic onslaught like the Japanese attack of 1941-2. They do not appreciate the possibilities of political and economic pressure from populations already grown beyond their means of subsistence and seeking any spillway.

The pressures of rising human tides in Asia have repeatedly changed the courses of history. Since the dim beginnings one outlet has been by Southeast Asia and the rich islands which curve like a scimitar above Australia.

Wave after wave of peoples have come out of Asia by the East Indies, driven by the press of peoples behind them. The remote ancestors of the Australian natives probably came that way; the Melanesians and the Polynesians took it to the Pacific; the Malays have been followed by recurrent tides of Hindus and Chinese. Through the last half-century the Chinese have again been flowing south and southeast. In Malaya, they outnumber the Malays. They are multiplying in the East Indies. If China succeeds in restoring her own political and economic structure, she must seek new fields and markets for her human overflow. Should China and India reach in this century the populations statistically possible, they will provide the whole world with a desperate problem. The present food-resources of the world would not meet their added demands. New resources must be found. Would public opinion in the United States or any other country support Australia in a persisting neglect of its tropical regions?

If war or famine do not destroy two or three hundred millions of Chinese and Indians in this century, their problems will have to be met. Hunger and desperation are notable organizers and disciplinarians, as the Chinese Communists know. A competent national Government in China would probably be forced to exert all its power to relieve the population-pressure on its resources. Indeed, no competent national Government is likely to appear unless it can offer its people relief by one means or other.

If the world could achieve peace and some reasonable measure of co-operation, the problem might be tackled by a combined effort. It could not exceed in cost another world war; and if the man-power of Asia could be put to profitable work and the purchasing power of 200,000,000 families raised by even a few dollars a year each, the economy of the whole world would benefit enormously. China especially is hopelessly short of capital now. It needs a transport-grid. People sometimes starve by millions while there is rice in the next province which cannot be moved to them. Soil-reclamation and irrigation works are essential. China and India have the man-power. A sane world would help with capital. It would provide capital also for the archipelagos about Southeastern Asia. The region from the Philippines to Australia and from Sumatra to the Solomons has, with the possible exception of South America, the richest undeveloped areas of the world. Java is one island which is carrying more than its human complement. Although overwhelmingly rural, it is among the most crowded areas on earth; but it is an example of what can be done with capital and irrigation and hygiene and the other resources brought it by the Dutch. The Dutch demonstrated in Sumatra and Borneo methods of colonization from Java; and though few of the myriad islands have the fantastic richness of the Java soils, the East Indian area could with technical developments, social discipline, and capital provide probably for treble its present eighty millions. I suppose that people who can think of these areas only in terms of imperialist exploitation will flinch at the notion of capital investment. Let us think of it then in terms of health and engineering services, irrigation works, agricultural schools and people's credit banks.

In a wiser world, the Dutch, British, Australians, and Americans might have gone back together into this vast area with a program to raise the living standards of its peoples and to create for them the economic and social bases of the political liberties they have claimed: which are quite meaningless and unreal unless the matrix of their lives is transformed.

No one who understands the fundamental problems of the East Indies (the engineering as well as the social and political problems) could seriously believe the Indonesian peoples capable of creating without great aid from abroad a modern democratic political-economy. They lack the technical and capital resources and the social morale and machinery. In Java they were unable to maintain the irrigation systems on which their expanding population had been fed. Millions in the outer islands still follow grossly wasteful and destructive methods of agriculture. The Asian world is faced with rising populations and (in their present phase) shrinking food resources. The world's interest requires the world's attention to these gigantic problems of population and sustenance.

In the absence of a general attention, the Australians should look to their own interests. They should make every contribution that they can to the solution of the Asian problems. They should tackle their own tropics, their tropical islands as well as their tropical main, not only to defend these but to breed there a race of white men who can work in the tropics and master the techniques of tropical economies.

Australia's own tropical regions may never carry great populations and may properly be left to the white man if the white man will use them. But he should use them in an orderly development of the whole region, and as a bridge for partnership with the peoples to his north: as a field for technical and social experiment and a school for skills which he might contribute, together with his meat, wheat, fish, fruit, vegetables, manufactures, and capital goods to the economic elevation of all this quarter of the world.

A healthy political economy in Southeastern Asia and the islands would be Australia's best assurance against aggression from these parts. The whole job in Asia calls for aid on an international basis and gigantic scale. Australia might profitably promote the idea and begin by educating her own people and shaping her own economy to the immediate tasks. In the years before the First World War Australia

did make a beginning in her own North. She settled some
thousands in North Queensland, mostly on sugar-lands. The
North Queenslanders have demonstrated that white men
can live and work at hard physical labor in the tropics if
the tropics are kept clear of their fouler diseases. They have
proved that white men and women can propagate in the
tropics. North Queensland gives Australia one of its best
birth-rates and the world its largest babies. But there are
still only thirty or forty thousands of tropical Australians.
The great ambition flagged in that fateful period between
the wars when Australia had lost the best of a whole generation and the careful men took over: the slothful men,
the men who wanted the easy life of the cities rather than
the tasks of creation, the men who sought security in the
State rather than in their own brawn and brains.

In World War II, roads, air-fields, bases, installations of
all sorts were put into the North. Huge truck-farms were
developed to grow vegetables for the Australian and American forces. The North for a moment was allowed to show
what it might be if human energy and capital were applied
to it.

Two years after Japan's surrender the vegetable farms
were mostly running to riotous seed; installations were rotting and rusting in the tropic rains; roads were sinking
back under the scrub; and the first priority to immigrants
was for building workers to make more houses for more
and more civil servants in Canberra, two thousand miles
south from the coasts that look at Asia. The population of
Sydney jumped in a few years by 400,000 to 1,500,000 of
a total Australian population of less than 8,000,000; and the
political situation was dominated by the demands of urban
workers for a forty-hour week and by the dislocations which
followed when they got it.

Australia and New Zealand have generally been accepted
as social laboratories for men of our sort; as in the van of

social experiment. In the post-war period they were engaged in the most dubious of all human experiments, less
plausible even than the pursuit of the philosopher's stone
or of perpetual motion: how to have your cake and eat it.

The effort should be instructive to other peoples who still
have cake.

* 2 *

The Second War was a brisk stimulus for most Australians and New Zealanders. The world rudely intruded.
Their military and economic response was remarkable.
Their mobilization and industrial expansion were by head
of population passed only by Great Britain's, among the
United Nations whose statistics are dependable. Australia
came out of the war like Canada with the material potential of a major Power. As one of the four chief exporters of
food she had at once a great opportunity and responsibility,
to which her farmers on the whole responded, although
they were of all productive elements the most neglected by
the Federal Government in their problems of manpower,
renewal of equipment, and rehabilitation of neglected lands.

The Australian secondary industries had all Asia at their
doors in desperate need of manufactured goods: textiles,
tools, machinery. Australia was producing through the War
the best and cheapest steels in the world. She had created a
notable aircraft industry from nothing. She had handled her
financial problems skillfully. Costs had been controlled
(the index number of wholesale prices rose from the 100 of
January 1939 to 141 in January 1947; in the United States
and Great Britain the rises were to 189 and 188). The budget
position by 1946-7 was strong. A fine force of skilled industrial labor had appeared.

Hundreds of manufacturers in Britain and America, looking at Australia's costs, conditions, workmen, and her opportunities in Pacific and East Asian markets, contemplated

moving in. On the eve of peace, Australia seemed launched on a new era of economic expansion and power.

Two years later the opportunities had been largely dissipated by industrial disturbances in the coal-fields, and in transport and the heavy industries, and by the economic drag of inflated public services, largely non-productive, which by June 1947 were using almost one-quarter of all persons employed. The President of the Associated Chambers of Manufactures estimated in July 1947 that Australia had lost orders from abroad worth hundreds of millions of pounds because her rate of industrial output had fallen till it hardly met her own needs; and while some allowance should be made for special pleading, he evidently stated a substantial fact. It was a tragic fact for peoples in desperate need of aid.

The few countries which emerged from World War II with a surplus of resources and expanded economies (the United States, Australia, Canada, New Zealand, Argentina, South Africa and one or two more) had enormous opportunities. Apart from the moral and humanitarian obligations, they had an acute self-interest in doing everything within their powers to help their neighbors. They were a handful of "haves" in a world of "have-nots." Hungry eyes were on their plenty; to hungry millions they could play either Providence or Dives. They could make friends or bitter enemies. They could help themselves by helping to restore a general prosperity, or they could bring on themselves the inevitable consequences of a spreading ruin. Ernest Bevin was the one world statesman who saw this and said from the first what he told his own trade union once more in July 1947: that the political, racial, nationalist conflicts had been intensified by war; that the only answer to them was in economic and social efforts. "I want an extra hundred-weight of coal per man out of the pits, a quicker turn-around of shipping, a bit of overtime when you are asked for it—

anything which will help give Europe the things it is asking for."

That is what every Labour leader, politician, and industrialist concerned for peace and order in the world should have been hammering home to his people. The attitude of democratic leaders in this matter is brief but sufficient test of their competence, courage, and honesty.

The "haves" did make some effort. The contributions of Australia and New Zealand, the United States and Canada in public aids and private charities might have seemed remarkable in any earlier emergency. But their national economies fell far short of the possible; and this was particularly disquieting in Australia and New Zealand, for in both the Labour movement was in power and Labour might have been expected to make a supreme effort for the workers of the world on whom the tragedy had come. This was a moment above all moments to put out a supreme productive effort. It did not appear.

The primary-producing countries could all have grown more food. A few thousands of extra workers on their farmlands could have grown food for tens of thousands more. In Europe, hundreds of thousands of agricultural workers stood idle in D.P. camps and in groups like the western Polish armies. In the first two years after Germany's collapse only Canada made any considerable effort to use them.

In Australia the chief interest of the Labour movements seemed their drive for more leisure. The general agitation for a shorter working-week at this crisis of the world was a renunciation of responsibilities. The Australians seemed prepared to sacrifice even their own prospects from an expanding economy to potter in their gardens and sit in the sun. The production and movement of commodities for which the world was desperate were repeatedly hampered by industrial disturbances. The economy was hamstrung at the moment of its greatest moral responsibility and material prosperity and possibilities.

On any count, including that of Australians and New Zealanders themselves, the scene was tragic. We are far from a coherent world system while the more fortunate of peoples can have as little kindness for the rest.

The causes are various. Men uninformed by powerful moral values are selfish, short-sighted, and given over to disorders which have ruin and wretchedness in their wake. Democratic government falters and ultimately fails where it cannot call on a moral consensus. The peoples of the new countries have lived much at ease and mostly lack an immediate sense of what war and famine mean. Horror has been piled on horror until faded imaginations no longer respond. And an awful cynicism has crept across our world in the decline of morals and of moral sanctions.

Cynicism may serve awhile the children of this world in their alliance with the mammon of iniquity. But moral blindness spreads to the intellectual faculties. The cynics cease in time to see even their own main chance. They mistake the realities of the universe: for whether it exists by God or by chance it does move in an order. Its parts must accept their functions, and men ultimately pay in misery and fear and blood for their refusals.

* 3 *

I allow for human preferences. During the Pacific War, when strikes went on much as usual in the New South Wales coal-fields (coal-fields elsewhere in Australia had a remarkable record of sustained work during the War), I talked with an Australian miners' leader. I was in a mild mood of protest. "Listen, son," he said. "If you could make enough money down the pit in three days to go surfing or fishing the rest of the week, what would you do?"

Anyone who has spent an hour or two at a coal-face

underground will understand the attitude, and a people has some rights to these decisions. Many peoples in warm climates long ago plumped for the minimum of work and found comfortable places to squat under the palms and bet on beetle races. They have had to accept the consequences of a gradual ebb of intellectual and moral energies and ultimately of domination by more virile races.

Australia is not a lush and easy land. It was developed by desperately hard work. Its soils are thin, its natural flora mostly inedible. Its aborigines lived mostly on roots and snakes and kangaroos and fish. They had to work hard at their hunting to get even these and to concentrate their intellectual and physical energies in a sheer struggle for existence.

The white man found nothing to his hand. He had to bring in his seeds and useful animals and breed both to a difficult environment. Perhaps he grew tired of the struggle. It certainly induced (as Australian literature reveals) a queer streak of bitterness. After World War I, he had practically abandoned his effort to occupy the continent. A vast part of it is waste and never could be occupied for agriculture or even for the hardiest cattle. But there is room still for many millions.

The Murray Valley, Southeastern Australia, and much of eastern Queensland could take much closer settlement with adequate irrigation and soil-conservation.

But with the progressive mechanization of agricultural methods the numbers actually working on the land may not much increase. The rural growth will come from tertiary industries or services, as Colin Clark has argued. For many years, primary prices should be high. With peace and prosperity, the world will need ten or fifteen years to recover its pre-war levels of consumption in food and raw materials. A real effort to raise the living standards of the

Oriental peoples would require all that the food-exporting countries could produce for generations.

The farmers should earn large and steady incomes for their peoples if they are properly supported by the general economies. With money in their pockets and increasing harvests, they will draw to the rural areas more carpenters, mechanics, insurance agents, dentists, cinema operators, storekeepers, schoolteachers, clergymen, wheat lumpers, barmen, veterinary surgeons, truck-drivers.

The extension of electric-power grids should spread light industries and their workers across the landscapes; and this is now desirable for military reasons and because the Australians and New Zealanders, like the Americans, get their biggest birthrate and their lowest death and crime rates in the country towns.

The large Australian cities, like the industrial wens elsewhere, eat population. None reproduce themselves. Perhaps their populations are just too tired in the dreary clatter, dirt and confusion to bear children; as they are growing too tired to work.

While habits of industry decline, the masses become more and more dependent on the State. Social security has become a fetich in Australia and New Zealand. It will continue so while anything of the cake survives or until the diminishing and overburdened groups who make it refuse their thankless tasks. The strains in the Australian economy are already evident. With them comes a deepening hostility between countrysides and cities and between New South Wales (which has most of the black coal, heavy industries, and industrial troubles) and the other States.

* 4 *

New Zealand has been something of a paradox. She is commonly accepted as the most British of the Dominions in population and sympathies, and her economy has always functioned largely as a dairy and sheep farm for the Mother Country. In each World War she has raised from her population prodigious forces; [1] and her fighting men have won from Anzac Cove to the Gothic Line a record unexcelled by any troops the world has known. In World War I, she had 26,688 killed and 41,315 wounded; but only 356 made prisoners-of-war.

Her great military efforts have conformed with her highest interests. The British Commonwealth has been the essential frame of her defense and her development; and her service to it and the Allied cause has given her a weight in international councils more than any other nation of her size.

Yet this energy and heroism abroad has been accompanied by an increasing lethargy at home. The New Zealanders are in possession of a remarkably rich country which could support many millions. A people charged with energy and imagination would be much less concerned with social security than with the expansion of their economy, the creation of new and abounding wealth.

An American publicist has argued that New Zealanders are excessively in-bred. But that in their few generations is biological nonsense. They do suffer, like the Australians, in social habit from their long ease under the protection of the British power. They lack the racial variety which has unquestionably made for the energy, the competitive spirit, and diversity of gifts in American life. Australia and New Zealand are in comparison with the United States a human monotone and in sad need of French cooking, German industriousness, Slavonic gusto, and Italian joy in life and family affection. They have perhaps the English and Irish laziness which is countered in the home countries by sheer

[1] Over 200,000 in 1939-45 from a population of 1,600,000. The Maoris were not made subject to conscription, but contributed their quota in volunteers.

necessity, the climate, and the Scots. In New Zealand there has been an easy sufficiency and even the Scots succumb.

But it has been sufficiency only for restricted numbers; and the trades unions between the wars saw to it that the numbers were restricted. And it has been only a material sufficiency. The lethargy which has come on the British nations in the South is most evident in the intellectual and social life. Here an increasing privation appears in Australia and New Zealand. Both peoples are much given to sports and watching sports and listening to sports on the radio. They live outdoors a great deal and swim and sail and sunbask, like other peoples of the seductive Pacific climates. In the lackadaisical habit they dream of easy money, and millions of man-hours go each week in unprofitable efforts to outguess bookmakers. Although both countries have a curious collection of blue-laws, they are much given to lotteries and the like. But beyond these activities, their social life is poor and undeveloped. They lack the normal civilized resources in good hotels, restaurants, and places of pleasant public entertainment. A once flourishing theater has long been moribund. Politics actively interest only a few despite the universal dependence now on political machinery and measures. Literature and art are lean and dry.

One may perhaps make overmuch of these deficiencies. But they are all too evident. Perhaps they are from the unease of adolescent growth. Against them must be set the strength revealed in war.

Time probably is needed for the new circumstances to educate peoples who had in all their histories until 1941 no vital issue to settle. But will time be allowed them? Peoples usually call up their reserves of energy under pressure or great inspiration. Political and social leadership has not been in Australia or New Zealand notably inspiring; but under pressure Australians and New Zealanders have as individuals shown great powers of response. The general behavior of Australian prisoners-of-war in Japanese hands was superb. The men produced a corporate loyalty and self-discipline of the highest quality. History may with menaces call up from sluggish depths the power which seems to be there.

The general lethargy has given excessive scope to subversive influences in the economy. Australia has been a special object of attention from Communists who have understood its significance in military and political strategies.

Immense prestige would accrue to Communism everywhere if a British Dominion could be brought to heel; and a breach in the Commonwealth would do inestimable damage to British prestige and authority, and weaken the general front of the Western democracies. The prospects of reducing Australia to Communist control may be slight; but Communists do not count their agitation wasted if it produces dissensions and doubts and difficulties.

They have already had formidable influence in the situation I have described. The post-war difficulties in Australia and New Zealand are in part the product of their careful plans. But they found a social and moral situation apt to their purposes.

Communism grows where it can feed on grievances, corruption, and moral indifference. The democracies get in this sense the Communists that they deserve.

Australian workers through the 19th century had cause for grievances. Labour first gathered strength in a period of intense bitterness in the 1890s when strikes had been smashed and the small tradesmen and farmers were ready to join the industrial workers against the financial power. Their bitterness still stains the Australian mind, although Labour has held power in the States and Federation for many of the last forty years and there is less class-distinction in a social sense than anywhere else in the world. Employers and employees are at much the same cultural levels and they mix freely in social life. But sour suspicions and hostility persist in economic relations.

The Labour Movement sought and still professes among its objectives a rule of law and reason in the economy. Australia and New Zealand both created a massive system of arbitration and conciliation courts and industrial law. But it is questionable whether the methods of the law-courts are generally appropriate to the whole field of labor relations. They put employers and employees always at issue and in roles corresponding to plaintiffs and defendants; whereas both have urgent common interests in the well-being of their industry even if immediate issues may for the moment cloud their views. Labour and capital have become less and less partners in industry, more and more competitors for its profits. In the struggle its potential increment has never been achieved. Modern techniques could with industrial peace and co-operation provide much higher returns than they have to the community at large.

Yet the effort to free industry of strikes and lock-outs by a form of legal process is very characteristic of the sober British way; and it had a marked influence on British political thought and practice. In Britain itself the intervention of the State was less than in the southern Dominions; and better calculated perhaps (especially in the recent Joint Industrial Councils) to cushion the collision of the classes which Marx thought would smash the capitalist structure.

* 5 *

The power of the Labour parties rests primarily on the trades unions. With Labour in office, the trades unions have immediate influence on Government policies. The unions have been a tempting field for Communist penetration; and with the mass of trades unionists careless or apathetic, the small, highly disciplined groups of Communists have rapidly reached in many unions the executive controls. They have proved very difficult to shift. The Australian Labour Party grappled belatedly with them and an intense struggle has developed within the unions. But Governments have been slow and weak in meeting their proper responsibilities. Powerful trades unions under Communist control were by the middle 1940s much a law unto themselves. Though they might, when occasion served, go to the Federal or State Arbitration System for their awards, they frequently flouted decisions which did not suit them; and they could exploit against the general interest the traditional loyalties of trades unionists to their officers and organizations.

The Labour Governments which presided in the Federation and most of the States were merely flaccid. The reign of law was obviously endangered. But the alternative parties could make little head. The Right in Australia has seldom shown much sense of positive policy. Australia has suffered from the malaise of the Right which has been a curious feature of modern politics elsewhere. It has suffered especially, as I have already noticed, in social balance from its losses of the First World War.

The major parties are by and large agreed on the need to co-operate with the British Commonwealth, on the need for population and production, on the general problems of defense. The chief difficulty is to get things done.

Immigration is a case in point. The Federal Government and the Opposition agree that population should be built up as rapidly as possible. The Minister for Immigration in the Chifley Labour Government talked of 20,000,000 people before the century's end as essential to the country's defense. He worked hard at his program. He persuaded the trades unions and employers' federations to some co-operation. His publicity attracted over half a million applicants in Europe during 1946 and 1947. The mass of Australians, if they thought much at all about the matter, gave grudging recognition to the need. Yet somehow, the thing would not go. There were obvious difficulties in ships and housing. But these could have been met if the people had really wanted to meet them. In the pinch, the limping economy was resistant.

A small community can absorb large numbers of arrivals only if it is prepared to work furiously and set them to work. The economy must be expanding. But economies will not expand while effort and production drag. The United States grew great because it threw its lands and resources open to the free and full play of ideas and energies from half the countries of the world. The Australians were not prepared for that. They wished to drill their immigrants to the local disciplines, and hold them to the established tempo.

Many have thought this the triumph of the common man. A reasonable security is certainly a proper ambition and the State may properly promote it. Australian and New Zealand workers have achieved a measure of control in the economy and their conditions which workers nowhere else have reached. Yet oddly, they do not seem especially happy. They have in old age, unemployment, sickness, a security that other peoples lack at present. But these are bought at a heavy cost if they obscure the imperative necessities of population, production, and defense.

Australia and New Zealand have yet to demonstrate that they have the answer to the dilemma. In Russia, the masses have been dragooned and deprived to build a Great Power. In France, a Great Power has declined in the selfish play of faction. In the tropics men have put greatness off to loll at ease. Australia and New Zealand have tried to entertain greatness, faction, and the sun in a compromise that as yet never was on land or sea. They may prove to have the

necessary magic. It is more likely that they will be recalled
to harsh realities.

* 6 *

In external policies, Australia and New Zealand have
made some move for themselves with their Anzac Pact,
which establishes a special relationship between them
within the Commonwealth. It is one outward sign of the
inward trend towards re-integration which will be a character of the Fourth British System if it matures. The United
Kingdom has beamed beneficently and given evidence that
she will co-operate in the defense of the Pacific regions of
the System as best she can. She has joined with Australia
in a rocket-development project. A Pacific Fleet has co-
operated in training with the local naval and air forces;
and staff relations are intimate.

Australia and New Zealand have few friends other than
Great Britain and the United States in the two-thirds of
the world between Panama and Suez. They have conducted
their affairs with some brashness. There was a moment
when the United States might have been committed to
some joint arrangement for defensive bases under the
Equator. But it indicated in mid-1947 that it was no longer
concerned to keep up bases in the Australasian area. The
decision provoked some amusement among connoisseurs in
these matters, because the Australian Government had
been prepared for stern bargaining; but the American with-
drawal left it with all its arguments and the huge, costly
base at Manus entirely on its hands.

Yet the United States cannot be indifferent to the strate-
gic significance of Australia, which is except for Japan the
only highly industrialized economy between California and
India. Modern wars must be mounted on modern economies.
In World War II, Australia was an essential base. The United
States would have had to fall back to the line from Dutch

Harbor through the Hawaiis to Bora-bora but for the Australian base and its resources. Australia may not seem very relevant to the strategic problems of the North Pacific regions. Yet MacArthur went from Australia to Japan, and Australian ports on three coasts are nearer than San Francisco 'to Vladivostok. The north coast of Australia commands the narrow passages (vital to a world-strategy) between the Pacific and Indian Oceans.

If Australia were joined with a Power great in Asia and hostile to the United States, America might be cut off from her westward access to all southern and southeastern Asia; and her communications even with the Philippines might be threatened from the south as from the Asian main. In a war of long-range rockets, the immensities of the Australian interior, New Guinea, and the island complex about it would offer countless opportunities for concealed launching-sites. All this may seem highly improbable (one hopes that it is): but in 1940 how many Americans foresaw that two years later they would be heavily embattled in New Guinea and the Solomons, and fight a fierce sea-air action off the Queensland coast? A major war in or across the Pacific can no longer be confined to one corner of it. The United States may have no immediate uses for bases south of the Line; but their control by a friendly Power will henceforward be an American interest. Of this Americans can be reasonably assured while a democratic regime and the present inhabitants survive in Australia. Neither can be taken as a certainty.

* 7 *

Australia and New Zealand have normally been closest of the Dominions in sentiment to the United Kingdom. Unlike the Canadians and South Africans, they are almost entirely (over 90 per cent in each) of English, Irish, Scots and Welsh stocks. Economically, they are closely linked to their Mother Country.

In 1938, Great Britain took 84.7 per cent of New Zealand's exports and 54.2 per cent of Australia's.[2] They were the last of the Dominions to set up their own machinery for the conduct of foreign policy.

Yet both are strongly nationalist. In Australia, isolationism had a lively vogue especially among Labour politicians and some Federal public servants. Australians or New Zealanders generally had until 1941 little sense of foreign policy or the harsh realities with which it must grapple; and history's lessons since have been slow to take. Political interest was obsessed with domestic issues, often of a minor sort. The basic problems of population and soil-conservation were neglected. Erosion was appallingly advanced in Australia before either politicians or people would notice it.[3] To argue for more people in 1939 was to be convicted of treachery to the standard of living. The attitude was child-like and would have been pathetic if these people had been children instead of adults in a dangerous situation.

The Australians and New Zealanders are in a situation more exposed and dangerous than almost any other people of their blood. Something of England would survive as Poland has survived repeated catastrophes. The European peasant clung to his fields through the barbarian invasions and the Dark Age which followed, and somehow lived and bred to restore again his faith and culture.

But the few millions of Australians and New Zealanders might conceivably be wholly overrun, uprooted, and as

---

[2] And 72.8 per cent of South Africa's, 40 per cent of Canada's.

[3] I speak with feeling. I was roundly abused in Australia (and by men professedly expert) for writing of advancing erosion in a book published as recently as 1939. The Professor of Agriculture at Melbourne University confessed in 1944 that he had only lately begun to take erosion seriously: presumably when he was blanketed in dust blown down on Melbourne from wheat-lands hundreds of miles away.

living communities destroyed. Their future primarily depends on themselves: on their energy, their virility, on their capacity to meet their own problems according to their own needs and judgments.

Their polities must be rooted in the facts of their own situation and not in alien ideologies. They must prove all things for themselves and not as the easy tools and fools of alien purposes. Plain speaking is the merest courtesy in their case.

Their state is of extraordinary interest to all the democratic peoples. They are the most advanced in a way which has been widely thought of as social progress. They have often been posed as models, notably to the British electorate; and they have provided materially for the common man as no other people has. They have not produced the standard of living of American skilled workers; but their average standard much excels that of the "poor white" and the mass of American Negroes and Mexicans in the Southern States. They have given measures of social security which American workers lack; and an authority to Labour organizations unapproached elsewhere. These to my mind are specific goods; but they must be related to the general good of the living society and to its future as well as to its present needs. The social benefits which have been won can be retained only if the whole body remains in health. Golden eggs are not laid by a dead goose; and the Australians sometimes seem ready to cook theirs. A high standard of living is possible only with a high level of production. Men must work if they want wealth. Governments must be allowed and made to govern if there is to be good order. Moral values must count for something in public and in private life if coherent goods are to be sought. The Australian scene has all too many lessons for its neighbors; and I could not decently shirk them here.

These are my own people. I come of families which sweated to pioneer Australia and which have given more lives than most to her defense; and I claim the right of my stock to speak to her necessities.

I have known the men and women of the wide brown land: long, gaunt men who broke the soils and brought them to plow, women who bore and bred the great battle-divisions of the Australian Imperial Forces. I have seen Australians come from three years of brutal captivity and terrible labor under the Japanese, but I have never seen men who carried themselves higher as soldiers. Australia has promise of a new sort of man steeled in the task of his hard country and under his strong suns. He is meant, I believe, for greatness. But he must refuse to cower before alien superstitions and foolish or sinister temptations which would pervert and corrupt the Australia we have known. The Australian must be his own man. To be your own man, you must learn to examine your own conscience and consciousness. And that has been the effort of this passage of my book.

FIFTEEN

NEW ORDERS IN THE BRITISH

SYSTEM

INDIA is the great incalculable of the British System. There forces and passions work which no European adequately understands; and there the problem of poverty bears on all political issues as nowhere else in the world. China is poorer and the lot of her peasants harder. But in China poverty is a massive fact about which politics merely swirl. It has no practical solution in things as they are. Poverty and all the problems which come with it cannot be countered until order is sufficiently established. Poverty must be fought with adequate communications and stable currencies and markets and sufficient safety for lives and goods. These require effective government and great capital resources. But almost every social condition which China needs for progress except the industry of her people is missing.

India was in quite other state. In India under British rule the peace was kept as it had not been before in her history. Communications were developed, currencies and markets were stable, and there was a slow growth of capital and industries to relieve the pressure on the land which has constantly increased with the increasing population under the British peace.[1] India's public debt is now practically all owned in India and she has thus acquired the capital assets of "reproductive" public works originally built by British capital. Britain's remaining investment in India is not more than £250,000,000; much less than India's own investments in commerce and industry. The enormous human tide beats heavily on the country's resources: even so the level of life has been slowly rising. Famines and epidemics still follow droughts and floods and dislocations in the world economy. In 1944 and 1945 they killed their millions. But in China they could still kill their tens of millions.

The British controls in India have passed. But as they were lifted a surging tide of passions which had been controlled under the British regime was loosed. India was being swept, it seemed, not towards nationhood but into chaos.

The dissolution of India would bring down all Asia in unimaginable catastrophe. War between Hindus and Moslems would rouse all Islam and might spread through Southern and Southeastern Asia. It would pile horror on horror in the waste of provinces and cities. The outer world in some way or other would have to intervene, and there would be much fishing in troubled waters. From India, as from China, could rise the world-crisis.

---

[1] During War II India was able to build hundreds of vessels and to repair nearly 40,000,000 tons of shipping. She provided over 100,000 miles of cotton cloth to the Allied Forces, produced 1,500,000 tons of steel a year. She supplied to the United States Forces in India materials to the value of $516,720,000.

By May 1947, this was at last clear to those in India and Britain who had hurried on the event; but apparently the resources of the doctrinaires were exhausted. It was left to Mountbatten (by a pretty historical irony, a great-grandson of Queen Victoria, Empress of India) to produce a plan. The British Prime Minister evidently had several fingers in it. It bears some marks of Attlee's character as the perfect chairman. But Mountbatten first had to catch the hare. His task when he took office was to find a method of transferring all power to the Indian Legislature within the fourteen months which the British Government had set as a term to its own authority. Mr. Churchill thought the task impossible in the time; and as Mountbatten came to office it seemed that reason and order would be drowned in a blood bath. But he swept aside all barriers between himself and the Indian leaders. In a few weeks he had produced a plan. and brought seeming irreconcilables to agreement on it. At the least calculation, it was a brilliant *tour de force;* it may prove immeasurably more.

Mountbatten shaped his plan within the terms of the British Commonwealth, with Dominion status for each of two great hostile groups. It revealed that the hope for peace and for some measure of community in India was still within the broad and generous frame of the Commonwealth concept. Whether it endures or not, the Plan reveals the peculiar genius of a System which seems beside all other polities vague and intangible, but which yet can restore order in chaos and raise men to new perceptions of their responsibilities.

The shape of the Fourth British System must wait on events in India. If the two new Dominions remain within the Commonwealth (the choice is with themselves) as freely co-operating nations, the Fourth British System will offer to the world a great instance and example of political sanity and wisdom; and Mountbatten's plan will seem one of history's shrewdest strokes. For if the Commonwealth can continue as a free fellowship of Hindus, Moslems, Australians, Canadians and the rest it may open the real road to a world order. The appointment of Ministers for Commonwealth Relations by both Dominions (they were thus the first to follow this British precedent) was a happy portent. The Commonwealth can aid the Indian peoples, and the Indian statesmen can bring new values and perspectives to the Commonwealth.

* 2 *

While the old Empire was passing in Asia, the British were turning more attention to Africa. The Colonial Empire in Africa had little public notice until World War II. It had mostly been acquired in the late 19th century and first opened by the Chartered Companies; and though Kenya had been discovered by several women novelists, few Englishmen could have placed Nigeria, Uganda, or the Tanganyika Territory on a blank map.

Sierra Leone was purchased from native chiefs to establish a settlement for freed slaves (and especially for Negroes who had served with the British in the American Revolution); and Gambia comes from the old trading-posts established in Charles II's reign, the great creative period of the Second Empire. But the vast West African territory of Nigeria came to the Crown only in 1900, twelve years after the Royal Niger Company was chartered.

Nigeria is one-third the size of India; larger than Spain and France combined. Its history for its first twenty years as Crown Colony and Protectorate is largely the achievement of Frederick Lugard who broke the immemorial slave-traffic and built the base and frame of the political economy.

In East Africa, the British established in 1884 a protectorate in Somaliland, at the northeast corner of Africa where the Red Sea comes to the Indian Ocean. In 1888, a British East Africa Company was chartered to acquire by lease the mainland properties of the Sultan of Zanzibar. The British Government had refused his offer of the Tanganyika area; but when the Germans laid claim to it, the Company was allowed to acquire the area north of it which is now Kenya Colony. The Crown took it over in 1905. Uganda to the east was acquired by the Company in 1890 to keep the Germans from the sources of the Nile and the influence control of them would give in the politics of Egypt and the Sudan. The Crown reluctantly took Uganda into its charge four years later.

German Southwest Africa was captured in a brief campaign by General Botha and his South Africans in 1915. Smuts with British and South African troops conquered German East and German West Africa. South Africa received German Southwest Africa in mandate; France, the Cameroons; and Britain, Togoland in the West, and in the East the Tanganyika Territory to form a bloc with Kenya and Uganda. These three in East Africa, Nigeria in the West, and the Rhodesias are the massive elements of the Colonial Empire in Africa; and with them the United Kingdom now proposes to launch a new phase and effort of the British System.

Kenya and Southern Rhodesia, which has long been in all but name a Dominion, have considerable white populations. But the effort now is to bring the Africans to their full stature as partners in the Commonwealth.

The Fourth British Empire will probably have as one great character the development of tropical regions. The British have created a Colonial Development and Welfare Fund which is to spend £120,000,000 by 1955 on health and education and services for agriculture, forestry, livestock, game, fisheries, and secondary industries, on rural development, communications, water control and irrigation, on marketing, housing, and loans to local authorities.

In June 1947, the Government of the United Kingdom announced the creation of a Colonial Development Corporation with an initial authority to spend £100,000,000 on projects to increase colonial production and the facilities necessary to it: roads, railways, markets, research stations, and the rest.

The Corporation is to do for the Colonies much that the Marshall plan implies for Europe. It is not to create a monopoly, but to encourage and assist local enterprise and provide conditions to attract private initiatives and capital.

The greatest part of its effort will be chiefly in the African colonies where a generation or more of settled administration has established the political and social order and machinery necessary to social and economic growth.

British Colonial Officers have worked patiently for these conditions. They can only come slowly; and for many years the British may have to plow back proceeds of their investments and be prepared to increase their stake. But this is the way in which the System grows. India showed little profit for many generations. Some petty profits are taken from local trades. But the real wealth of the British System has come from long, slow, careful cultivation of resources, human and material.

The fact that Britain in the difficulties of 1947 could turn again to a gigantic enterprise of the sort is token of her persistent virility. The new Corporation is in the grand style: a renewal of the Imperial effort which has sown half the world with British ideas, money, and values and spread the reign of British order in every continent.

It should not, one hopes, be necessary to explain how men and money can be provided for enterprise of the sort while Britain's domestic difficulties seem extreme. Britain's poverty is chiefly in dollars. If she could use her own money or sell enough of her goods in the United States she could spend freely there. In the Colonies, she does not need dollars and their economies will grow on imports from the United Kingdom: of British machinery and manufactures.

The possibilities have long been foreseen. General Baden-Powell, the founder of the Boy Scouts, once put them thus (the imaginative response to shirtings is exceedingly British):

"It has been said that in Africa two-thirds of the natives are unclothed and one-third half-clothed, and that it is England's mission to clothe the half-clothed and half-clothe the unclothed. Even a rough statistical estimate of the number of yards of grey shirtings and other mysterious cloths of commerce needed for such a purpose would far and away outrun the capacities of all the mills of Lancashire and India combined. It has also been asserted that if these many millions or even any large proportion of them could be prevailed upon to wear flannel next the skin Australian squatters no less than Bradford manufacturers would have unprecedented cause for rejoicing."

The basic fact of colonial enterprises is that they can be substantially profitable only if the colonial standard of life is raised. In spite of all the talk of exploitation the British have not merely mined their colonies. They have made of moneyless peasants and hunters moneyed customers. The British System has grown on principles true for any market. You cannot sell your products unless the customer can buy; and, as Henry Ford observed, the producer's normal interest is to promote the purchasing power of the market.

West Africa provided about 165,000 men to the Services in War II; East Africa raised over 200,000 men. The development of East and West Africa as Allied bases quickened the tempo of social and economic change. In the

Services and civil life large numbers were trained as crafts-men or clerks or transport drivers. The British program is designed to employ their new skills.

The mass of Africans remain on the land. The peasant, like his fellow in most Asian areas, has immemorially been oppressed by debts; and the first problem of agrarian policy is to free him from a system which has eaten all his usufruct. The social advantages of peasant proprietorship have been preferred by the Colonial Administrations to the conveniences and quick profits of mass-employment on large estates; but the peasant requires a slow and painstaking process of education in methods of cultivation and soil conservation.

The soils of Africa have suffered extensively from primitive methods of agriculture. Erosion and exhaustion of the land become urgent problems with the rapid rise in population. In East Africa the population pressure on the land is already excessive. Light industries and services must be developed to relieve it. The African tradesman has begun to hold his own in spite of competition in East Africa from Indian immigrants. New towns with their crafts and markets must be brought to being in the British program; and the Rhodesias are giving the lead.

There are new political difficulties. The Indians in East Africa under Congress influence have agitated for years on the drearily familiar lines; and their sound and fury have reverberations among the half-educated African "intelligentsia." Askaris returning from the wars and accustomed to Service rations and equipment and a widened view of the large world are often restive in their villages. The Government is drawing Africans into the administration as fast as they can be trained and used. The bases of the Legislatures are being broadened. But much must wait on education and economic growth with local revenues enough to provide adequately for social services.

Political advance must not be pressed too far ahead of social progress. In regions where the schools have worked outside the prevailing social pattern, the literate or semi-literate has too often become a mere misfit, a nuisance to himself and an object of hostility to his fellows. The functionless *babu* of any breed rapidly becomes a malcontent. Peoples cannot be carried overnight from a tribal or pre-tribal life into the modern world; and their education should be designed within the orderly growth of their communities and not to the prescriptions of a European or American school-system. The British have gone too fast in many colonial areas, attempting to telescope into one generation an advance that elsewhere has needed centuries. Moral and intellectual confusion inevitably follows the impact of Western life on the static cultures of Africa and Asia. Cushions are needed. The backward peoples must be equipped for new roles in an advancing world. But they must not be forced (any more than children) to responsibilities they cannot meet and into political controversies they do not understand.

The essential problem is to build bridges from the minds of the native peoples to the modern world, and to bring to them meanings and moral values which will sustain their lives and societies as their own traditional beliefs, superstitions, and modes decline under Western influences.

The peoples of Africa and the Pacific and of much of Asia had lived time out of mind by customs and beliefs which enclosed the individual and the society but also sustained them. Men were begotten, born, lived, married, died within the antique patterns which embraced their whole world-view. When these are broken the whole shape of life dissolves. It loses values, meanings, sanctions, and leaves the man literally demoralized. He cannot be restored to moral and intellectual order by a course in the three R's or a job in a garage. His naked soul must find new binding-cloths, new sense, new meaning. His life must find new compass and new reference; and time must be allowed.

Religion has here a vital role. As Lugard (speaking from an incomparable experience of Africa) said, the missionaries could do more for its development, even in mundane affairs, than any other agency: for they could provide an essential cement and they could build bridges for the native mind. They could bring to Animists obsessed with tabus and superstitions the fundamental concepts which have given to Western man his belief in his personal responsibility and power. Without it, talk of democratic systems is the merest nonsense. Without belief in the dignity and value of his own personality, man is fit only to be the slave of arbitrary power and of superstition. We can recognize among ourselves the consequences when that belief declines in the cultures it created. We must see that Western dominion is justified in the outer reaches only when it carries to them the best that it has; and its best has been in its great sense that man comes from the Hand of his Creator a being responsible and free.

The notions of trusteeship defined in the United Nations Charter, the goals of development and welfare to which the British by statute commit their colonial policy have sense only in the fundamental context from which they derive. Loss of this basic belief is the major danger now not only to the dominion put out by Western man but to Western man himself, to his own cultures, civilization, and life.

* 3 *

While Britain makes this new effort across Middle Africa from east to west, the future part of South Africa in the Commonwealth is still unsure. Some Boers of the Nationalist Party came into World War II reluctantly, and perhaps they might not have come at all but for the determination and influence of Smuts.

Smuts became a legend while still an active politician. He seemed to some the indispensable link between South Africa and the Commonwealth. South Africans of British stock were inclined to mutter, "After Smuts, the deluge." In his own country and before the world, Smuts became the chief interpreter of the Commonwealth Idea. No man has expressed it better than he, as at New York in 1946: [2]

"Britain and the other Dominions are not a bloc of states pledged to follow common policies. Nor are they a group in which the most important member—Britain—dominates the others. They are all free sovereign states, all equal in status, each with full power to determine its own policy and destiny. Their common bond is the common crown or king, who is in fact the hereditary president of a number of sovereign democracies. They meet for common consultation without being bound to follow any resolutions taken, and recognize therefore no right of veto. They need not even support each other in war, as the recent case of Ireland has shown.

"But under the common king they cannot go to war with each other without secession from the Commonwealth. As co-members of the Commonwealth, there is therefore perpetual peace among them. They follow their own fiscal and economic policies, which show wide differences. But all follow certain fundamental principles of government which, as copied from their practice, have been largely embodied in the Atlantic Charter. Here is therefore an entirely new phenomenon in human government, quite unlike the old empires or the newer federations of today. Safeguarding as it does both the sovereign freedom of its members and peace among them, it is the most novel and unique experiment in constitutions ever made. And this unique system is not a vision in cloudland but an actually existing working system which has survived the storms of an era, in which great empires have foundered.

[2] At the annual Forum conducted by the *New York Herald Tribune*, 1946.

"Nor was it planned by constitutional lawyers or theorists, but has grown up empirically in the constitutional practice of a free group, which lies scattered over all continents and among diverse races of men. It is the most interesting, if not the most promising, evolution yet seen in the constitutional relations of large masses of mankind.

"It is a freer and looser system than the American Federal Union, but likewise preserves internal peace and fundamental principles of government.

"It is much closer and more effective than the Pan-American Union. It is not so tight as the Soviet Union, which is dominated by the most powerful member of the U.S.S.R. It is unique in its combination of the freedom of its members with the peace and security of the whole. Perhaps it points to the type of government which will best suit the twin ideals of freedom and peace for which mankind is undoubtedly making."

But over against Smuts and those who think with him in South Africa stand Malan and the Nationalists with their demand for a republic and their determination to restore the unqualified supremacy of the Afrikaans culture and language and of the Afrikaner. The Boers have much the tenacity and toughness of the French Canadians, but unlike the French Canadians they outnumber their British compatriots.

Both Boers and British have in South Africa a problem paralleled only in one or two of the Southern States of the U.S.A.: they are a minority in a population predominantly Negro. But the population also includes large communities of Asiatics, mostly Indians and Malays.

The Boers' corporate loyalties are strengthened by their general determination to stay on top of this human pile.

The Nationalists' dislike of the British connection derives in part from British interventions on behalf of the colonial races. The Nationalists insist like many Southerners that they be left alone to manage their difficulties in their own fashion.

If they could be sure that they would be left alone, many Boers might be willing to leave the British Commonwealth tomorrow; and if the Nationalists come again to power we may expect a formal declaration for a republic, perhaps on Mr. de Valera's model. But a special relation with the British System will almost certainly remain. Botha and Smuts may have provided the essential links in the generation after the Boer War. But history (as the Field Marshal has well understood) has steadily been forging others; and some are in South Africa's necessities.

At the Assembly of the United Nations in the fall of 1946 the Indian delegation made bitter protest at the treatment of South Africa's Indian minority. The South Africans, whatever the justice of the issues, have raised enemies against them in Asia who may make formidable trouble. Further indication of it appeared at the Assembly when the Indian delegation with Russian support led the opposition to South Africa's request that the mandated territory of Southwest Africa become a province of the Union.[3] The Russians had remembered that the Boers have been long and bluntly hostile to Communism and stiffly attached to their ancient faith and traditions. But the attitude of the United Nations Assembly was a sharp reminder to the Boers that they might yet need good friends in the outer world. The Nationalists could threaten to withdraw South Africa from the United Nations if they came to power; but they could not promise to withdraw it from a difficult and dangerous world however much the old farmers of the veldt might have considered that a consummation devoutly to be wished.

South Africa cannot afford even to withdraw her commerce from the world. It is chiefly with the British Com-

[3] The Russians' attitude, in view of their performance in Lithuania, Estonia, Latvia, Poland and elsewhere, seemed somewhat inconsistent.

monwealth and predominantly with the United Kingdom. Nor can the Nationalists wholly ignore the English-speaking population which is still warmly attached to the British connection. It is true that many South Africans of British stock incline to the Boer attitude on racial questions. It is equally true that the Boers cannot sit forever on that seething cauldron.

Taking one thing with another, the Nationalists in power would probably be much more restrained than their vocal efforts out of power suggest. Their wing of Boer opinion had power before, with Hertzog's Afrikaner Party which found the Statute of Westminster, the reduction of the Union Jack in a new flag, and the appointment of a local Governor-General sufficient to its *amour-propre*. A Nationalist Government might think some further political gesture necessary or desirable; but the basic realities of the System are not in political gestures. The South Africans need the frame of the Commonwealth as they have never needed it before. Their more hard-headed men understand that very well. Smuts has pointed it for them:

"It is said that of the Big Three the British group is not the equal of the other two in respect of war potential. Even if this should be so, it does not tell the whole story. True, it has not the vast economic and industrial resources of the United States of America, nor the immense continuous land-mass and defensive position of the U.S.S.R.

"But it has something no less valuable and precious in what is essential to world power. It has the large background of history, the maturity of outlook and purpose, the long experience of human government in all parts of the world, the practical acquaintance with human nature in its political aspects, in short the know-how in running world affairs. It has a certain moral quality which its critics deride but is none the less real. These imponderables weigh up against very heavy assets of a more tangible character."

But if South Africa needs the Commonwealth, the Commonwealth also needs South Africa. The way by Good Hope is essential to its communications when the Mediterranean and Suez route is closed or seriously threatened as it was for three years in World War II. The British forces in the Middle East were strengthened and supplied by the routes about the Cape from 1940 until we had cleared the Mediterranean. The routes from Britain to India, Burma, Malaya and China were protected from the naval bases at Simonstown and Port Elizabeth and the new yards at Durban. South Africa is an essential link between Australia, New Zealand and their European allies and markets; the three Southern Dominions may yet together have to keep a rendezvous with history.

As the Fourth British System begins to appear we can now detect one element in marked contrast with the Third System. The Third System revealed between the wars strongly centrifugal tendencies. Even so, it came to the Second War in unity and fought to the end without any serious departure from its common purpose and effort. But in the Fourth System, as it enters a world grown very small and dangerous, the interests of the Commonwealth are working for stronger ties. The forces are not centripetal. But they are no longer centrifugal. They are working through the pattern with new threads.

We cannot say that the new Dominions in India or the Union of South Africa will stay in the Commonwealth. But in 1947 their collaboration seemed more likely than in 1946 and much more likely than in 1945.

If the Commonwealth survives it will grow, and it will take new shapes and forms. The Fourth System cannot wear the slough of the Third.

It will not grow a new central authority. This was the reject of the Third System.[4] Its instruments of authority and responsibility must be distributed, not centralized. It must produce political and social relations of a sort new to the world. If it succeeds we shall have seen some real advance towards a world society; which can come only with the increase of organic community.

[4] For motions toward centralization in the Third Empire, see Appendix, Note 5, page 396.

SIXTEEN

THE POPULATION PROBLEM

AS isolated units, the various countries of the British Commonwealth would become second-rate and third-rate powers. All, including the United Kingdom, gain much of their strength and influence from their general system: from the pool of experience and skills as well as from material resources.

This is immediately evident in matters of defense. In both World Wars, each member of the Commonwealth has been able to draw on a world-wide system for its resources, and its men and material have moved on a world-wide frame of bases and communications. Sea-power, in Bacon's phrase, made it possible for them to take as much of the war as they would.

The new techniques of war do not diminish the strategic strength of the System. They increase it. Modern war demands the distribution of industries and populations. The

British Commonwealth and Empire is of major Powers the most widely distributed.

The possibility of war with long-range rockets is not infinitely remote. The distribution of its sites about the world would give the British System an obvious advantage. The Government of Ruritania contemplating a surprise attack on London might hesitate if it had to expect in return rockets from the directions of Bulawayo, Sierra Leone, Alice Springs, Edmonton, and the Scilly Isles.

The development of rocket-ranges in the empty desertlands of Central Australia is a combined project; and the Staffs of all the Commonwealth countries are now in close and constant consultation.

Modern war, which tends to sweep about the world, requires forces highly trained for every sort of climate and condition. The Commonwealth has vast empty areas most suitable for training, from the Canadian Arctic to the sand and stone deserts of Central Australia and the jungles of Africa and New Guinea. In World War II, the Empire Air Training Scheme functioned as one great school from Saskatchewan to Rhodesia for air-crews from all parts of the British System.

In another major war, the United Kingdom might find the training of her Forces within the narrow island extremely difficult. Already the Forces, especially the Naval and Air Forces of the Commonwealth, have much co-ordinated training. The methods obviously will be developed.

Modern war requires an immense variety of materials; all of consequence except oil are abundant in the Commonwealth or Empire, and conceivably oil will be found in one or other region where the search is being pressed. The Commonwealth has a large proportion of the world's known uranium.

Distribution of essential industries is the first defense against the new weapons. Four of the Commonwealth countries have already highly developed heavy industries. A co-ordinated program is technically feasible and militarily desirable. But a planned expansion of the industries essential for defense will require a planned distribution of skilled manpower.

The population and migration questions are immediately relevant; and they are the crux of much else.

* 2 *

The Dominions all need population urgently to exploit their present opportunities. South Africa needs more white population in face of its color problem. Australia and New Zealand need it as a condition of survival.

The United Kingdom, on the other hand, has in one view too many people. They are dangerously concentrated for the chances of modern war. They are excessively crowded for a healthy and wholesome life. They cannot all be fed even at the most meager rations from domestic food-production; and their dependence on foreign fields and harvests gives constant hostage to fortune, and creates the economic difficulties which have beset them in the post-war period. If ten million mouths could be removed from Britain there could be food and drink in abundance. But ten million mouths mean twenty million hands, mostly active; and Britain cannot export active hands unless she has compensating benefits in return.

Emigrants are usually from the young and active levels of a population. Every Western country now has to take account of its age-levels. With the increasing population of elderly and inactive people, the weight on the economically active increases. But while the Dominions are ready to welcome young Jack and Jill, they show no enthusiasm for their aged grandmothers or maiden aunts. Yet who is to provide for grandfather and grandmother if Jack and Jill depart? For the aged and sick and young must still have their sustenance from the economically active whether grandmother in her chimney-corner has it direct from the family pot or draws it in the guise of social benefits.

With these, grandma may happily imagine that she is not a burden on her Jack and Jill, but blessed by bureaucratic bounty: actually the busy Jacks and Jills are providing not only for grandmother but for the bureaucrat who takes their money to give it to her after appropriate deductions for his own provision. He may encourage grandmother and her industrious grandchildren to think of him and the State as providence. But he knows very well that if Jacks and Jills depart in considerable numbers, the dependents (bureaucrat as well as grandma) will have shorter commons.

In other words, as the State multiplies its mechanism it enmeshes more and more its active citizens.

Someone has to earn wealth enough to pay for old-age pensions and all such bounties not in themselves productive, and for the cost of administering them. As their demands increase with advancing social benefits and age-levels, more is required from the working population. The United Kingdom already lacks manpower to provide for all its needs even though the island has more people than it can feed. We seem to swim in paradox and vicious circles as soon as we touch these problems.

Though our industrial economies have produced the machine to save incalculable hours of manual labor, they have also immensely multiplied the demands on manpower. The old village communities ate from their neighboring fields, and grandmother could be fed with another potato or two in the pot. They lived in houses built to last for centuries and their furniture withstood the generations. They managed without deep drainage or electric light or buses or the vast tribes of salesmen, stenographers, and public employees we have acquired. The emigrants who peopled the new countries were chiefly supernumeraries of simple peasant populations or the unemployed of industrial slums before social controls and security pinned them down to local labor markets by unemployment relief, doles, or insurance. These may be miserable pittances, but they are enough to keep most men from the chances of going farther and faring worse.

The modern State in these and countless other ways is hostile to the migration of its manpower, and especially so when it is inflamed by militant Nationalism. Italy is a case in point. The flow of Italian emigration was checked by restrictions raised in the United States and Australia, but also by Mussolini's dislike of losing his potential bayonets. Although he could not feed them all, he wanted them under the Italian flag as servants and soldiers of his new Roman Empire. Hence his excursions into Abyssinia and North Africa. The Russians would seem to have land and men enough for reason in these matters; yet they have kept at home even a few women married to foreigners. They are reluctant to lose one woman who might bear a baby.

The new regimes in Eastern Europe are of like mind. Ireland was rebuffed when she offered to receive and feed Polish orphans. Tito does not encourage the departure of his poverty-ridden State-fodder. The Monstrous State wants all its children if only to devour them. They may before the sacrifice grow lean and hungry. But hunger will make willing soldiers for Nationalisms on the march.

This is the way the world goes; and living in it, the British also must hoard their manpower for their defense and sustenance. The Dominions should not expect the British Government to encourage emigration unless the Dominions are prepared to provide political and military and economic compensations.

As matters stand, the United Kingdom is being asked to present the Dominions with human assets which have cost much to produce and have each a high productive value (for the Dominions want no unprofitable servants).

The United Kingdom might at least begin a process of education if it hinted that, as each emigrant represents £1,000 or more in nurture, education, and capital value, it will exchange him for an appropriate quantity of wheat, meat, citrus fruits, or maybe a machine-gun.

If this seems absurd, it merely reflects the absurdities into which our world has come. Yet if any group of nations can break through the tangle of Nationalist nonsense, it should be the British Commonwealth. Certainly the Commonwealth must slash the knots of its population problem if it is not to come to an end, literally a dead end.

Two basic factors appear. The Dominions all need more people to protect and develop their great estates; and the United Kingdom would be a more comfortable place if it could send some of its people abroad and still give protection and provision to those who remained.

If methods could be found to meet this last condition, the re-distribution of population would be an evident general interest. Britain would not necessarily suffer a permanent diminution. With less pressure on her resources, her birth-rate might conceivably rise.

A British subject may remove from Birmingham to Plymouth and remain a useful member of the British community. Is it beyond the wit of man to devise a method by which he could go on to Brisbane or Bulawayo and still retain his responsibilities and privileges? Does he pass necessarily through some mysterious sea-change when he crosses the ocean? Does the man who takes a steamer instead of the Great Western Railway become a different man?

The difficulties are not in Nature, though a Christian might find in them fallen Nature and evidence of the

darkened understanding and the weakened will. Nature
does not draw the lines of frontiers or set up barriers to
pen hungry masses into overcrowded corners. Nature does
not contrive currency controls and regulations, tariffs, import and export quotas. It is even doubtful whether the
dog in the manger was behaving naturally for a dog; his
performance seems almost human. The difficulties primarily come from the exclusive political, social, and economic arrangements of the Nationalist State.

There seems little prospect even within the British Commonwealth that the National State will be absorbed into
the larger community. People who talk easily of world
government forget what is implied. The problems of the
British Commonwealth are instructive.

The redistribution of population and industry within
the Commonwealth, for which so many urgent interests
argue, would be possible only if its political structures
were transformed. If it were, for example, one single State,
it would have a single system of defense. The United
Kingdom then would not need to be concerned at a soldier
lost if a man removed from Manchester to Melbourne. In
a single State, Jack or Jill gone from London, England,
to London, Ontario, could still contribute to grandmother's
old-age pension. In a single State, Britain could move hungry mouths to the Murray Valley without losing from the
general economy the use of their hands. But what prospect is there of a single State or political economy?

One can conceive other political and economic arrangements which might meet part of these problems. The
United Kingdom could give to the Dominions a million
potential fighting-men if the Dominions would guarantee
their support in war. The United Kingdom might distribute
essential industries abroad if she could be sure of their
disposition in crisis and if she could freely draw their
profits home.

A new Commonwealth might gradually appear from special accommodations of one sort and another merging to create a new community, a new sort of supranational political economy.

Much would have to change in men's minds before we could come to it.

But if appropriate provision were made to compensate the United Kingdom for the departure of potential defenders, the practical problems of large migrations should be soluble.

Several millions of men were moved overseas in each year from 1942 to 1946. One million people could be moved from Britain in each of ten or fifteen years.

The capital investment would be colossal: perhaps a third of the cost to the Commonwealth of World War II. But it would have return, an economic and human increment. It would not go to death, waste, and destruction.

Paper plans are easy. They do not have to contend with stubborn soils and tempers, prejudices and special interests. But let us assume for purposes of provocation that the politicians, public servants, trades unionists, employers and the peoples generally of the British Commonwealth were prepared like Descartes to face *ab initio* their basic problems. We should have among the premises for a policy these considerations:

The Dominions need and could comfortably support ten or fifteen millions more people than they have. They support most of them now by shipping across oceans food to eat and raw materials to work.

The United Kingdom has to pay for much of this supply by frenzied efforts to produce and market exports enough or by raising credits. Her loans and credits in countries which will not buy her goods to cover them are unredeemable. If we were squarely facing realities (often a salutary exercise) we would recognize and call them gifts.

If ten or fifteen millions of people were moved from the United Kingdom as families or social groups (carrying their young and old, their social responsibilities) the remainder could make do fairly well on home production and the imports they could afford.

The millions gone abroad would enrich the Dominions, which all need more minds and muscles to develop their resources.

The emigrants would reinforce markets where Britain has always found *per capita* its best customers.

Ships would have to be provided, and many specially built; but the British shipbuilding industry is a national asset and money spent on ships is well spent.

Vast housing schemes would be needed in the Dominions, because emigrants are no longer ready to make do with tents or huts. But houses usually bring back their price and more, in rent and purchase and in human values. Moreover, an active building program stimulates the whole economy, for its ramifications reach into scores of industries; and housing is the best counter economically and morally to slumps and depressions.

Money spent on ships and houses mostly goes into the pockets of workers, contractors, manufacturers and back to the Treasury in taxation.

The immigrants must have jobs, so capital would be required for land, factories, machines, roads, railways and all the developments necessary to an expanding economy. The initial outlay would be huge, but most would be productive, and capital would flow with the people and to the prospects of profitable investment they would create.

Though the Dominions might have to increase their national indebtedness considerably they would be increasing the population which bears it and developing the wealth to meet it.

A program of this general character is not beyond all reason. The United States grew as rapidly through decades of the 19th century; and although no Dominion has the natural resources of the United States, they all have technical means which the 19th century lacked.

The great difficulties are not material, in fact. They are in the minds and wills of men. The Dominions want only young people (and they want only their own selection of them). They suffer in this from a penny-wise delusion; because the workman with his established family and responsibilities is a better social buy than a youngster on the loose. The trades unions are afraid that immigrants take jobs from the native labor, forgetting that jobs multiply in an expanding economy. The British Government is aware that its elaborated machinery of social services and administration might be seriously dislocated by large population movements. British Labour would be reluctant to see a subtraction from its strength in the electorates and in trades unions. British employers would resent the loss of workers and local customers however straitened. All the mesh of Nationalist feelings and interests vested or in shirt-sleeves would resist. The thing could be done only slowly and quietly; and it would need a development of political relations and machinery of which there is yet little promise.

But some political development is necessary if the Fourth British System is to survive: and it will need to be a new growth, though rooted in the living experience and precedents of the Commonwealth.

SEVENTEEN

THE FOURTH BRITISH SYSTEM:

THE POLITICAL PATTERN

POLITICAL development within the Commonwealth cannot be an abrupt departure from the living System. It must meet the conditions which are still vital in men's minds and it must not overset or gravely dislocate the existing orders. It must accept the principle of growth and avoid the mechanists' delusion which drew into the blueprints for the League and United Nations evident and fatal flaws.

The essential point of this book is that the British Commonwealth is a Society of Nations which has worked: a visible instance. It represents the only practical experience men have had of an enduring and peaceful association among sovereign states. As a working model it should be developed for the further instruction and experience which the world needs in supranational organization.

The problem of the Commonwealth, like the problem of the world at large, is to reconcile a supranational community with the existing facts of national and racial loyalties. Power is distributed among sovereign governments. A few might willingly surrender sovereignty to some sort of federal arrangement. But no one can seriously think that the Kremlin or the mass of Americans would enter a World State in which they would be small minorities, and submit their economic and social systems to its governance. Would Americans accept even a customs union or the abolition of restrictions on immigration? Yet these would be conditions of a World State in any serious sense.

Movement towards world organization must work within the possible. Time and growth may transform the facts and produce new possibilities. But prevailing facts must be recognized if only to deal properly with them.

So we must recognize the fact of many centers of local power. An attempt to create a single center of sovereign authority merely invites nations and blocs to struggle for its controls, and to seek in precautions like the veto protection for their autonomy. This is still humanly inevitable, as every American will recognize who would not have his tariffs thrown down and his national income pooled with the world's for the taxation purposes of a World State. The World State would have to accept a thousand millions of impoverished Asiatics as citizens of equal status with the rest. It would have to make equal provision for them in its social services and its franchise. They would dominate any representative assembly elected on a democratic basis. In a World State the one alternative to a democratic method would be dictatorship by the more powerful elements: an empire of the old and more sinister sort. In either shape, a World State would have to undertake the social and economic elevation of the African and Pacific peoples and of the poverty-trodden masses of eastern Europe. Its wealthier citizens would have to find the funds as in any other political economy.

Plainly, we cannot hope for a World State until we have sufficiently developed a world economy; and until the general level of income can provide for the essential services of a State. This is true also of our working-model, the British Commonwealth; and the reason why I have argued its population and production problems before approaching the matter of political machinery.

In our stage of development, distributed power is not only inevitable but in many ways desirable. The resistance of Canada to centralization in the British Commonwealth was sound. Government should as far as possible be local in any democratic system. The effective resistance to Totalitarianism and the Monstrous State is to leave as much as possible of government to the people most concerned; and most matters which touch people in their daily lives are local matters of which they are usually better judges than some remote authority. The old local schools of Scotland and the English grammar schools have not been surpassed in the national systems. The wider interests of communities must, of course, be met by wider authorities, and some needs of the community as a whole must be governed by the political machinery which expresses the general will and which we call the State. But democratic method requires the distribution of powers and responsibilities as they can be best ordered and directed and controlled by the people. We must accept Canada as the judge of Canada's specific interests even if we think her judgments mistaken specifically. We must accept a town meeting in Ridgefield, Conn., as better instructed than a bureaucrat at Washington in the local needs of Ridgefield. The bureaucrat may be letter-perfect in the social requirements of all the Ridgefields; he may know (he will probably believe that he does) better than themselves what is good for them. But a healthy democratic system will not function unless the people of Ridgefield are themselves convinced. It is better that the inhabitants of Ridgefield make their own mistakes on their own responsibility than that they should be dragooned. The higher authority should see that Ridgefield's mistakes do not injure neighbors who have no responsibility for them.

The democratic pattern is ultimately one of personal and community decisions and responsibility. It assumes that men are free and responsible beings, competent to shape their lives to proper ends. It recognizes that they make mistakes and that they are sometimes vicious. It recognizes Original Sin; and we have yet to see the philosopher-king or enlightened bureaucrat who can counter that. It knows that all men are often fools and sometimes knaves; and that we do not work in a medium of perfection or of perfectibility. But it still insists that each man has a unique personal value and personal rights and responsibilities. It is in fact the political expression of the Christian Idea of Man. It rises and falls with the rise and fall of Christian belief.

Totalitarianism grows with the invasion by the Great State of the proper responsibilities of the lesser societies, political, economic, social, and religious. It has its opportunity in their abdication of their proper responsibilities; and when the sense of man as a free but responsible being declines. The complexity of modern life and the interdependence of communities favors both processes. But the new conditions must be reconciled with a sturdy assertion and acceptance of local rights and personal duties if democracy is to persist in tomorrow's world. The local and personal interest must also accept the common good: as the national interest must at last accept the universal good. The effort to find the proper balances and proportions in all these relations is the fundamental and crucial problem of politics. They can, of course, be found only in judgments instructed by the general interests of men, by all the sciences, including the moral sciences.

This instructed judgment now reveals common interests in the British Commonwealth which need political expression: the problems revealed by the sciences concerned with population, production, consumption, health, military defense and the rest.

Consider health as an example. When travel was slow and difficult and medical science not much advanced, the sovereign state did not recognize its interest in health conditions beyond its own frontiers. But now influenza caught in London may be spread from sneezes the next evening in New York; and plague may travel from Karachi to Sydney by air in two days. Clearly interest requires the nations to co-ordinate health measures. But arrangements for health or any other matter between sovereign states require a political frame: they inevitably touch at some point on political policy and require political machinery.

The British Commonwealth (as distinct from its several members) has always tried to meet its problems as they arise and *ad hoc*. It has created machinery only when it was needed. It has not elaborated its political machinery because its Governments have generally concurred in matters of high policy and political principles; and when these have had to be defended they have moved together to defend them, creating again *ad hoc* the machinery for the occasion. This has been an admirable method because it has always resisted machinery for machinery's sake and acted only when the general will demanded action.

Now it is faced by new conditions and necessities which demand new machinery, including new political machinery; for the great questions of defense and population now emerging can be answered successfully only in long, clear, and coherent programs involving political policy at the highest levels. A new political frame has at last become essential.

Yet, let me repeat, it must conform to the conditions prescribed by Mackenzie King and Smuts, because these statesmen are speaking not from their personal whims but for the living context of the System.

Mackenzie King's insistence on the autonomy of each member has been developed by Smuts to the concept of leadership by each member of the team in regions of its special interests. Thus Australia and New Zealand have special interests in the Pacific, South Africa in its continent, Canada in the Americas. Smuts conceived that each Dominion should accept sympathetically the special interests of others and give (though not with formal obligations) its moral support. Dr. Evatt of Australia took the theme further but also brought it round. "An entirely new concept," he said in March 1946, "of British Commonwealth relations is emerging which tends to reconcile the autonomy of the Dominions with full co-operation within the Commonwealth, and envisages the possibility of the Dominions acting on behalf of all other members of the British Commonwealth. This principle suggests the possible integration of British Commonwealth policy at a higher level."

One Government or local center of authority might thus represent the general will of the Commonwealth (or the world): acting for the whole and aware that it may draw on the support of the whole. The community elects one of its members to fulfill a special charge; he may, if necessary, call out the posse.

This is a familiar phase in the growth of all democratic communities; a primitive phase, if you like. But the international community does not escape the principles of growth and development which govern all social life. We cannot manufacture an international community any more than the 16th century could manufacture the 20th century or

the Vigilantes of early California construct to a blueprint
the social organization of the present San Francisco.

This is the lesson men must learn before they can come
to world order; which can only be an expression of their
moral state and develop with their moral effort.

Evatt's concept has obvious implications. If one Government is to act for many, it must have the best means possible for exchanging information with them, for discussion,
consultation, and development of common policies and the
general will.

The existing machinery is inadequate. The press of problems in the modern world will not be met by meetings of
Prime Ministers at odd or occasional intervals. The problems flow in an unbroken stream: they cross and intercross
and shuffle in a continuum, one merging with another.

The exchange of information and views must be constant. Representatives must sit together watching, working, talking, arguing. Policy must be in a constant process
of distillation from the application of principle to the stream
of facts and interpretations. But it must always be related
to the special, local, regional interests of particular Governments.

Each Government thus needs at its center of authority the
opportunity for constant consultation with its fellows; with
agents or representatives especially alive to the local Government's interests and problems, but bringing to bear upon
them the interests of their own Governments to produce
agreements which balance the special interests with the
common good.

Australia, as an example, must shape its policy in the
Pacific to its essential interests of survival; but one condition of its survival is the support of its friends and allies.
Therefore its policy must have room also for their interests
and for the provisions which secure their support.

An apt illustration appeared with the Occupation of

Japan. The Australian representative with General Mac-Arthur was also the representative of the British Commonwealth. The Commonwealth Occupation Force composed of Australian, New Zealand, Indian, and British troops was a single command.

The United Kingdom, however, sought no similar arrangement in Germany, Italy, or Austria; and this was extremely curious. The Occupation had borne heavily on the United Kingdom's resources of men and material and even on her own domestic food-supply (bread-rationing in Britain in 1946 was necessary to meet the demands of the British Zone in Germany). The Forces and resources of the Commonwealth might well have been asked to contribute more and to share the responsibilities and consequences of policy: especially as the fantastic program which emerged from the Yalta and Potsdam Conferences was certain to sow the German fields with dragon's teeth.

But the United Kingdom was maneuvered into a false position at the Big Three Conferences. The Commonwealth had stood to her from the beginning. She should have insisted that the Commonwealth be represented. The Dominions could hardly be expected to share the responsibilities of a German and European policy which had been shaped without them; whether by the neglect of the United Kingdom Government or pressure from the other Two. Their natural resentment was expressed in the Canadian House of Commons on the 4th March 1947. Canadian Forces had shared in the Occupation of Germany until mid-1946. Mr. St. Laurent said that they were withdrawn because Canada had been "left out" by the Big Three. "We were told," he said, "by the Great Powers that there would be three Zones; that there would be a fourth, if France wanted one: but that there were not to be any others. I suppose the Russians might perhaps have accepted our co-operation. The French might have accepted our co-operation. The United States might have accepted our co-operation. The United Kingdom might have accepted it. But we would not have had any Occupation Force of ours taking any separate part in legal occupation of Germany."

Canada evidently desired her own separate zone and responsibilities; but she might have accepted the arrangements like those by which Belgium and Holland contributed to the Occupation Forces.

If the whole matter had been handled with more discretion from Yalta or before, Canada might have continued with a Commonwealth Force or a Commonwealth-United States Force in the combination of the actual campaigns. But the thing does not seem to have been attempted; and in the event, both the United Kingdom and the United States have carried burdens which they might have shared with the virile Dominions if they had been sufficiently sensible of the Commonwealth relationship.

Russian influence explicit or implicit was largely responsible for the neglect of the Dominions. This appeared clearly with the drafting of the European Treaties. The Russians then proposed to allow a larger part to countries like Albania, Luxembourg and their own constituents, the Ukraine and White Russia, than to Dominions which had contributed vastly more to the German defeat [1] than any but two or three European countries.

Before the Moscow Conference of March 1947, Australia took up the problem again, and proposed that the United Kingdom and the Dominions should appear there as a team whose spokesmen would represent the general views of all the Commonwealth Governments. But the proposal died.

We can recognize what might be called a lack of energy in the United Kingdom attitude. Fearful, perhaps, of cries

---

[1] And to Russia, as St. Laurent pointed out, Canada gave war supplies valued at $167,000,000.

against "a British bloc" in the United States and Russia, it allowed diplomatic wedges to be driven between the Dominions and itself. The process has weakened also America's position in the world; for the British Commonwealth is a great stay of order.

British Governments are timid in pressing the Dominions to co-operation. But they should not have been timid in demanding effective Dominions representation at major conferences. It was not Britain (though she made the greatest effort and suffered the most) which held the Axis pinned in 1940-1941. It was the British Commonwealth. The Dominions in both wars had been the staunchest allies. As a mere matter of policy, the United Kingdom might well have fought tooth-and-nail for the Dominions' partnership with her to be carried from the battlefields to the conference tables. Mr. Churchill once declared that he had not become the King's First Minister to preside over the dissolution of the British Empire. The phrase would have kept more force if he had taken the Dominions with him to Yalta. The Labour Government was not more sensitive.[2]

Its manner at the Imperial Conference (if it could be called such) in April 1946 was depressed and depressing. It perhaps felt that little could be done to quicken Commonwealth relations while the machinery was weak; and the joint representation in Japan had not been highly successful. But the experiment in Japan was compromised from the beginning by the lack of effective means to a policy developing with the flow of events. Thus difficulties, as in the matters of Japanese whaling and phosphate-mining in Angaur, popped unexpectedly under Commonwealth noses; and far too much was made of them by novices in Canberra.

[2] I make no suggestion whatsoever against the gentlemen's capacities and merits; but it does seem a trifle curious that Mr. Attlee should in 1945 have allotted the great portfolios of Dominion Affairs and India to the elders of his Cabinet, and to the House of Lords: Lord Addison becoming 76 and Lord Pethick-Laurence 74 in the year of their appointment.

If the United Kingdom Government clearly recognized the character of these new Commonwealth arrangements, it should have pressed at the meetings of 1946 for better methods of sustained consultation.

Australia and New Zealand would surely have agreed. Field-Marshal Smuts made it clear that he did not want new methods; and Mr. Mackenzie King was presumed to take much the same attitude for Canada. But the 1946 Conference agreed that some matters might concern only two or three of the Governments; and that these could be developed among them.

An evident instance is the South and West Pacific areas, where the interests of the United Kingdom, Australia, New Zealand (and the Indian Dominions, if they remain with the Commonwealth) are obviously more considerable than the interests of Canada and South Africa.

A flat declaration against centralized machinery appeared in the official statement at the end of five weeks of conversations in 1946:

"The existing methods of consultation have proved their worth. They include a continuous exchange of information and comment between the different members of the Commonwealth. They are flexible and can be used to meet a variety of situations and needs, both those where the responsibility is on one member alone and where the responsibility may have to be shared.

"They are peculiarly appropriate to the character of the British Commonwealth, with its independent members, who have shown by their sacrifices in the common cause their devotion to kindred ideals and their community of outlook. While all are willing to consider and adopt practical proposals for developing the existing system, it is agreed that the methods now practised are preferable to any rigid centralized machinery.[3] In their view such centralized machinery would not facilitate, and might even

[3] In other words, the British countries repudiated for themselves central machinery of the sort they accepted for the world at large in the United Nations.

hamper, the combination of autonomy and unity which is characteristic of the British Commonwealth and is one of their great achievements.

"They reaffirm their belief in the efficacy of free and constant consultation and co-operation, not only within the British Commonwealth but also in the wider international sphere."

But the official statement did not propose an alternative to centralized machinery which would meet the new needs. And as Dr. Evatt pointed out, the process of decentralization is paralleled by "the almost equally important practice of integration where this is necessary for the purpose of carrying out specific functions involving all members of the British Commonwealth, for example, in such matters as telecommunications, wool disposal, and civil aviation." [4]

One can conceive of matters even more important than wool disposal which involve all members of the British Commonwealth.

The meeting convened at Canberra in August 1947 to discuss the views of the different countries on the peace treaty with Japan is a case in point. A brief, occasional conference much publicized has its uses. But time does not stop and the tempo of history now is enormously accelerated. The diplomatic methods of the 19th century can no longer pace events. The British Commonwealth and all Governments with great, common, and persisting interests should be in constant consultation. The machinery of any one Government or State would break down hopelessly if its responsible Ministers and high officials met only at long intervals and on critical occasion; world problems are not simpler than domestic issues.

We cannot hope to develop a proper flow of policy in which the interests of Governments will be always known to the others and reconciled in a coherent pattern unless there is constant exchange of views and information. This

[4] Statement of 23 May 1946.

is the first essential of united action in the world, the rudiments of any growth towards One World. The integration of Commonwealth policy among its own members and its neighbors of like mind in major matters is the only obvious line of growth now before us.

* 2 *

The alternative to the abhorred centralized machinery is already coming to being. The scheme advanced at the 1946 Conference for military links is an instance. The notion of a central imperial defense council or general staff was rejected. The Chiefs of Staffs Committee proposed instead the creation of combined Staffs in the United Kingdom and in the Dominions. Each should include officers from each country's Services, and each would be primarily concerned with the local problems; but, by the constant exchange of information and appreciations and policy proposals with the others, these would be related to all other problems and to the general interest and pattern.

In 1946, a combined Staff already existed in Australia to administer the Commonwealth and Empire Force in Japan. It was, as the London *Times* (usually very careful in these matters) suggested, adaptable to the common problems of defense in Southeast Asia and the South Pacific basin.

In Canada, a Staff of this sort would offer a potential link between the whole Commonwealth and the United States. The advantages of this to the United States would be very real; and there seems indeed no reason why consultations should not be extended to any other Power which feels that it has common objects and concern.

The United Kingdom's Chiefs of Staff are free to discuss problems and projects with their opposite numbers; it being understood that Governments are not committed. Economic and social as well as military problems and policies might be similarly examined, tested, and shaped. The

methods agree with the principles of the United Nations
and present no obstacles to co-operation in the broader
international field. They are actually essential to support
of the police-action which the United Nations may require
and which will be a necessary feature of any supranational
authority.

The methods evolved by the military staffs could be
adapted to other common concerns. They already have for
many. But as such instruments multiply, the need for more
order in them and for a frame in which they can be related
to political policy becomes urgent. They touch politics
at countless points. They provide the information in which
policy must be shaped. But only the political authority can
correlate them in the terms of national policies.

* 3 *

Consultative machinery is needed in each capital of the
Commonwealth of Nations to cover the whole range of
common themes.

The first step might be to create a portfolio of Commonwealth Affairs [5] in each Government: the precedent being
the Dominions or Commonwealth Office in the Government
of the United Kingdom. The portfolios might be conveniently held with the Prime Ministerships or the Ministries
of External Affairs if separate Cabinet Ministers were not
desired; though the press of business would be great.

The second step should be the transformation of the High
Commissionerships. The High Commissioners are appointed
by Commonwealth Governments to one another. They are
not like ambassadors accredited to the Head of the State.
They are rather agents of the Prime Ministers, and not

[5] The United Kingdom has substituted Commonwealth Relations for Dominions Affairs; Commonwealth Affairs would have been a better description if co-operation in common problems is the objective. The two Indian
Dominions have created Commonwealth Ministries.

flesh, fish, fowl or good red herring in a diplomatic sense. They cannot carry policy responsibilities unless they appear as Resident Ministers; but they could be charged to initiate and examine proposals for policy and within broad terms to conduct accepted policies. In urgent matters of great consequence, they might be supported or replaced on the occasion by their own Ministers for Commonwealth Affairs.

These High Commissioners or Ministers could in each capital form a consultative body under chairmanship of the local Minister for Commonwealth Affairs. Thus in each capital (and consistent with the principle of distribution) would appear something like a Permanent Standing Committee advisory to all the Governments: a delegate committee of the Imperial Conference.

The committees would constantly relate the flow of information to political considerations and give political guidance to the special committees and groups working under them.

These would be formed for every sort of common interest (for defense, agriculture, health, migration, education and so on). Their members would be specialist attachés to the High Commissioners with local chairmen.

Each Government would presumably provide for a suitable Secretariat; and with an interchange of members these would in fact, if not in form, evolve a Commonwealth Public Service.[6] With careers opening to broad fields of enterprise, the Public Servants would make the thing go. Commonwealth and International relations have both suffered because they were nobody's particular business or career; though within the restricted ranges where they were allowed some initiative, the officials of both the League

[6] An International Public Service will be needed for any effective World Organization: here the Commonwealth might by trial and error establish a more effective model than the Secretariat of the United Nations in its nature and limitations can hope to develop.

and the United Nations have shown what might be done with a ball set rolling.

A precedent for Inter-Dominions Secretariats has been given by the Australian-New Zealand Secretariat brought into being by the Anzac Pact.

Organization of this general character would avoid the difficulties of centralization; and its distribution, capital by capital, would be in tune with the problems of population, production, and defense which require a widely distributed mechanism. This would meet the ideas of Field-Marshal Smuts and the Australians on regional leadership: each local consultative group would be primarily concerned with the problems of its region, but always in relation to the whole.

The ultimate reference, of course, would be to the several Prime Ministers and Governments: the constituents of the Imperial Conferences.

The machinery need not lie too heavily on any one Government. It could take as much of it as it wished. Canada might not find use for some committees which would appear in Australia. The structure could be modified to local needs and preferences.

Nor need it be an exclusively Commonwealth affair. Representatives of other Powers might join at points and levels appropriate to their interests or attach observers. A committee in Australia concerned with tropical health or development might well include in one form or another spokesmen for the East Indies, the Philippines, the United States, or the British African Colonies.

The essential is to establish growing points for international co-operation wherever these are appropriate and possible.

* 4 *

A system of this sort would possess much of the institutional character of a federal system but not its central instrument. The machinery would be distributed about the several local sources of authority.

The conception is clumsy. In a rational world a common authority for common interests would appear. Mr. Lionel Curtis was (to my mind) right when he insisted that the failure of the Commonwealth Governments to develop in peace common machinery for foreign policy and defense was a cause of the World Wars. A united British Commonwealth governed by clear-headed men who understood the nature and responsibilities of world power would have produced in politics a system corresponding to the British Economic System which spread across the world. Other States and especially those already close linked with the Economic System (Belgium, the Netherlands, and the Scandinavians, for example) would have been drawn about a strong central pillar of order. A powerful group acting together could perhaps have made the League of Nations work. It might have checked Hitlerism before it grew too large. It might even have checked Hitler's course before it had begun, by facing the troubles in Germany on which he fed.

These are not unprofitable speculations; because a British Commonwealth effectively united could still be the surest guard of peace. The Americans must recognize that their interest in world order would be much better served by a strong Commonwealth than by its several States weakened in isolation. The smaller democracies throughout the world, but especially those with highly developed industrial and commercial interests, would still group about the Commonwealth if it was sufficiently charged with magnetic energy. When Mr. Bevin went to Paris in July 1947 for the first conference on the Marshall proposals, he should have appeared (on Dr. Evatt's principle) as the representative of the whole Commonwealth. But again no instrument for swift and sustained consultation was available. The Dominions undoubtedly were informed; but no coherent policy appeared.

The difficulty before and between the World Wars was largely in the Nationalistic temper of the Dominions and the excessive readiness of the United Kingdom to lump the major costs of defense. The British Government might have insisted from 1926 that equality of status meant equality of responsibility and demanded that the Dominions should contribute to the general defense in their appropriate proportions. But the issue was evaded. Perhaps Great Britain felt that the ties would not stand the strain. They have taken it in war; but the ruck of politicians in the democracies are shy of defense expenditures in peace. The bigotry of Nationalism persists in the Dominions. They will not yield yet a tittle of sovereign authority to a common creation. Their attitude is an interesting commentary on the prospects for a World State.

The Dominions might deny that their interests were, in general, common. Canada pointedly refrains from initiatives in Pacific policies although she has a longer and more vulnerable Pacific coastline than the United States. Australians feel little community of interest with South Africans.

The best we can do now is to develop the relations where common interests are recognized and trust that the sense of common interests will grow with consultation and experience and knowledge.

The System in one view might be seen as a series of concentric circles. The United Kingdom and the Colonial Empire is the innermost. The United Kingdom, Australia, and New Zealand is the next. Canada and South Africa are in another. Eire and other democracies whose political and economic interests are closely related to the British countries might appear in another.

But other circles intersect and overlap. The relations between the United Kingdom and the United States and between each and Canada all hook into one another. Each of the Commonwealth countries might provide a center of growing relations with its neighbors. We are seeking not mere machinery but growing-points of international life and order. We need not be afraid of complexity. Organic life is complex and grows by the constant multiplication of its cells. We must abandon the idea of the National States as fixed and static forms. A World Order is not to be built like a wall of separate bricks. It must grow in the terms of organic life.

This has been the lesson of the British System, and it stands in the sharpest contrast to set-pieces like the League and the United Nations.

These constructions have sometimes been compared to the creation by Constitution of the United States. But the Constitution was the political expression of a living society, of a social commonweal in being.

Political machinery does not create community. When it represents realities, it is as an expression of community, of common needs and interests understood.

Any true community must be not of the letter, but of the spirit; for the letter killeth, but the spirit giveth life. The text might have been inscribed above the meeting places of the United Nations.

EIGHTEEN

THE CONTINUATION

IF we are to grow towards a world order we must obviously encourage in every way possible the development of the world community.

A world community cannot grow in pious professions only. It requires the growth of a world economy and the extension and intensification of cultural, scientific, humanitarian, moral, and philosophic relationships. Mechanical contrivances like the United Nations are mere distractions and confusions unless there is organic growth.

The world economy must be in its primary character an open economy. It should give protection against gross exploitation to peoples economically, socially, or politically backward. But it must permit all peoples a sufficient access to world markets. It must allow for a free flow of trade and capital. It must return towards the ideal of the old free-traders. For a world economy is not compatible with a persisting conflict among the various national economies.

A world community implies a free movement and exchange of ideas, peoples, and goods. Unless we are prepared to face this evident fact it is the merest nonsense or hypocrisy to speak for One World or to expect a new international order.

Here at once appears the immensity of our real problem. I do not believe that any National State is at this moment prepared to do what must be done if we are to make a real order and a permanent peace.

Some individual politicians and many economists recognize the fundamental contradictions in our present courses. But the general body of opinion (in those countries where the public may still hold opinions) remains uninstructed even in the simple fact that a world community is inconceivable without community of social, economic, and political interests.

The growth of the modern State wars constantly against the growth of a free international order. As the National State extends its reign over life and constricts its citizens to its own service, it obviously cuts across the interests which link them with the larger world.

The British Commonwealth as distinct from its members has been a supranational organization. The major threat to it now comes from the growth of the Nationalist and Socialist State within it: for Nationalism, Socialism and all that tends to inflate the Great State is in conflict with the terms of supranational community.

In face of the political and economic prejudices and superstitions which now dominate the actual situation, the Customs Union tentatively suggested by Mr. Ernest Bevin in 1947 is not "practical politics." Yet only in a customs union or something comparable to it can a world system grow.

When Britain's overseas investments were liquidated the circulatory system of the world economy began to flag: for they were like a strong pump which in diastole and systole sucked and drove a great volume of world trade.

Somehow or other their part in the world economy has to be restored or replaced. It cannot be adequately replaced by loans or credits from the United States; for these are temporary panaceas, mere shots in the arm. They may for the moment relieve a local symptom. But the healthy flow of trade in the world can be restored only by the restoration of a steady, normal circulation. The problem now is primarily one for the United States. It has resources which Britain has expended in two wars. It has capital to export and markets and purchasing-power. It must if we are to make sense of our world now play the part which Britain played. Its particular, as well as the general, needs of the world demand this of the United States.

America must export if her export industries are not to be thrown into confusion, dislocation and unemployment. America may presently have six or seven million unemployed if her exports flag: and six or seven million unemployed mean a crisis through the whole economy. Her exports will flag unless she permits her customers to earn dollars. They cannot buy from her if she will not buy from them.

The economic key to the present distresses is as simple as that.

If America will not use that key she forces all the other peoples of what was the Western Order to desperate competition for the shrinking markets still open and to even more desperate efforts at self-sufficiency. These efforts require, as we see in Britain, social controls and disciplines of a sort which startled us in Nazi Germany, but are now become commonplace in most countries. These efforts compel Governments to the courses of National Socialism. The present bent of the Western World towards National Socialism is a far more sinister and dangerous threat to the United States than the U.S.S.R. alone could be. It threatens the United States because it threatens to Balkanize the Western World: to reduce what was a supranational economy to a group of politico-economic baronies each in conflict with the others.

As a member (and the leading and essential member) of a supranational economy and of a developing international community of nations the United States would have nothing to fear from Russia.

The West will not fall before a Russian onslaught, unless the democratic nations are corrupted from within. No great civilization in all history has fallen at the hands of a more primitive power while it was itself still sound in wind and limb. The barbarians did not break the Roman Empire. They came to loot it in its confusion, venality and corruption. The swords of its own mercenaries and hirelings were turned on it when it could no longer hold the sword or scales itself.

The West may die of its own excesses and the poison it secretes from its diseased members. It may in its weakness be struck down by its enemies. They will not attack while the West still has vigor in its limbs and faith in itself. But both are ebbing fast.

The West must be very weak before it falls; for the Russian social economy is far less strong than it seems. It is still backward and lacking in the energies of a highly developed modern community. It has not yet advanced sufficiently to break (or even much to modify) the autocracy which has ruled it for centuries from the superstition-shrouded Kremlin [1] by the instruments of secret police and standing armies. Dictatorships (whether National Socialist or Czarist) are

---

[1] The Court through several Czarist reigns was usually at Petersburg; but the Kremlin remained the symbol of power in the minds of the remote masses.

evidences of social weakness: the weakness of immaturity or of decline. Strong societies cohere by the power and energy of their common sense and common values. They do not need to dragoon and discipline reluctant or unenlightened masses or divert a large part of their manpower to police activities.

America's primary interest now is to work for the growth of a great supranational economy and community in which she can freely collaborate for their general good with all the peoples who will accept its conditions.

A free economy in the world at large is in the natural course of American expansion and tradition. It implies from the first economic collaboration with the British System and all the communities associated with it.

Elements within the British System and in the United States would, of course, oppose it: manufacturers in protected industries; trades-union leaders with their members tied to a tempo and strategy of their own. Marxists would fight, some in the invincible ignorance of their superstition, others because the bases of their growing power would be broken (and nothing else now will break them) by an open world economy. Many bureaucrats and politicians who have their fun (if they have fun) from trying to enclose all the rich life of man in their blueprints and boxes would be hostile. But their opposition would fail if America moved to her opportunity and charge. For the Open Society would mean that not only were America's economic frontiers advanced to Hudson's Bay and Cape Town and Whyalla; but that America would open her economy to a marriage with the world. The Open Society must be a fair and free trade. Economically, the peoples must be one community and they all partners in it.

The people of the United Kingdom and their Government would not refuse such a partnership if their present and prospective miseries weighed with them; and if the Government meant what it has repeatedly said of the need for world order. The Dominions, especially Australia and New Zealand, might be more resistant for they have stubborn and powerful elements bent on the destruction of economic liberties. The Australian Labour Government in August 1947 was embarked on a program of National Socialism; but the Australian people will sweep this aside if they have a clear alternative. The Pacific Dominions will in any case go much as the United Kingdom goes, unless their Governments are prepared to tear their economies apart.

The security and influence of the Dominions in the world are still much dependent on their association in the Commonwealth. Their security and influence would be enlarged in a Commonwealth and American combination.

In an Open Society, the Americans and British could freely help the Dominions to take the immigrants they need. President Roosevelt was in his last years working at a plan to settle 20,000,000 Europeans in Alaska, Canada, Australia, and South America: where they could contribute to the world's resources instead of rotting in the sullen confines of D.P. camps or dying industrial towns. The United States might profitably promote his ideas again among the community of nations, if it appears.

This (like so much else needing to be done) cannot be done by the United States alone; it does not have means enough. But it could be done in a world ordered by British and American collaboration. This could in alliance with the local Governments, economies, and peoples seriously approach the problems of areas still awaiting adequate development: Africa, the South Americas, Australasia, Northern Canada, and the incredibly rich region between Sumatra and the Solomons, Mindanao and Northern Australia. These countries and India and China could be gradually provided with the men and money needed for irrigation, soil conservation, transport and the rest.[2]

The British peoples can be shown that a combined operation now does not mean American political domination. The resources of the British Commonwealth are comparable to those of the United States. Theirs will be an equal partnership or approach it. The United States has not the resources or men to monopolize the scene. But it can set the ball rolling.

The Americans and British can save the world together. Neither can do it alone. Their success would demonstrate to peoples harassed and uncertain that the democratic ways, the methods and ideas of the Open Society are the nearest answer men can have to their temporal problems. Even the Kremlin might be impressed. The Kremlin has worked hard to check the combination of British and American intelligence and power and resources. It seems to have had a clearer view of the possibilities than the two themselves.

The firm association of the American and British Systems would combine American strength with the strength of four of the first ten industrial States in the world: with 80,000,000 whites of the most vigorous stocks and 500,000,000 Asians and Africans, if the Indian Dominions came with the rest of the Commonwealth (and the Indians could not match its prospects elsewhere).

It would bring to British dispositions America's industrial and financial strength, her energy and élan and ideas. It would bring to America (with its dangerously concentrated industrial regions) a screen of bases and communications girdling the earth. In an age of rocket warfare, America (like Britain) could be usefully covered from Australia, Africa, Southeastern Asia, and Canada as well as from her

[2] The quickening of the Australian and New Zealand economies in war with the aid of American resources and energy was very notable: the Allied Works Council in Australia was a model of the method needed.

own bases. But in fact these would not be needed once they were assured. No single enemy would risk attack on a defensive system organized as a world-wide screen. Peace would be guaranteed by an overwhelming combination of strength; and provocations to war would sharply decline in an era of economic growth and rising prosperity.

* 2 *

Arrangements so far-reaching need a sufficient development of political relations and machinery. Here we cross at once the dragon of the National State. For my part, I feel that he has long outlived his uses and that humanity should find a less dangerous pet. But he still breathes fire and has a large circulation even at points remote from Chicago.

The issue is squarely up to the United States. They and they alone have the power to restore the Open Society in the world at large and in its several parts. They and they alone can apply the American Idea to the international order. If the American Idea is valid for them in their domestic affairs, they should have the courage to rest their foreign or international program on it.

I believe that if the United States would play now the role which Britain played in the 19th century and until the Second War, the world economy (or the economies of all those parts of the world which did not persist in their economic and political superstitions) could be restored within two years. With its restoration would come positive prospects of peace and of a rising and expanding economy which would properly employ the immense technical resources now at our disposal.

It would require a considerable effort from the Americans. They would have to face large economic changes. But the human and material cost would not approach the cost of another war or of continuing economic dislocation or even of the loans and credits with which the Americans must now plaster local symptoms.

Nor need the American economy be immediately or drastically reconstructed. A clear declaration of America's intentions to modify her economic order to the needs of the world would immediately restore confidence and stability.

A social and economic conference of the peoples still inclined towards a free society might lay down the general principles by which each would abide and provide the necessary machinery for the progressive restoration of these principles.

But a conference of the sort must move far beyond the Geneva meetings of 1947. It must begin with a clear statement of principles and purposes, of the ends to be sought. And the particular interests must be subdued to these ends. The prospects of a world community must not again be wrecked by the selfish interests of special and local groups who can organize powerful local lobbies. Both American capitalists and British Socialists must be prepared to throw off the economic superstitions and the political lusts which now corrupt their national orders.

But in all this we face the evil spirit of the Monstrous State which informs all modern politics, however its shapes and works vary from one community to another.

It is begotten (we cannot emphasize too much) from moral and intellectual confusion. It can be reduced only by a moral and intellectual renaissance.

The future fortune of mankind now hangs upon the possibility of that renewal.

* 3 *

Competent American publicists and politicians generally recognize with Mr. Walter Lippmann that from the Napoleonic to the World Wars the British System regulated the conditions of peace and prosperity. But most have their eyes excessively fixed on the political pattern. They do not see sufficiently that the supranational social economy of which Britain was the central organizing element stands over and against the National States, even its own National States. Aggressive and militant National States have taken arms against it. The nationalist temper rising in its Dominions and Colonies has repeatedly checked its development towards political and social unity. Economic nationalism outside and within the System has confused and diverted its movement towards a world community of trade.

Publicists who interpret the world scene only in terms of the National States have much to excuse them. We have organized our political life in these curious closed compartments which are in form and theory as self-contained and self-supporting as a brick or a brick-bat. But if we shift our fascinated gaze from the National State to the National Community or Culture or Economy we see at once that these are not self-contained or entirely self-supporting. They are in constant interplay and exchange with their neighbors. Only the State entertains and exudes the delusion of exclusive grandeur. Politics is but one of man's activities and the State but one of his social projections; yet only as subjects of this projection of their own are men packed into their separate national boxes.

The chief significance of the British System to the world is not in the sovereign polity of the United Kingdom or of Canada, Australia, India and the rest. It is in the shape of things promised, in the energy which strove through the British System to make sense in the larger world. It is in the strange power of the British to create in the teeth of their own nationalisms a larger unity which for a century embraced peoples of every color and creed. This is the phenomenon which America should study; for it has clues to the supranational society that is now the one alternative to chaos.

We are obsessed by the political structures and patterns which produce the crazy-pavement effect in the maps. If the map-makers would make a popular atlas which illustrated not the political frontiers but the economic, cultural, or religious systems within which a modern community lives and works and reads and thinks and prays, we should have quite another picture of the world. An atlas of the sort might be a job for the United Nations Educational, Scientific and Cultural Organization. It would reveal to bigoted nationalists that they were working in an economic system spread like a web across the world and sustained by many other than their local threads. It would reveal that science, invention, music, painting, language, worship, race have no necessary relation to the National State at all.

We must distinguish the National State from the National Community and culture. Each developed people possesses distinctive characters, values, experience and traditions which inform its arts and crafts, its cookery and consciousness, and all that we call its culture and its way of life. They are the organizing element, the indwelling and creative spirit of a true society. They bring their several savors to our common earth. We distinguish the special merits and distinctive characters of English music and German, of French and Chinese cooking. We recognize in the stones of Wells an English mode of praise; and only the French genius could have shaped the hymn in glass and stone at Chartres. But the Englishman who knows at Wells or in Purcell the peculiar harmonies and humors of his people does not refuse to pray in Chartres or to listen and to learn from Bach and Beethoven. A Frenchman may relish Chinese food and not be held in treason. Until lately Nationalism has only in its political expression run to strait-jackets and closed frontiers. But as the political arm reaches out to clutch at the whole of life, it seeks to crib, cabin, confine, and distort all these other phases of man's activities.

The National State has already crammed much of the economic life into boxes whose walls are tariff barriers and the like. It now in many countries strives to confine in the same fashion the cultural and religious life, the arts and sciences. A man in one box may not read philosophers his bureaucrats dislike or hear of progress elsewhere which he might compare with his own condition. He may come to believe in God at his peril and discover that delight in Swift or Mozart or Oliver and Hardy represents right-wing deviations or dangerous thoughts.

The Nationalistic State is not by its nature creative in any but its own political province. It can properly perform, like all things else, only according to its nature. The State's role is one of order and discipline and law. The State may provide bread and circuses, but it cannot create an art. At the most it may sometimes be persuaded to build galleries or library buildings or even to subsidize an artist it approves. It has silenced philosophers and it has turned some into its propagandists, but it has never inspired a system of thought or even produced an adequate philosophy of its own existence. The scientists are constantly telling us they cannot properly do their work under the controls and inhibitions the State imposes when it employs them on its pet projects. In war, to which the State in our time has devoted most of the resources it can command, it may lay hands on the results of scientists and mobilize them, but their essential work is done to serve not the State with atomic bombs but pure science.

Art provides the material for a criticism of life; and criticism seldom appeals to men in power. Science advances knowledge and therefore produces the conditions and courses of change. But men in power prefer things as they are; for in things as they are, they have their power.

Established governments and governors are always resistant to political change even in democracies, where they are sometimes forced to accept it. Are they likely to encourage the free play of thought which calls up the processes of change? Wherever the State grows too powerful, it begins to control and conduct and restrict and restrain, to drop its iron curtains and impose its censorships. It is thus under the Caesars and the Czars, under Hitler, Mussolini, Stalin; in war and social crises and wherever it has room or excuse to extend its reign. The State has one response to all problems: to establish its own overriding and overruling authority. The British Labour Government in the economic crisis of 1947 would not turn to the institutions, men, and methods which had built the British economic structure. It laid hands on their works and reduced their liberties.

State instruments have here and there promoted or taken over economic and social activities and operated them with some skill, especially (as with the British Broadcasting Corporation) where a measure of autonomy has been allowed. Here and there the State has to the general benefit opened or conducted public works which private enterprise could or would not have developed. But economic institutions of a representative character rather than the polity would better fill such economic gaps.

State services show all the evils of monopoly in service and competence (who ever bought good tobacco from the State monopolies in Europe?). Lacking competition, their equipment and discipline and morale progressively decline. The balance-sheets of State enterprises are fascinating studies when they are honestly presented (they seldom are, because almost every Government has developed tricks for off-loading deficits and depreciations to general revenues or consolidated funds).

But the real evidence against the State's intrusions in

the economic field is in their effect on national and world economies. The tariff and customs barriers piled up in this century may have had specific benefits for special groups; but we see their whole effect in the ruin they have brought on the world economy and in their provocations to war and poverty and depressions. The trail of the National State lies slimily across the wreck of Germany and Japan and the starved or broken bodies of uncounted millions of mankind.

An industry here and there may exist because of tariffs. Some have waxed fat and sluggish on them. But no industry which has real strength, vitality, and social usefulness needs to continue sheltered in maturity. Tariffs are iron curtains in their kind. They are restrictions on liberty. And in the world's overall account their local benefit is little to set beside war's waste and wreck.

We have yet to see the full effects of the identification of the political and economic life in the modern totalitarian state; but evidence enough is displayed in the ruin of half Europe and in the paralysis slowly creeping over all economies where the State's controls advance.

Men must be free to work and think and pray and trade their talents in the light and energy with which God or nature endows them if there is to be health and activity in all the organs of the social body; and the State must have only its natural and proper functions. St. Paul had the rights of it: "For the body also is not one member, but many." There are diversities of ministries and diversities of operations. "And if they were all one member, where would be the body? But now there are many members indeed, yet one body." This is the law of all organic life, of everything more complex than the unicellular structure; and men belong to life, living by the laws of life not of mechanics, however planners would have it.

* 4 *

The social body like the individual organism must be constantly readjusting itself to new needs and conditions. Political life is constantly in the flux produced by social movement; and the political organizations which we put out are normally (unless they master the whole social body and impose a cult of death or stagnation) the least stable of all social projections. Frontiers and the forms of government change (as we have seen) from generation to generation. Yet we allow our lives to be dominated and confined more and more by this unsteady device; whose claims have come to rest in part on a legal fiction, the curious doctrine of sovereignty.

We can see that there is in reality no such thing as a sovereign and self-sufficient economy, unless among the Eskimos or Australian aborigines before the world reached them. There is no such thing as a sovereign and self-sufficient political-economy. And the sovereign polity is a legal abstraction produced by lawyers who wanted to be rid of God and Moral Theology and the older sense of the Natural Law but who were still aware that authority must have some final center, source, and frame of authority. We might have done better to stick to God and keep the State in its proper place; for the State as God is obviously a dangerous delusion.

No polity is sovereign because none is completely self-sufficient; and wherever is dependency, there also is constraint. The British Dominions are not absolutely sovereign. If they depended on their own power alone they would never have been born or if they had been born they could hardly have survived; and their weight in the world now is largely from their association with Great Britain and one another. The United States and Russia are as nearly sovereign as any Powers since the Roman Empire; but both must sometimes bend to the necessities of their neighbors and to elements within their frontiers. The sovereign polity of Russia would have been an extremely groggy polity in 1943 if it had not sought and hurriedly accepted support from its Allies. The American economy must now trade its talents in the world if it is to avoid catastrophe.

The modern State rests on an illusion. No highly developed polity lives of itself alone, and none is entirely its own master, whatever the Kremlin, *The Chicago Tribune*, and other political primitives may think. And it has no proper authority over the other phases of life except as these bear on the political well-being of the social body. Nor are these rightly constricted to the political patterns we see drawn on the map. If the State imposes or tries to impose its yardstick on the cultural, moral, intellectual, and religious life, it is by harsh and perverse tyranny. But even then it moves in delusions. The whole life of man cannot be thus confined; unless indeed the iron curtain becomes a guillotine and the body is trimmed to the box.

We must shake off the notion that any State is in fact absolutely sovereign and independent. The doctrine may serve in a lawyer's argument, but it is more than time that the peoples of the world and their publicists dropped a fiction which has obscured the facts. We have been seeing the State through a fog of nationalist sentiment; and it has like a Brocken Shadow grown across the skies and fed on our substance.

* 5 *

When Mr. Lippmann and others of his quality argue that the United States must play the part which Britain has played in the world, they should make it clear that the United States is not being called to some fantastic political role or to the responsibilities of the British State (which are in rapid change). It is being called to a lead in the social-economic system which the British developed: to the support and growth of the world's social and economic communities, which are as much America's interest as Britain's.

Americans must understand their role, not in terms of nationalist politics but as of a part and partnership in a world community. They must resist in the economic and social orders the political passions of the Nationalist State which have prompted its efforts to chop up the larger cultural and social life of men and cram its severed quarters into several bloody boxes.

The peoples must learn to work (and to grow a new polity maybe) in the vast field of social and human relations which pass the national frontiers and reach out to mankind. If we fail, we shall continue in maniac quarrels all the more murderous because they have no rational motives and can reach no rational conclusions.

The United States and the British Commonwealth are already interknit by countless and rapidly increasing common interests. But the organization of their political relations is reminiscent of a world where communities were divided by wide seas or mountains, where communications were slow and difficult, where each lived of its own, like primitive tribes in isolated valleys.

As we have seen, this is true of the British Commonwealth itself, whose political confusions still cross its social and economic growth. The British Commonwealth has no political instrument to compare with its Imperial Shipping Board (established in 1920 to organize cheap freights and improve communications).

This political weakness at the international planes may seem a paradox beside the excessive strength of the National State. But it is precisely the strength of the Nationalist State which prevents the growth of an international or supranational order. And the Great State has been an aberration of right order. It is itself a crashing paradox for it defeats the proper purpose of its being: the peace, protection, and good order of its people. What peace has the Monstrous State given, what protection can it now promise?

Modern communities have developed by the gradual knitting of smaller units. As the social and economic life of ancient little lordships or colonies spread, their governments also expanded to express politically the developing community. The French and German feudal lordships were ultimately organized in unitary States; the American and Australian Colonies formed their federal Unions. But while the economic and cultural life of the advancing communities grew on out into the world to form new syntheses with others, their political life did not. Its energies were perverted into morbid growths at home. The State did in fact become monstrous because it was no longer one healthy organ of the whole social body. It spread like a cancer within each community, usurping the place of other organs natural to the body and gradually strangling them.[3] Every great modern war has come from this disease.

Our paradox is resolved into one problem. The State must return to its proper province and functions. It must again be seen not as an end in itself but as a means to the larger good of man. We are again confronted with the confusion of ends and means: the intellectual and moral disorder which has worked through all our social life and institutions. When the polity is returned to its proper functions within the national community, it may begin to grow in right order towards an international polity.

Within the national community it must again permit and encourage social and economic institutions responsible

[3] St. Thomas More, the greatest lawyer of his age, saw the beginning of this evil growth. He died in protest at the usurpation by the national political authority of a supranational and suprapolitical order and authority. But his protest went unheeded: and the National State began its monstrous aberration.

in their several provinces. It will require that these institutions also serve the general good of the community with which the State is properly concerned. It will if necessary discipline them. But it will not usurp their functions. It will insist that they work within the rules of general order as the members of a team. *Laissez-faire* let the economy run wild and pursue its economic ends without reference to the greater ends which these should serve. The State must allow the economic player to carry the economic ball. But it must check the ball-carrier if he tries to jump on other players' faces in his rush towards his goal. The political authority should be the rules committee, and its judiciary, the referee. It gives the law and polices it and guards the ground. But it does not join in the game.

It must in its rules conform to the general sense of what is fair and just; otherwise it produces dissension and confusion. Its sense of what is fair and just must come from beyond itself if different teams are to agree on the rules and play ball together. But whence are the several States to have enlightenment on what is fair and what is just? This is the dilemma of modern man and the root of his difficulties. Is the State the sole arbiter of morals? If so, does each separate State create its own morality? Do Mr. Truman, Mr. Taft and their colleagues proclaim *ex cathedra* and infallibly what is just, what is true, what is fair, what is virtuous between the 49th Parallel and the Gulf of Mexico; and is Stalin equally infallible, in his contrary dogma, across the Bering Sea? Are Stalin and a shifting majority of Congressmen each God in their local reigns? Or was Theodore Parker perhaps right when in giving form to the American Idea he saw all States like other mortal creations subject to "the principles of eternal justice," to a law beyond their own?

We cannot have it both ways. Either the State is subject to a moral law higher than its own or it is the sole arbiter of life and conduct; and Stalin and Mr. Truman and Senator Taft are the nearest we can know to a God. When we accept the State as sovereign in an absolute sense that is precisely what we imply. When modern man dismissed God, he left no higher authority than the State. Modern man (it now seems clear) was a frightful ass. For when he invests a bunch of people with the attributes of God, he should not be much surprised if they begin to fight for God's prerogatives.

We still assume in the West (even when we deny the premises) that the State must, as in Parker's American Idea, legislate according to the principles of eternal justice. We should therefore be able to see its proper part in the hierarchy of authority.

When States agree that their programs must conform to the principles of justice they can live and work together because they can accept a reference higher than their own. If we want a League of States or a Society of Nations we must first have this moral consensus. We must agree in fundamentals on what is right and what is wrong. Otherwise a United Nations Organization can be only a temporary expedient, an accommodation which States accept while it suits them. It has no real authority or life in it. It draws its being and authority only from the will of its member States. It will inevitably reflect and exacerbate all their confusions and contradictions; and they will each strive to use it for their own purposes.

No team can play a game unless it agrees within itself and with those it meets on the rules. The team must also know at what goal it is aiming. It must have an end. And it must accept the rules and the coach's training which define the means to its end.

These are obvious conditions which appear in any form of social organization. We cannot organize our activities or govern them until we know the end we seek and the means proper to it. Yet we constantly confuse these evident necessities when we approach the problems of national and international politics.

We mistake the end and confuse the uses of the political instrument when we permit it to intrude in every phase of life. The State is not properly concerned to conduct our economic activities any more than it is concerned to paint our pictures or to feel our pulse. It may encourage us to paint pictures. It should see that the man who feels a pulse is qualified. But it is not itself the artist, doctor, butcher, banker, or candlestick-maker.

The State's function is to preserve law and order and peace, not to turn Jack-of-all-Trades and universal employer and entrepreneur. When men were active in small local governments, they would never have conceived that politics could perform or cover all the duties of man. But this is what is proposed for the vastly more cumbrous and remote machinery of the modern State: which like Wilberforce's corporation has no soul to be damned, and no body to be kicked.

In Abraham Lincoln's lately opened papers were notes on the legitimate function of government. "In all that the people can individually do as well for themselves, Government ought not to interfere." This is not the perfect phrasing of what was evidently in Lincoln's mind; but the sense is clear. The State should not try to run with everybody's ball. If no player is fit to carry it, the State should find a proper substitute. The State itself is not a player. It is the grave signior in the judge's box, the policeman on the pickets. The performers in the field must work out their own plays within the rules. Lincoln was expressing the meaning of all right order with its proper distribution of functions and responsibilities. But the State now declares:

"*I* am the batsman and the bat,
 I am the bowler and the ball,
 The umpire, the pavilion cat,
 The roller, pitch, and stumps, and all."

From this monstrous usurpation comes our evil; though, like the devouring cancer, it is an effect of evils more profound.

The Open Society is the only way to peace, because only in a world economy can the national communities be knit together by interests active in the daily lives and livelihoods of all the peoples.

People live at peace together within national frontiers and in their own communities because they recognize their interdependence. The butcher, baker, postman, and insurance agent may dislike one another intensely; much more than they could dislike Germans or Japanese they may have killed but never knew. But they do not kill one another: murders (in spite of the provocations) are remarkably rare in almost all societies. People hack at one another's reputations or pocket-books but seldom at one another's heads. They have long learnt that their personal safety and their livelihoods depend on sufficient measures of co-operation and good order. This is true for Covington, Ky.; it should be true for all this little ball that dangles beneath its star.

The urban area of New York would fall rapidly into economic chaos, privation, and perhaps civil war if its boroughs behaved in the fashion of sovereign States. We should think it somewhat absurd if the Bronx threw up tariff barriers to protect its spaghetti market against the spaghetti-makers of Brooklyn. Some confusion would follow if Manhattan put quotas on migrants from Queens and required passports and visas of commuters from Connecticut. New York would rapidly go hungry if the Sov-

ereign States of New Jersey and Ohio refused to take
dollar-bills current in New York or New York's shoes and
hats and shirts for their milk and eggs and pork. Why
should there be a tariff wall between Windsor and Detroit
across the river but none between Detroit and San Diego,
thousands of miles away? Why should there be a fence
between Armagh and Monaghan but none between Edin-
burgh and London?

When the world was very wide and communities were
small and isolated, the exclusive polity was a convenient
and sometimes a sufficient instrument; though we may
recall that it grew as we have known it in the decline and
fall of an imperial civilization in which Scythian and
Briton, Goth, Persian, and Spaniard had claimed with
Cicero and the great Jew from distant Tarsus: "Civis
Romanus sum."

The National State as a political form is a secondary
growth, a tangle of wildwood where the tall tree was destroyed. It springs from the decay and defeat of a much
greater thing; and it has the bitter taste and sour fruit
of the dark humus whence it climbed.

As the wide spaces were filled and the peoples pressed
on one another and the lives of their communities were
interlinked, they should again have grown together politically. For what exactly are the uses of the curious boxes
in which we still persist?

We cannot dwell too much on the absurdities we pursue; if only to chasten the conceit we have of ourselves.
Peoples as diverse as the English, Scots, and Welsh with
their thousand years of war behind them merged in a new
polity. Why could not others?

The answers are in the history of politics but not in
reason or good sense or any useful interest.

The whole conception of the National State is in the

modern world turbid, confused, illogical; and the thing itself is deadly dangerous.

I have traversed this ground at length because we cannot be too clear about the nature of the beast we must train and domesticate to the use of mankind, if mankind can make any real use of it. The major obstacle to peace and prosperity is the determination of the large majority of men that this chimera shall still wander on the loose while its victims await their sacrificial day in its several pens.

Unless we free ourselves of this superstition of the National State, we shall die of it, devoured by our own fantasy, hoist with our own petard.

Our major difficulties are with ourselves, here and not elsewhere. They are in mental and moral sluggishness and inertia, in our failure to see what must be done or to do it. These probably will defeat every effort towards a peaceful, ordered, prosperous world: modern man does seem to have on his forehead the mark of the sin against the Holy Ghost, which is surely to refuse to save one's soul alive though all the means are at hand.

APPENDIX

Note I. STRUCTURAL DIFFERENCES IN GOVERNMENTS OF BRITISH DOMINIONS AND COLONIES

AUSTRALIA formed its Federation of six States on the first day of the 20th century. The residuary powers remain with the States, and the Federation, with Senate and House of Representatives, exercises only those specified by the Constitution. Canada, whose Constitution (the British North America Act of 1867) provides for a federal, parliamentary state, salutes both Westminster and Washington with its House of Commons and Senate. New Zealand is a unitary state, like the United Kingdom, with a House of Representatives and an Upper House of Nominees. South Africa is a Union with a House of Assembly and a Senate. As in all the British Dominions, Ministers are members of one or the other House. Newfoundland, given responsible Government in 1855, preserved Dominion status until 1934, when, as a result of its desperate economic plight, its administration was vested in Commissioners appointed by the United Kingdom. The Irish Free State came into being with Dominion status in 1922. Under the Constitution of 1937, it took the old name of Eire. Its structure is republican, with President, Senate, and Representatives. The chief executive is the Prime Minister, who sits with his Ministers in Parliament. Like the United Kingdom, the six structures noted above combine the legislative and executive functions, as distinct from the American system of checks and balances.

Of the group which, aside from the Dominions and the Colonial System, conducts its relations with the United Kingdom through the Home Office, Northern Ireland has its own Constitution, Governor, and Parliament of Senate and House of Commons. However, it still elects members to the Parliament of the United Kingdom, the relationship possessing something of a federal character. The Isle of Man has also its own Governor and Parliament, the Court of Tynwald with two Houses, the Legislative Council and the House of Keys, which make local law. The Channel Islands are governed under the King as Duke of Normandy.

Southern Rhodesia is a further curiosity. It has representative and responsible government and deals with the United Kingdom through the Dominions Office. It is in fact a Dominion like Australia and Canada, but no one has yet thought to elevate it formally.

The Colonies are variously organized under the Colonial Office. Burma, detached from the Government of India in 1937, became then a self-governing unit of the Commonwealth with its own Constitution, Senate, and House of Representatives, though powers resembling those of the Viceroy of India were vested in the Governor. Under the 1947 Treaty, it becomes a republic maintaining special relations with the United Kingdom. In 1931, Ceylon's existing Legislature was replaced by a State Council, elected by adult suffrage, to deal with both legislative and executive matters. The experiment was not successful, however. Now, Ceylon goes toward Dominion status under the constitutional proposals of 1945-6. As of World War II, the other Colonies, greatly diverse in their societies and economies, ranged from such self-governing Colonies as Burma and Ceylon to military garrisons like Gibraltar, administered by its Commander as Governor. Pragmatism and constant recognition of local problems and prerogatives have been the guides to a growing distribution of responsibilities.

Note II. LOCAL GOVERNMENT IN INDIA

In 1892, Legislative Councils, established in the Provinces and at the Center, were enlarged. The "non-official" members were increased and empowered to discuss budgets and to question Executive Members of the Council. In 1909, the powers and membership of these Councils were again enlarged. In 1911, an impulse to nationalism was given by the proposal for a new capital of all India at Delhi. In 1919, a new constitution distinguished the functions of the Provincial Governments and gave them a diarchic character. Matters primarily of local concern (education, health, agriculture, excise, public works, etc.) were put under Ministers responsible to the elected Legislatures, while responsibilities such as law enforcement were reserved to the local Governor and his Executive Council.

This constitution (the Government of India Act of 1919) provided that the Indian Legislature should consist of the Governor-General with two Houses: the Council of State and the Legislative Assembly. The Governor-General's Executive Council remained the chief administrative authority in India and responsible ultimately through the Secretary of State to the British Parliament, but the Budget and legislation henceforward were submitted to both chambers of the Indian Parliament.

The British India Act of 1935 was based partly on the immensely valuable survey of India which appeared in the Simon Report of 1930, partly on Round Table Conferences of Indian and British leaders during 1930-33. The Act provided for new Provincial Governments and Legislatures of one or two Chambers with responsible Ministries. The Governors retained special responsibilities for good order, the protection of the rights of minorities and of the Indian States. The Act provided also for the creation of a Federal India from the Provinces of British India and those of the Indian States which chose to enter: the plan to operate only when Indian States representing half their aggregate population agreed to join. The Federal Legislature was designed for two Houses and for a Council of Ministers responsible to them.

A Federal Court was established in 1937, but the general scheme of Federations had to wait on the assent of enough Princes. Most were repelled by the demand of Congress Party leaders that they should all first create within their States representative and responsible institutions similar to those of British India. Some already had advanced democratic forms.

Note III. CO-OPERATIVE MACHINERY IN BRITISH COMMONWEALTH BETWEEN THE WARS

THOUGH Imperial Conferences and Imperial Economic Conferences came at odd intervals, they produced machinery of more permanent character. The Dominions Office grew out of the Colonial Office to serve as a secretariat and a center for disseminating information among the Imperial Governments. The Dominions themselves developed External Affairs Departments to deal with London and appointed to Great Britain and in time to one another, as Great Britain appointed to them, High Commissioners and Trade Commissioners. The Foreign Office supplied Dominions Governments with its information through the Dominions Office, and the Dominions reciprocated. Also, the Prime Ministers deal directly with one another in "matters of cabinet importance" requiring consultation and decision.

The Dominions, or Commonwealth Relations, Office includes an Overseas Settlement Department for joint planning of migration. The Department of Overseas Trade has an Empire Division which informs and advises on everything apt to commerce and plants out its Trade Commissioners from Winnipeg to Bulawayo. The Dominions High Commissioners in London have their Migration Services, Trade, Press, Publicity and Commercial Divisions; political officers for contact with the Dominions and Foreign Office; and Naval, Army, and Air Officers for liaison with the United Kingdom's Services. The Canadian Provinces and Australian States also have their own representatives, the Agents-General, distinct from the Federal High Commissioners. Australia, for example, has seven separate Missions in London, all busy.

The Committee of Imperial Defence promotes throughout the Commonwealth and Empire common methods of organization, weapons, etc. The Imperial Defence College trains officers selected from the fighting and civil services of the United Kingdom and Dominions. The Naval links throughout the Commonwealth are very strong, and the Air Forces have also followed much the same organizational and training programs.

The Commonwealth is still linked, although in different ways and degrees, to its old legal centerpiece, the Judicial Committee of the Privy Council. At the economic and scientific levels, the British System had long before World War II, which multiplied them, a tremendous range of co-operative instruments, classified by the Imperial Committee on Economic Consultation and Co-operation under the following main heads: (1) Bodies, the main function of which is the dissemination of information; (2) Bodies engaged in *ad hoc* investigations; (3) Specialist Advisory Bodies; and (4) Bodies for the improvement of marketing conditions. And in addition to these, the Departments of Scientific and Industrial Research, the Medical Research Council, and many more work out the pattern of a co-operating Commonwealth.

Note IV. WAR EFFORT OF BRITISH COM-MONWEALTH IN WORLD WAR II

IN WORLD WAR II, the United Kingdom mobilized in its home islands nearly 23,000,000 people: 93.6 per cent of its males between the ages of 14 and 64, almost 45 per cent of its women between 14 years and 59. Some 6,000,000 (including 500,000 women) went to the Armed Forces, which took 57 per cent of men between the ages of 18 and 40. The Civil Defence Forces had a little less than 300,000 men and women. Munitions took 5,000,000, essential industries 4,700,000, and 6,000,000 were left in other full-time employment ordered to the war-effort.

Great Britain built over 125,000 aircraft and more than 2,200 naval vessels, including 750 major ships, and about 4,000 lesser naval vessels, landing-craft and the like. Although, by agreement with the United States, it concentrated on naval construction after Pearl Harbor, it had built from 1940 to 1943 more merchant-tonnage than it produced even under the tremendous pressure of 1915-18. It increased iron-production by 50 per cent, and the light metal industries grew beyond all precedents (magnesium production by 1,100 per cent, for instance). Although large areas had to be given over to the training of the British and American Armies, to the new air establishments, and to industry, the Kingdom increased its tillage by 62 per cent, becoming able to reduce its pre-war imports of food by 50 per cent.

The British effort represented also enormous reserves of moral and intellectual capital mobilized in circumstances of unprecedented difficulty. Britain had in the crisis of the war no foothold or effective ally on the Continent, and for five years she was the one base on which the major offensive against Fortress Europe could be mounted. Here invading American and British Forces had to have most of their training and to be fed, supplied and kept at a high pitch of morale for months and years, under conditions of utmost strain to the civil population.

In the year when the British Commonwealth fought alone, the victory was sown—first by the blockade which cut Germany off from all non-European sources of oil, natural rubber, cotton and wool, and most of the copper, nickel, molybdenum and the like essential to a war-machine. The blockade forced Hitler to attack Russia, to the war on two fronts he had dreaded and repudiated. Meanwhile, the British had to meet the counter-blockade. Their losses were enormous, but they held effective control of the sea-routes to Africa and Asia, Australasia and the Americas. Before the end of 1940, the Germans were turned aside from the attempt on England—six months before the attack on Russia, twelve months before Pearl Harbor. And even before this, the British had moved to the first great stroke against the Axis.

When Italy declared war on 10 June 1940, the British Fleet in the Mediterranean put immediately to sea; and Admiral Cunningham seized overnight the strategic initiative which was never lost, though for months and years he had but one battleship at each end of the Mediterranean and often only one aircraft-carrier. A campaign of three years unsurpassed in naval history for moral courage, skill, endurance, and sheer gusto ended when *H.M.S. Warspite* led the Italian Fleet into Valetta Harbor, under the guns at Malta.

In September 1940, British, Australian, Indian and New Zealand reinforcements were pouring into Egypt. The decision to build strength in the Middle East at that moment of crisis at home was heroic; but, more important, it was superlatively shrewd and long-sighted. If the Middle East had not then been held, Russia would have been isolated when her day came; the Axis would probably have joined hands across Asia; and the War would on all human calculations have been lost. Wavell's offensive in North Africa, begun in December 1940, forced the Germans to turn southward to help their Italian ally. Henceforward, they were desperately involved in the Mediterranean. By December 1941, the British had held their own island, had destroyed an Italian Empire, had forced Germany into its fateful war with Russia, and were out-bombing the Luftwaffe from the Atlantic to North Africa. The Germans had in general been out-thought, out-fought, and out-built.

The British Dominions and Southern Rhodesia mobilized in the Armed Forces approximately 2,500,000 men; India, 2,560,000; the Colonial Empire, something over 300,000. The Dominions employed over 3,000,000 workers in war industries, built 20,000 aircraft, approximately 5,000 naval vessels and special craft, over 4,000,000 tons of merchant-shipping. They spent about $30,000,-000,000. India employed 5,000,000 men in war industries and spent approximately $2,400,000,000. The economic and financial effort of the Colonial Empire (as distinct from India and the Dominions) is still difficult to calculate because it often merged with other accounts, but it supplied to the United States $220,-000,000 worth of food and raw materials.

As a direct contribution of the British System to the American war effort, the United States received some $5,294,000,000 in Reverse Lend-Lease—all but $306,000,000 of their total receipts from this measure. In addition, Britain spent in the United States probably $6,000,000,000 on supplies; and gave to the United States after Pearl Harbor great quantities of ammunition, barrage balloons, machine-tools, and anti-aircraft guns, as well as designs for the Liberty Ship, for rockets, Bailey Bridges, radar, astrographs, and jet-propulsion engines. In fact, the resources of the United States and the British Commonwealth were actually merged for war, each contributing what it could best provide. Though humanity is slow to learn even by the hard ways of war, we may assume that such great lessons as this are never wholly lost.

Note V. MOTIONS TOWARD CENTRALIZATION IN BRITISH THIRD EMPIRE

IN 1905, Alfred Lyttelton as Secretary of State for the Colonies proposed an Imperial Council with a permanent Commission and Secretariat. Sir Wilfrid Laurier of Canada opposed it, fearing that a Council might develop executive functions and trespass on the sovereign ground of the Dominions. He preferred the method of consultation in Imperial Conference. Alfred Deakin, the Australian Prime Minister, liked the idea of a permanent Secretariat, however, and returned to it at the Conference of 1907. He saw the Secretariat as "an agency for carrying out the instructions of one Conference and for acting as an intermediary at the suggestion of any Prime Minister or any Government or Governments, in order to prepare for the next Conference or between its meetings." He wanted it appointed by the Conference and attached to an appropriate Department in London. Laurier again objected. But the Conference (1907) approved the principle of a Secretariat, and the Colonial Office was charged with its shaping.

The Imperial Conference of 1911 considered on the initiative of New Zealand a Standing Committee, advisory to the Governments and meeting regularly. The Australian Prime Minister (Mr. Fisher, the Labour leader) supported Sir Joseph Ward of New Zealand, but Laurier again felt that the Committee might grow too formidable and the notion was dropped.

In 1924, the Ramsay MacDonald Government raised questions concerning the machinery of consultation. Australia, pointing out that between Imperial Conferences no effective machinery existed for keeping the Dominions continuously informed as to developments, suggested a permanent Secretariat responsible to the Prime Ministers for all matters of common concern other than those of foreign policy. Such a Secretariat would provide not merely a connecting link between the individual Dominion Governments and the British Government, but also among the Governments of the various Dominions themselves.

This reference to communications among the Dominions themselves is notable. Until they began to appoint High Commissioners to one another during World War II, they had little direct association: as the phrase ran, they all talked to mother but little within the family.

The Labour Government went out and the Conservatives came in. The discussions lapsed. But Mr. Curtin, the Australian Labour Prime Minister, in 1944 returned to the theme, with new proposals for a Central Secretariat. They were firmly quashed by Mr. Mackenzie King, in the full succession to Sir Wilfrid Laurier.

Repeated efforts have been made to find a method by which the Governments could rapidly confer on urgent occasion. When decisions of high policy must be reached, only Cabinet Ministers are competent to commit their Governments. But Cabinet Ministers cannot or could not until lately be swiftly assembled from the opposite ends of the earth. The Dominions have not kept Ministers regularly in London, and their High Commissioners normally are only their Agents, lacking policy responsibility and even the precedence of foreign Ambassadors.

The problem has thus become to find a method for the review of common problems by each Government in intimate relations with the rest but on its own responsibilities and ground.

INDEX